THE OBJECTIVE PROOF FOR
CHRISTIANITY

THE PRESUPPOSITIONALISM OF
CORNELIUS VAN TIL
AND
GREG L. BAHNSEN

DR. GREG BAHNSEN
MICHAEL R. BUTLER

EDITED BY JOSHUA PILLOWS

THE
AMERICAN
VISION
A Biblical Worldview Ministry
POWDER SPRINGS, GEORGIA

The Objective Proof for Christianity:
The Presuppositionalism of Cornelius Van Til and Greg L. Bahnsen
Copyright © 2024 by Joshua Pillows
First printing.

Published by:
The American Vision, Inc.
P.O. Box 220
Powder Springs, Georgia 30127
www.AmericanVision.org

Cover design and typography: Justin Turley
Cover image by Daniel H. Riedel

Scripture quotations noted KJV are from the King James Version.

ISBN-13: 978-1-936577-88-0 (Paperback)

Printed in the United States of America

In loving memory of
Dr. Greg L. Bahnsen
1948-1995

Table of Contents

Section 1—Background

CHAPTER 1
Covering the Prerequisites 13

CHAPTER 2
Four Types of Proof.. 21

CHAPTER 3
Why I Believe in God: Readings and Analysis 35

CHAPTER 4
A Survey of Christian Epistemology: Readings and Analysis 45

CHAPTER 5
Kant in Context 57

CHAPTER 6
Non-Transcendental Attempts to Answer Skepticism 71

Section 2—Contemporary Transcendental Arguments

CHAPTER 7
Contemporary Transcendental Arguments 81

CHAPTER 8
The Contemporary Debate 93

CHAPTER 9
Analysis and Overview of the Contemporary Climate 99

Section 3—Van Til's Transcendental Program

CHAPTER 10
Summary of Transcendental Argumentation 115

CHAPTER 11
Commendations of Van Til's Transcendental Method 131

CHAPTER 12
The Uniqueness of the Presuppositional Use of
Transcendental Reasoning 145

CHAPTER 13
Back to Basics: Readings from Van Til 163

CHAPTER 14
Van Til's Critics 183

CHAPTER 15
Van Til's Critics: John Frame 197

APPENDIX
Answering the Transcendental Criticisms of Van Til's TAG ... 209

INDEX
Subjects 265

INDEX
Names 269

Glossary 271

References 275

Preface

Dr. Greg Bahnsen was perhaps the most brilliant philosopher and apologist that the Church has procured since the Apostle Paul. Greg always possessed a deep intellectual acuity, even in his elementary years. In high school and throughout college he won numerous awards for his high academic achievements, always residing at the top of his class, and that intellectual rigor did not subside after his graduate years. In the short time that he was here, his contributions to the Church and to the Reformed faith in particular are second to none. In his 47 years he left behind numerous articles pertaining to philosophy, apologetics, ethics, and theology, six books in apologetics (four of which were published posthumously), and over 1,500 tapes containing lectures, seminars, sermons, debates, and entire courses in philosophy, apologetics, theology, ethics, socio-political theory, and logic.

What Greg accomplished in his relatively short lifespan most people could not do over multiple. He was an ardent defender of the faith, in particular, of the method formulated by his instructor, Cornelius Van Til (1895-1987), and worked tirelessly to defend what he argued to be an absolutely certain, objective proof for the existence of God and thus by implication an absolutely certain, objective proof for the truths of the Christian worldview as a whole.

In recent years, The American Vision (with the help of Greg's friend, Gary DeMar) worked to publish his first official posthumous book. Greg had done a short seminar in apologetics with a group of high school students who were soon heading off to college in order that they would be able to defend the faith against the secular onslaught on college campuses (both then and now). Based on these videos, The American Vision published Greg's first posthumous book, *Pushing the Antithesis*, in 2007, twelve years after his death. A year later they would go on to publish another book based on manuscripts Greg had written that had been lost and only discovered after his death titled *Presuppositional Apologetics: Stated & Defended* (2008).

Within the past couple years, The American Vision had worked to publish a new trilogy of apologetics books based on other lectures Greg had recorded on tape: *Against all Opposition: Defending the Christian Worldview* (2020); *The Impossibility of the Contrary* (2020); *Pushing the Antithesis* (2021) (this book being the same as their first publication in 2007 but now updated and conformed to synchronize with the other two books). We truly owe a tremendous debt of gratitude both to Gary and The American Vision's diligent work to keep Bahnsen's legacy alive.

While many have benefited greatly from Greg's lectures in presuppositional apologetics, not enough work has been done to elaborate more on the argument within the apologetic itself: the Transcendental Argument for Christian Theism (or God)—TACT/TAG. Proponents of presuppositionalism know how to pose a reductio argument against their opponent's worldview to show its futility while also knowing how to express that Christianity can make sense of intelligibility. But exactly how many can formally state the argument? What if a more philosophically-astute opponent attacks the apologetic, specifically criticizing the nature of transcendental reasoning and its legitimacy? While the enterprise of apologetics is to be done by both the Christian philosopher and layman, the issue over transcendental reasoning must not be ignored by either class of people, despite its more philosophical nature.

In the Summer of 1995, just a few months before Greg passed away, he gave a wonderful three-day seminar surveying both the history and contemporary climate of transcendental reasoning, as well as expositing the transcendental program passed down from Van Til and how it relates and withstands the transcendental charges of its critics. Does Van Til's TAG succumb to the same problems of modern transcendental arguments in secular philosophy? Does Van Til's TAG actually prove the truth of Christianity and Christianity *alone*? Does Van Til's TAG actually prove that all other worldviews are false? Does Van Til's TAG actually prove that the Christian worldview is metaphysically (or objectively) the case and not that it is indispensable to simply have to think that it is? These sorts of questions are answered in the most incisive way by Greg, and these tapes are an invaluable source of information not just for the proponents of Van Til, but also for his opponents.

Greg, however, was not the only one who taught in this seminar as he had required his pupil, Michael Butler, to teach on the contemporary climate of transcendental reasoning. While Butler teaches for two-and-a-half-tapes worth of time, Bahnsen still interjects periodically when the subject matter becomes more rigorous with an all-too-known incisiveness and profundity.

Finally, footnotes will of course be implemented throughout this work when further clarification is needed either from Bahnsen or Butler. Moreover, in the same way that The American Vision altered the transcript of Bahnsen's words in order to suite the purposes of a book setting, so, too, will I alter the transcript at various points to fit it into a literary work. However, none of the alterations will of course affect the content of the seminar; it is strictly for grammatical formality (e.g., omissions of irrelevant parts, grammatical corrections, inserting remarks such as "In the previous chapter," adding emphases, etc.).

Above all, may this work glorify God and continue to champion Dr. Bahnsen's legacy.

Joshua Pillows

SECTION 1

BACKGROUND

(Dr. Greg L. Bahnsen)

CHAPTER 1

Covering the Prerequisites

Why Study Transcendental Arguments?

Why talk about transcendental arguments? In certain narrow areas of philosophical study there is discussion of transcendental arguments going on, but I would not expect a broad cross-section of the Christian Church to be interested just because some philosophers are talking about something arcane like transcendental arguments. I am going to take a few moments to try to explain why I think it is so important that we as Christians take a look at this subject. It's not just because there is a narrow interest in it in philosophy. In fact, to be honest, I am a little surprised that there is any interest in it at all among philosophers. To the degree that you get involved in transcendental reasoning you are going to be forced to worldview considerations—what our basic perspective on the nature of reality is, how we know what we know, how we should live our lives—that network of assumptions in terms of which we organize all of our experience, make sense out of our lives, guide our lives, and so forth.

Modern philosophy is almost allergic to worldview considerations; it is really out of touch and out of style today. Many philosophers would consider it amateurish or gush in some sense to even think about the big questions in philosophy anymore. Philosophy has taken such an analytical turn in the 20th Century (which is what I've specialized in) that you have philosophers who focus very narrowly not even on a broad field like epistemology, but some subsection of epistemology or metaphysics or ethics[1] or meta-ethics, philosophy of science, philosophy of language, etc.—they focus on these subsections because the analytical approach is to break down bigger problems into smaller ones.

> Modern philosophy is almost allergic to
> worldview considerations.

So when you come along and start talking about what the broadest consideration is in terms of which (or what is the framework in which) all of that analysis makes sense, philosophers often chuckle or ridicule and think it's old fashioned, silly stuff. So again, it really is surprising that there is any philosophical interest in transcendental arguments at all.

Now, I am convinced that the existence of God is not only objectively *true* but is also objectively *provable*. This is politically incorrect. You have to understand that this is *not* what apologists say today. The existence of God might be shown to be probable or preferable, but very few apologists today are going to say that the existence of God is objectively provable, and I do believe that it is objectively provable.

Proof and Persuasion

The question of the truth of God's existence has nothing to do with the psychology and/or character of those who are arguing one way or another about God. We have to be very careful of the genetic fallacy and ad hominem arguments; we do not want to say either in favor of God's existence or against God's existence things which really have nothing to do with the merits of the case, but only have to do

---

1. Epistemology: The theory or study of knowledge; Metaphysics: The study of the nature of reality; Ethics: The study of human conduct. These three areas form the constituent parts of a worldview.

with the subjective origin of the opinion being discussed or the man himself who is doing the discussing. It is important to remember that an objective proof for the truth of something really has nothing to do with the man who is arguing for it. We want to make clear to the unbelieving world that we are not defending ourselves or the character of our compatriots; we are defending the objective truth of God's existence.

The fact that these are objective matters, however, does not take away from the fact that they are personal. The existence of God is obviously a very personal question, and it is personal because it touches us deeply, it touches our lives vitally. Indeed, even the most important aspects of human experience are affected by what you think regarding God (i.e., who are we?; the enigmas of suffering and evil; love and death). All of these things are affected by whether or not you believe in God.

Additionally, an argument need not be accepted by everyone for it to be conclusive and I'm tempted to make reference to the O. J. Simpson trial. Should we just say, "Well then why don't we just give up courtroom protocol—calling witnesses, garnering evidence, arguing with one another—because, you know, you can't get everybody to agree one way or another so it's really just a crapshoot. So why don't we get together, throw the dice, decide whether or not the guy is guilty and just get on with it?" In our whole way of life, even in our culture, we know there is a difference between proof and persuasion. Not everybody will be persuaded but we think proof is available, and as Christians that is a very important thing for us as well. *When we say we can objectively prove God's existence we are not saying we can universally persuade people.*

I am told that it was Plato who said it first, but I am not really sure: "A man convinced against his will is of the same opinion still." That is true. If I can prove something (in the sense of being convincing) and yet the man does not have a heart to go along with it, he is not going to cry "Uncle!"; he is not going to give up and we have to recognize that. If you don't, then you are really going to be strung out working on your Christian apologetic because over and over again what you are going to do is use an argument and see that somebody does not just fall immediately and say, "Oh, well I have to revise the argument." That is not true. Sometimes you have to repeat the argument. Sometimes you just have to keep coming back and back until the coin drops for that person. But even when you have the greatest of arguments, if a man's heart is not changed then he is not going to have the coin drop.[2] So when I say that the existence of God is objectively provable, remember:

1. I am talking about an objective matter, not just personal desires or ad hominem and genetic considerations.

2. I am talking about proof, not persuasion.

Metaphysics and Epistemology

Metaphysics deals with what exists, what is real, the nature of reality, relationships between the things that exist and so forth. Epistemology deals with how we know what we know, what the nature and limits of human knowledge are. There is a difference between metaphysics and epistemology in the sense that something can exist (something can be real) without us knowing it. For millennia DNA existed without us knowing it. So there is a difference between *existing* and something *being known* to exist. But there is also a difference between something existing and a person being able to prove it. You can believe it is possible that something exists which no one has proven. The planet Uranus existed and was suspected to exist before there was proof of it. So existence is different than "knowledge of,"

---

2. Especially from a Reformed perspective where it is God alone who changes the heart of the unbeliever, it would be all the more inconsistent for the Calvinist to revise his or her argument on the grounds of alleged impotence of persuasiveness. One might as well accuse God of not doing a good enough job of performing miracles since some still doubted when they saw the resurrected Christ (Matt. 28:17).

existence is different than "proof of," and something can exist even when someone offers reasons against it. Sometimes we have reasons that we think show that something doesn't exist. I think I can give good arguments against the idea that I have diabetes. My doctor thought it was interesting that I felt that I had good arguments against having diabetes when he was giving me the lab reports that show that I do, so here I am arguing doctor-to-doctor about this matter. Do you think that had anything to do with whether or not I had diabetes? Of course not.

When I say that the existence of God is objectively true and objectively provable, I am not at all suggesting that I can persuade everybody, I am not talking about psychological considerations, and I realize that there are people who think they can offer arguments against God's existence. But I would like to show you how you can prove the existence of God (that is, a metaphysical truth) and you can epistemologically in an objective, provable fashion demonstrate this conclusion even though not everyone is convinced and people may argue against it.

Faith and Reason

If we can get worked out this notion of an objective proof for God's existence along the lines of transcendental reasoning, I think that it will really open things up and enlighten your minds with regard to the relationship of faith and reason.

I think it is mistaken and misleading to think that Christian faith takes over where reason leaves off. Many people have the idea that we can reason about things such as science, medicine, industry, economics, history, etc., and reasoning will take you really far, but at some point reasoning stops and then faith begins, so that we as Christians agree with everyone else when it comes to natural matters, but then what we do is add another story to the house of knowledge, and that is the story of faith. I think this is misleading and mistaken. Faith is not without reason, faith is not above reason, and faith is not contrary to reason.

To put it simply, I do not in any sense endorse *fideism* (lit. faith-ism).[3] I do not believe that. I not only believe that Christian faith is reasonable, but I maintain that Christian faith is demanded by reason.

Reason can be affirmed without endorsing what is known as rationalism.[4] In the broad sense rationalism says that man's mind is the highest authority, or that man's mind is at least autonomous. It never bows to any outside authority. The autonomous man (that is, the man who says he is intellectually self-sufficient and the final authority) might grant that there is a god. Usually he doesn't, to be sure, but you need to recognize that in order to understand the *character* of autonomy, he could grant there is a god. But it could never be the Christian God. Why is that? Because the Christian God doesn't bow to the authority of the servant; the servant is to bow to the authority of the Lord.

Faith is not without reason, faith is not above reason,
and faith is not contrary to reason.

Now, there are people who want to promote autonomous reasoning to get people to believe in the Christian God, and I think that is just so fundamentally wrongheaded to *try to say to somebody that they need to have faith in this God and that you will prove to them, to their own satisfaction as being the ultimate authority, that God is the ultimate authority.* You can't do that. I have been in university training in the past and I continue to pay attention to higher education in our culture as well, and it just boggles my mind that anybody could believe

---

3. Meaning that Christian faith is independent of considerations of reason; that Christian faith is a personal choice—a blind, voluntaristic leap which has nothing to do with reasoning and argumentation.

4. Bahnsen delves into the etymology of the term 'rationalism,' rightfully pointing out that the term has been subject to a number of different definitions. Here, he is referring to it symbolizing the primacy of human reasoning in all matters.

in the autonomy or the self-sufficiency and independence of man's mind. If that were true, why is there still such massive disagreement in the universities? What's wrong with man's mind? How does man's self-sufficient mind not get things worked out? And it's not just that psychologists differ from political scientists. Political scientists can't agree among themselves, and psychologists can't agree among themselves either. There are even huge disagreements in issues which seem incontrovertible such as math or logic or the laws of physics. There are huge disagreements in schools of philosophy, mathematics, science and so forth. So, the self-sufficiency of man's mind, just on the face of it, is a silly doctrine.[5]

Rationalism, as we have talked about it, is different than rationality. I affirm with all my heart and soul rationality, and I affirm it because God made us to think. He expects us to think. Indeed, since we are made in the image of God, and He is supremely rational and coherent (He is the Truth Itself as Jesus said), then we ought to be concerned about the truth and about reasoning and using our minds to glorify God. Paul put it this way: we are to bring every thought captive to the obedience of Christ.[6]

We're supposed to be using our minds and using them in a subservient way as a tool to glorify God. While some people use

---

5. One may be tempted to rebut this point and appeal to universally accepted and accomplished feats such as the moon landing, the efficacy of particular medicines, etc. (philosophically-put, inductive and pragmatic ends). However, such a viewpoint and rebuttal is too myopic, for these very feats themselves rest on philosophical assumptions, and, as Bahnsen pointed out, considering the huge disagreements within philosophical schools of thought, the rational autonomy of a *subjective* being attempting to cogitate and predicate truths of the universe *objectively* is futile. There may be objective truth, to be sure, but the autonomous man could never know with certainty if he obtains it. Thus, so far as fallible, finite, subjective, and autonomous man is concerned, these feats were (and are) only possible given the truth of the Christian worldview, not his autonomous and artificial system relegated to the relativistic level of pragmatism—truth is just what works for their particular, relativistic ends.

6. 2 Corinthians 10:5.

their mind as a tool to argue against God, we use our minds to argue for God. But we certainly affirm rationality. *We are not fideists.* We affirm reason, we do not affirm rationalism. In fact, this entire work is an attempt to show that the Christian use of rationality refutes rationalism. If we're going to use our minds in the best way, you cannot be a rationalist.

> You can't justify reasoning or rationality without a worldview, without a broader consideration of the knowledge that you have...

Against autonomy I argue that all reasoning rests upon faith. My first consideration was that faith does not go beyond reason. Now I'm going to turn the tables and say to the unbelieving rationalist that as a matter of fact, his rationality rests upon faith. You can't justify reasoning or rationality without a worldview, without a broader consideration of the knowledge that you have, and the only worldview that will allow for rationality or make intelligible the use of rational procedures is Christianity. This is pretty heavy stuff. We are arguing that if anybody reasons at all, ultimately, they are borrowing from, or working in terms of, the Christian outlook of life—that faith is foundational to all rationality, to all reasoning.

CHAPTER 2

Four Types of Proof

How are we going to prove this? How are we going to prove that rationality itself is only intelligible or rational within the Christian worldview? We first have to ask how we go about proving things. There are four general kinds of proof or reasoning: rationalist-type proofs, empiricist-type proofs, pragmatist-type proofs, and transcendental proofs.

Rationalist-Type Proofs

In the history of philosophy, some philosophers have argued that we prove things by showing that they can be deduced from more basic truths, and ultimately, the basic truths which are the foundation for what we are proving are known in a rational way because we have a concept or an idea that is clear, distinct, and self-evident to us. Here is a self-evident truth: "I exist." How could I think otherwise? Isn't that clear and distinct to me? In fact, Descartes[1] thought he had an interesting way of proving that it had to be because he said, "If I doubt that I exist, I have to exist in order to do the doubting." Now, Bertrand Russell (1872-1970), no friend to Christianity, was a sterner philosopher than Descartes. He said about Descartes's

---

1. René Descartes (1596-1650) was a French rationalist philosopher who is known as the "father of modern philosophy." Descartes was one of the three primary philosophers of Continental Rationalism along with Baruch Spinoza (1632-1677) and Gottfried Wilhelm Leibniz (1646-1716).

argument (which everybody should see) that it begs the question. The argument should be "Thinking is going on, therefore, I exist." Of course, once you put it that way the argument is a horrible argument; there is nothing about thinking in general that shows that you specifically and personally exist. Descartes had something which he thought was clear, distinct, and self-evident, but it turns out that disagreement is possible about that.

However, there were other philosophers at that time who felt that you could give a foundation in clear and distinct self-evident truths or notions from which we can deduce substantial conclusions about the nature of reality. Spinoza began with his notion of substance which he thought was a clear and distinct idea, and from it he concluded that there is only one thing that exists: the whole of nature (or you can call it God). He was a monist. That is, he believed that there was only one type of reality. Descartes felt like there had to be two types of reality: mental (which is not extended in space) and body/matter (which is extended in space). He was thus a dualist.

It would appear that rationalist-type arguments reduce to subjectivism...

So here you have one man claiming self-evident truths as a foundation for a metaphysic of dualism, another man claiming self-evident truths as a foundation for his metaphysic of monism, then Leibniz came along and accused both of them of being wrong. There is, he said, an infinite plurality of substances that he called monads, and he was therefore an atomist. The point of all of this is that such disparate conclusions make rationalist-type arguments very suspect. It would appear that rationalist-type arguments reduce to subjectivism or at least disagreement which is unreliable.

Empiricist-Type Proofs

Much more popular and easier for American and English students to understand are empiricist-type arguments because that is the culture in which we have been raised. We like this idea that seeing is believing. Empiricist-type arguments likewise appeal to foundations, but these foundations are perceptual, or at least commonsensical in nature. So to know anything is to be able to trace what you are claiming to know and every aspect of it back to some kind of observational certainty.

The empiricist tradition in the history of philosophy has always floundered, however, over considerations in cognitive psychology. That is, looking at the economy of thinking—how do we think?; what is the psychological process by which we cogitate?—and if the truths that we believe need to be verified by being traced back to our cognitive psychology to perceptual foundations, then we're going to have to have a credible explanation of that psychological process, and it has never really been offered. In fact, in the case of David Hume,[2] cognitive psychology was completely blown out of the water because Hume said that if everything is loose and disjointed then I don't ever find myself when I look at the world. That is, my observations never include an observation of me as a continuing, thinking person or substance.

Locke said that every judgment we make breaks down into certain kinds of other judgments (complex judgments into simple ones) and these simple ones can be traced to sensation and so forth. Hume comes along and, using the Lockean approach, says, "Well then where do I ever see myself as the one who is receiving these sensations?" It's not just that there are sensations that are coming to

2. David Hume (1711-1776) was a Scottish empiricist philosopher who used empiricism not to formulate a workable philosophy (which one would expect a philosopher to do), but rather to prove the inevitable skepticism that awaits anyone seeking to escape it. He was one of the three British Empiricists next to John Locke (1632-1704) and George Berkeley (1685-1753).

me, but there must be a receiver of these sensations, right? But what if there is no continuing receptor? What if there is just perception-1, perception-2, perception-3, and they have no connection with one another? That's possible, philosophically. If somebody says, "Well that isn't what happens. As a matter of fact, there is one continuing self-conscious receiver," Hume says, "Fine. Show that to me in my observations. Where do I observe the *self-conscious continuation* of my personal identity?"[3]

Hume's problem was that he thought every sensation was separate from every other sensation so that, rather than my perceiving someone as a human body or humanoid—that is, rather than taking you as a whole object—what I am perceiving is the color of your shirt, the shape of your body, the numerical quality of how many eyes, ears, and so forth that you have. All of these sorts of things are coming into my mind, but, according to Hume, I don't know that there is anybody here who can receive that and make sense out of it. So, you are loose and disjoint, and I am loose and disjoint. You can see now that that picture of knowing destroys the possibility of knowing anything.

The comeback to this is to say, as Kant put it, that the unity of apperception has not been dealt with well by modern philosophy at all.[4]

---

3. Bahnsen: Empiricism in our day and age has kind of shaded off into a kind of commonsense perceptual approach where, instead of looking at the cognitive psychology of knowing, we just begin with certain things that everybody knows. Everyone can hold their hand in front of their face and say, "I know that I have a hand with five fingers." But then if you deny that kind of thing, one will ask how you could be rational, how you could even talk to a person, how you could formulate rules of rationality for a person. I don't think that that is a very good argument, but that has been popular in the 20th Century. We do perceive certain things and people aren't being rational if they deny that.

4. Immanuel Kant (1724-1804) was a German transcendental philosopher and one of the most important contributors to modern thought. He will be discussed in more detail in Chapter 5.

Hume asked how it is that I am anything more than a bundle of perceptions. Of course, on Hume's approach he was cheating when he said we are bundles of perceptions. His argument was that we are nothing more than bundles of perceptions and that was enough to destroy science and the possibility of knowing; but, of course, we are not bundles of perceptions, are we? To call us "bundles" already assumes some kind of unity of perception, which is what Hume concluded that we cannot have.[5]

What happened to rationalism? It reduced to subjectivism and therefore skepticism. What happened to empiricism? It also reduced to subjectivism and therefore skepticism.

So what happened to rationalism? It reduced to subjectivism and therefore skepticism. What happened to empiricism? It also reduced to subjectivism and therefore skepticism.

Pragmatist-Type Proofs

The pragmatist sees the problems of the rationalist and the empiricist in terms of their theory of knowledge and essentially says, "I'm going to avoid those pitfalls by telling everybody that they're irrelevant." This is a bold move. They don't always come out and put it this bluntly, but essentially the pragmatist says, "Who cares about Hume's skepticism? We don't need to answer Hume because, after all, we are able to build bridges and cure polio and do all these things. If a certain procedure helps us to adapt to our environment successfully, then it's rational."

---

5. Looking past all of the more philosophical, abstract problems of empiricism as Hume has put forth, at base there is still the underlying logical problem that empiricism cannot live up to its own norms. To propagate that everything we know we know by observation is self-refuting since this idea or thesis itself is not something that is observationally perceived. It is, rather, a taken-for-granted assumption or starting point the empiricist must embrace by which he can operate his philosophy.

For instance, the reason we think inductively is because those who think inductively survive. It is just built into us; we don't have to worry about justifying induction as it is just a pragmatic matter.

Now, the problem with pragmatism is that it presumes to know what ends to seek. We know where we want to go and there is an obligation to go there, *but if you don't have a justification for the normativity of the end that is pursued by what we call rationality, then is rationality justified? No.*[6] So pragmatism reduces to subjectivism.[7] What seems to be the persistent problem in autonomous philosophy? It keeps getting reduced to subjectivism and skepticism.

Pragmatism not only reduces to skepticism in the way the others do, but I want to add that it also is the "chicken" approach to philosophy. It's just a refusal to face the tough questions…"Who cares?"

What seems to be the persistent problem in autonomous philosophy? It keeps getting reduced to subjectivism and skepticism.

Transcendental-Type Proof

The other approach to proof in this albeit very simplistic overview is what I'll call transcendental reasoning.[8] The transcendentalist is not

---

6. Bahnsen elaborates: "How do you justify rational procedure? How do you justify rationality? How do you make rationality itself rational? The pragmatist says because it accomplishes our ends. But you see, that doesn't justify rationality unless you can first justify your ends. And this is what the pragmatist is unable to do."

7. Pragmatism cannot justify whether our ends should be survival of the fittest, or egalitarianism, or anarchism, or hedonism, or scientific advancement, and so on. Since it cannot procure such absolute or objective justification for which ends to seek (and which to avoid), then the result is a subjective outcome: the ends we are trying to seek are ultimately predicated on a person-relative basis.

8. Bahnsen: Up to this point it would be possible for you to have the mistaken idea that when I talk about an empirical approach (for instance) that I am talking

talking about how we learn how to fix a carburetor or who won the war in 1776. *The transcendentalist is talking about how we show the rationality of our own presuppositions.* So I am drawing a distinction between how you justify your basic assumptions—how you show rationality itself to be rational—and what might be considered the higher-level considerations that we engage in intellectually to learn how to fix carburetors, learn about history, etc. I say this because sometimes people who don't like the transcendental approach will say, "Well, how does the transcendentalist give a specific answer to this particular thing over here?" Well, it's not calculated to give you a specific answer to anything; it's calculated to show how it's possible to be rational.[9]

We are talking about how you prove your ultimate assumptions...The transcendentalist is talking about how we show the rationality of our own presuppositions.

If I am a transcendentalist in my reasoning, do I reject empirical *methods*? Do I reject rational *methods*? Do I reject pragmatic *considerations*? Not necessarily. You are not understanding the question

about *particular empirical projects* so that some people would say, "Well, I would justify that particular conclusion by this empirical means," such that when I come along now and suggest transcendentalism as an approach that what I'm saying is I can justify that *particular conclusion* now by transcendental means. But that is *not* what we are talking about. We are talking about how you prove your *ultimate assumptions*. What is the nature of argumentation? What is the nature of proof? The empiricist says that when all is said and done, proof is going to be tied to observation. That means, even at the lowest level, my foundational assumptions have to be observational.

9. To illustrate this difference in simpler terms, a rationalist might argue why a Honda is better than a Ford. An empiricist might argue that a train coming his way is about 300 yards out while another may argue 200. The transcendentalist doesn't care about proving particular, experiential truths as the above; rather, the transcendentalist is asking and arguing for *what the philosophical foundations must be* in order to justify knowing any facts, such as the two given—it's a different plain of reasoning altogether.

properly if you think they all stand over against one another and you can only have one of them like flavors of ice cream. The transcendentalist says that if we know how to justify our ultimate assumptions, we have laid a foundation in terms of which we can now use, not empiricism, but empirical methods; now we can use rational methods; we can even use pragmatic methods. But it won't do you any good to be empirical, rational, or pragmatic if, in the end, the skeptic wins.[10] If someone approaches you and asks how we know ultimately what is and isn't the case, I believe it is only the transcendentalist who can give an answer. Transcendental reasoning seeks the preconditions for the intelligibility of experience in the broadest sense.[11] We are asking that for any kind of experience, how is it intelligible? How can it be that we can communicate and reason about it? How is it possible that there is objective truth in terms of which some of these things are imaginary and others are not? What would have to be true? What would be the precondition in terms of which my experience is intelligible? The transcendental-type arguments that we look at are an attempt to provide the precondition(s)[12] of intelligibility and defeat radical doubt, that is, to defeat skepticism.

---

10. There is a difference between a system of thought (ending with an *-ism*) and a method (*-al*). Empiric*ism* as a system: (a) says that we ultimately *know everything* via observation, and (b) is self-refuting. However, to be empiric*al* is: (a) simply to use your senses in order to draw specific conclusions, and (b) is only a method, not a self-refuting epistemology (in its extreme sense).

11. Bahnsen: Experience can be an internal thing. For instance, I can have an experience internally that has no connection with the outside world such as me imagining that right now I am on the beach in Hawaii even though I am not currently there. Bullet-pointed, experience can be: 1. internal, 2. externally-referent (experience of something), 3. conceptual, 4. visual/spatial, 5. computational, etc.

12. Talking about a singular precondition or multiple preconditions is merely a matter of semantics. The Christian worldview in its entirety being true is the single necessary precondition for intelligibility, but we can also talk about multiple preconditions within that "one" such as the causal principle, uniformity, reliable cognitive abilities, the existence of God, the self-attestation of Scripture, the Trinity of God, etc.

Transcendental reasoning seeks the preconditions
for the intelligibility of experience.

Transcendental reasoning is not an attempt to tell you what theory of childhood cognition is correct, or what theory for curing AIDS is correct, or who the person who made the "shot heard around the world" was. *It is not an attempt to settle any specific issue.* It is, rather, an attempt to show that issues are "settle-able."[13] The transcendental-type proof is an attempt to defeat skepticism, not by appealing to self-evident truths like the rationalists, or perceptual certainties like the empiricists, or to the success that is attainable as the pragmatists talk about, but rather *showing what would have to be true, what the preconditions for the intelligibility of all of our rational procedures are.*

Examining the Cosmological Argument from the Preceding Context

Earlier, I said I believe that the existence of God is objectively provable. Going back and looking at these approaches we've talked about, let's take a look at the cosmological argument for God's existence.[14] The argument tries to show that from a certain concept or principle that we have about the way the world is that God must exist. The specific concept or principle that is used in the cosmological argument is that of causation. Every event has a cause. We all know that. Now, since we have had an experience of causes (what we'll call "secondary causes"), the cosmological argument says that there must be a primary, first cause for this causal network or chain that we have experienced ourselves.

---

13. Bahnsen: We're asking if it is possible to have any settled conviction in the face of skepticism.

14. Here, Bahnsen is referring to the Kalam Cosmological Argument.

The argument thus begins with empirical premises (we have all experienced causation or origination in our lives) and from these observations we generalize that every event or object has a cause or origin. Therefore, the argument goes, the world as a whole must have a cause or an origin and that is what we call God.

There are so many fallacies in this argument, it is just incredible:

1. **Begging the Question**: Can I generalize from many observations that events have causes to all events have causes? No, that's a fallacy. I can't argue from some to all unless I assume the very thing I am supposed to be proving—that causation is a universal principle.[15]

2. **Fallacy of Composition**: Now, if causation is a universal principle, can I say that because each event has *a* (singular) cause that all events together have *a* (singular) cause? No, that is another logical fallacy. What is true of the parts is not necessarily true of the whole. And yet the cosmological argument commits that fallacy.

3. **Equivocation**: Can I argue that from what I know in my natural experience acts as a foundation for what must be true of the supernatural? No. This was Kant's argument: at best, the cosmological argument tells us something about a *natural cause* of all things. It couldn't tell us anything about a supernatural cause or else we would have the fallacy of equivocation. Our premises would mean one thing and our conclusion would mean another when we talk about "causes."

4. **Special Pleading**: If every event has a cause, then naturally we are going to ask what the cause for the event we call God

---

15. As a matter of personal testimony, I once brought this up with a classical apologist (who argures neutrally), to which he defended the universality of the causal principle by arguing "from the impossibility of the contrary," that is, transcendentally. One can't help but see the great irony of an anti-transcendentalist/presuppositionalist apologist arguing in such a manner.

is. Christians here will tend to just say, "Well it has to stop somewhere." To which Arthur Schopenhauer (1788-1860) said, "Why shouldn't it stop at the world?" If you're going to take this taxi and arbitrarily get out of the taxi, then you can just choose where you get out.[16]

So, what is this about? Again, I started out by saying that there is an objective proof for God's existence. Well, the cosmological argument and arguments like it are not going to do it.

A Transcendental Cosmological Argument

How, then, can we objectively prove God's existence? Let me go back to the cosmological argument and try to resurrect it. The argument as it is popularly used makes the mistake of trying to be neutral in our orientation (see previous footnote). "Everybody put aside their presuppositions and let's reason in a neutral way," they'll say. And then they proceed to take observational truths (which are then fallaciously generalized and pushed into the supernatural and such) to show that God exists. But now I am going to go back and give a cosmological argument; not one that says, "Let's put aside our presuppositions and go to our observations and draw

---

16. A few points must be made here: 1. (From the previous footnote) The classical apologist must utilize transcendental reasoning to circumvent question-begging (while presumably opposing transcendental apologetics for, among other things, circularity); 2. The classical apologist, embracing a neutral (or open-minded) perspective, must prove how their argument is exempted from the fallacy of composition *on philosophically-neutral grounds*; 3. The classical apologist must incorporate further premises so as to include the supernatural in order to circumvent equivocation; 4. in charity, a comeback to a Schopenhauerian criticism would be to introduce the delineation between contingent and necessary entities, but even then, the classical apologist must still resolve the above three frustrations, and given his *neutral* approach, he won't be able to in any absolute sense. His only escape would be to cling to an inductive paradigm, arguing only probabilistically (as Bahnsen has already remarked) such that any and all fallacies might be avoided (questionably).

generalizations neutrally," but one that goes back to the causal principle as the "engine."

The causal principle is the foundation of inductive reasoning.[17] But can that be justified? Is it reasonable to expect that we can generalize from particular cases to either properties or to future events? What if we can't? Well, I will take the cosmological argument, pick up its causal principle, and ask the unbeliever, "You need to use the causal principle and inductive reasoning, but is it rational for you to do so?" The general response is for the unbeliever to affirm that it is rational to use them because, after all, scientists use the causal principle and inductive reasoning. But we keep pressing them: "How do you know that it's rational to use the inductive principle? What would have to be true in order for you to use the inductive principle?" The best in the unbelieving world openly admits that there is no justification for induction. They cannot offer us some principle that itself is well-grounded by which we can (absolutely) justify the inductive principle.

What I am getting at is that I am going to offer a proof for the rationality of Christianity that goes like this:

> Without the Christian worldview, rationality itself is unintelligible. The methods you have been using to argue against me as a Christian themselves reduce to subjectivism and skepticism unless you have the Christian worldview as the framework or context for using them.[18]

---

17. Bahnsen: Inductive reasoning says that I can take instances from my experience and generalize from them either across time (generalizing in the present) or ahead in time (generalizing about future events).

18. The presuppositional approach takes the cosmological argument and, rather than pretending neutrality and ignoring the darkness embedded in the unbeliever's mind (cf. John 3:19), focuses solely on the "engine" of the argument—the causal principle. Rather than arguing directly that there must be a first cause, the transcendentalist asks what must be true, or which worldview can make sense out of the causal principle to begin with. It is not a rejection of this natural proof, but rather a reformulation of it to fit into biblical truth (i.e., acknowledging the total depravity of the natural man, acknowledging the antithesis that lies between

Here, I am not appealing to a rational, deductive argument (saying that I have a clear and distinct idea of God's existence), nor am I giving a cosmological deduction, and I am not appealing to empirical evidence or pragmatic success either (although you could rephrase the argument to look deductive, empirical, or pragmatic in various ways).[19]

My Christian apologetic is to this effect: that if you don't have the Christian worldview, you are not able to make sense of reasoning or prove anything at all.

My Christian apologetic is to this effect: that if you don't have the Christian worldview, you are not able to make sense of reasoning or prove anything at all. Ultimately, I am not assuming that the unbeliever is able to prove things rationally or empirically or what have you and now I'm just going to try and satisfy him by giving him enough grist for his mill. It is not that I am going to provide the raw material since he can use his reasoning process and prove God's existence. Rather, I'm going to say that your reasoning process proves God's existence because if God didn't exist, you couldn't even make sense out of reasoning.[20]

---

the believer and unbeliever, and not disregarding our Christian commitments in order to pretend alleged neutrality between the light and the darkness).

19. Bahnsen: Even though you can metaphorically talk about a transcendental argument in these ways, it is a distinct form of reasoning that is asking what the broader framework is in terms of which we do these other things.

20. In a primer logic course, you are introduced to the distinction between an argument and an explanation and what the key differences between them are. Critics of presuppositionalism who scoff at remarks like this all-too-often conflate this clear explanation by Bahnsen as the argument itself. Bahnsen here is *not* attempting to give his argument (in a premise-by-premise fashion).

CHAPTER 3

Why I Believe in God:
Readings and Analysis

Readings and Commentary on *Why I Believe in God*

Without using the language of transcendental proofs, Cornelius Van Til illustrates transcendental reasoning to prove the existence of God in his little booklet *Why I Believe in God*, and I would like to read and do some commentary on a couple of crucial portions from the pamphlet.[1]

In the booklet, Van Til is speaking with an imaginary unbeliever in a dialogue. He has already broached the problem of the unbeliever when he says, "You believe in God because you couldn't help it. You were just brought up to believe in God." At that point Van Til gives his testimony and basically says, "That's right; I was raised to believe in God." And as he goes through this he says:

> The telling of this story has helped, I trust, to make the basic question simple and plain. You know pretty clearly now what sort of God it is of which I am speaking to you.[2] If my God

---

1. The edition cited in this chapter is different from Bahnsen's: Cornelius Van Til, *Why I Believe in God* (Philadelphia, PA: Great Commission Publications).

2. Bahnsen: This is the crucial sentence. Van Til has not been wasting his time as an apologist telling his life story. Why? Because he has been trying to get out before the unbeliever his worldview. He says, "Now you know what kind of God…" Transcendental arguments, as they are used by Christian apologists, are not abstract arguments—they are not dealing with just formal considerations. Van Til is concretely talking about a specific kind of God. He has laid that out.

exists, it was He who was back of my parents and teachers. It was He who conditioned all that conditioned me in my early life. But then it was He also who conditioned everything that conditioned you in your early life. God, the God of Christianity, is the *All-Conditioner!* [3]

As the All-Conditioner, God is the *All-Conscious One.*[4] A God who is to control all things must control them "by the counsel of His will." [5] If He did not do this, He would himself be conditioned. So then, I hold that my belief in Him and your disbelief in Him are alike meaningless except for Him.[6,7]

As Van Til gets closer to the end of the pamphlet, he really starts digging in into the objections raised against his position. For a few pages, he's now going to take that argument of God being the All-Conditioner and drive it home:

It ought to be pretty plain now what sort of God I believe in. It is God, the All-Conditioner. It is the God who created all things, who by His providence conditioned my youth,

---

3. Bahnsen: What Van Til is claiming is that God is the condition behind everything. God is the One who makes things what they are; He makes you the way you are, makes me the way I am, makes the world the way it is—He is the All-Conditioner.

4. Bahnsen: There is nothing real of which God is not conscious. That includes future states and past states. God is the All-Conscious One because there is no area of darkness in His self-consciousness, to use the metaphor. He knows everything thoroughly.

5. Ephesians 1:11.

6. Bahnsen: Because God is the All-Conscious, All-Conditioning God, he says "my belief...and your disbelief...are alike meaningless except for Him." Van Til is now going to ring some philosophical conclusions out of this, namely, that it's not meaningful to argue as an unbeliever. It's not just untrue, but it's not even *meaningful.* And my believing in God wouldn't make any sense—wouldn't be intelligible, would be meaningless—apart from this sort of God existing.

7. Van Til, *Why I Believe in God*, 7.

making me believe in Him, and who in my later life by His grace still makes me want to believe in Him. It is the God who also controlled your youth and so far has apparently not given you His grace that you might believe in Him.

You may reply to this: "Then what's the use of arguing and reasoning with me?" Well, there is a great deal of use in it. You see, if you are really a creature of God, you are always accessible to Him. When Lazarus was in the tomb he was still accessible to Christ who called him back to life. It is this on which true preachers depend. The prodigal thought he had clean escaped from the father's influence. In reality the father controlled the "far country" to which the prodigal had gone. So it is in reasoning. True reasoning about God is such as stands upon God as upon the emplacement that alone gives meaning to any sort of human argument. And such reasoning, we have a right to expect, will be used of God to break down the one-horse chaise of human autonomy.[8]

Deep down in your heart you know very well that what I have said is true. You know there is no unity in your life.[9] You want no God who by His counsel provides for the unity you need. Such a God, you say, would allow for nothing new. So you provide your own unity.[10] But this unity must, by your own definition, not kill that which is wholly new. That really

8. Bahnsen: Van Til is saying here that if you want to argue, you're already resting upon God. Or, in the paraphrase I've begun using, if you want to be in the argument game, you're already assuming God's existence. *Any* kind of argument assumes God['s existence] in order to be intelligible.

9. Bahnsen: You may have many experiences, thoughts, and beliefs, but the unbeliever has no way of bringing them together.

10. Bahnsen: Van Til is saying that the unbeliever will object in that if God foreordains everything, then there is nothing new. Of course, for God there isn't anything new. It's new for us, though. But since the unbeliever doesn't want God to be the Principle of unity connecting all the events in the world and so forth, Van Til challenges him to try and provide that principle of unity himself.

means that it must stand over against the wholly new and never touch it at all. By your logic you talk about possibles and impossibles, but all this talk is in the air.[11] It can never have anything to do with reality.[12] Your logic claims to deal with eternal and changeless matters; and your facts are wholly changing things; and "never the twain shall meet." So you have made nonsense of your own experience.[13]

To pick up on this, if you have the laws of logic, the question is how they can apply to the realm of experience. The unbeliever says, "That's easy, we do it all the time." Yes, but the question is how can we do it all the time. I have a Christian answer to that; what's your answer? Because on your worldview, the laws of logic stand by themselves as unchanging abstract principles, and on your worldview the facts of the world are irrational, changing, flux matters. How do you get abstract unchanging things in connection with concrete, constantly changing things? You can't use both languages. That's like trying to talk German and English at the same time. If you're going to talk the language of abstract formalities, you can't talk the language of concrete details that are always changing.[14] On the unbeliever's worldview they never

---

11. Bahnsen: Again, Van Til is saying that if you have a principle of unity that deals with possibility (what is logically possible, scientifically possible, etc.), you want to hold on to those principles, but you also want to say that those principles don't determine what is going to happen since there would be nothing new, which is why the unbeliever objected to God being the principle that gives unity.

12. Bahnsen: Another way of stating this is that the unbeliever's principles of unity can only be abstract principles—formal principles of logic or statements about causality and nature—but nothing that gives you any detail about what is reasonable, what is natural, and what we know from observation.

13. Van Til, *Why I Believe in God*, 14.

14. This metaphysical problem does not exclusively apply to Platonism either, as the principles/laws/universals man appeals to must always be absolute (unconditioned) in order for there to be intelligible experience—whether abstract entities (Platonism), concepts (Conceptualism), or terms (Nominalism).

meet, but on our worldview they meet. Where? In the mind of God, and God's mind is what controls all the changing details of history as well. So we do know that they meet and we have a picture in terms of which it makes sense to reason in terms of logic and empiricism.[15] But Van Til is saying that on the unbeliever's worldview, *on his own approach*, logic and the facts of experience will never meet, which is why he says to the unbeliever that he has "made nonsense of [his] own experience."

> With the prodigal you are at the swine trough. But it may be that unlike the prodigal you may refuse to return to the father's house.[16, 17]
>
> On the other hand by my belief in God I do have unity in my experience. Not of course the sort of unity that you want. Not a unity that is the result of my own autonomous determination of what is possible. But a unity that is higher than mine and prior to mine. On the basis of God's counsel I can look for facts and find them without destroying

15. Or "empirically." Van Til's apologetic is not only Christian, but also Continental, referring to the past philosophy of Continental Europe. Contrary to analytic philosophy, Van Til's Continental philosophy is (a) more metaphysically-focused than what one would expect from an analytic perspective, and (b) broad in scope, as Bahnsen made reference to in the opening pages. Van Til is not so much concerned with how we're supposed to define "knowledge", or being meticulously analytic over other categories or subcategories of philosophy. Rather, it is aimed at painting the *broad* transcendental (as Bahnsen said) "picture in terms of which it makes sense to reason in terms of logic and empiricism." And with that broad picture captured (the Christian worldview), one can then proceed to be narrowly-analytic if they so wished, as Bahnsen, the analytic philosopher, was.

16. This excerpt is not found in the cited publication/edition above, but is still read by Bahnsen.

17. Bahnsen: Van Til was a very tender Christian man, but this is a very tough-minded analogy. What he is saying is that the unbeliever is at the swine trough *intellectually*. And it may be that he refuses to go back to the father's house, but he needs to realize that the only intellectual option is Christianity.

them in advance.[18] On the basis of God's counsel I can be a good physicist, a good biologist, a good psychologist, or a good philosopher. In all these fields I use my powers of logical arrangement in order to see as much order in God's universe as it may be given a creature to see. The unities, or systems, that I make are true because they are genuine pointers toward the basic or original unity that is found in the counsel of God.[19]

This is where we get Van Til's notion of analogical knowing. God has a system of thought in terms of which He's ordered reality, all truths: conceptual relationships, historical relationships, natural relationships, psychological, volitional. God knows all of these things, and then when I know things, I am thinking God's thoughts after Him.[20] I am discovering these things that God has already thought through (to use the human metaphor). I can find unity in my experience because there is an original unity that God has as the Creator and Controller of all things.[21]

---

18. Bahnsen: Here is a fact: quinine relieves malaria. Van Til says that if I know that fact, then I need to know the concepts of 'quinine,' 'relief,' and 'malaria' and their relationship. If I already know their relationship then I don't need to go look, right? But what if someone says that they don't know their relationship? We respond that if they didn't know their relationship, then they wouldn't know the concepts to begin with. Not fully, at least. Why? Because it could be argued that a person doesn't understand quinine as well as he or she could unless they know that it relieves malaria. So what Van Til is getting at here is that you have to first know it in order to find it *if unity is being provided by our own mind*. Van Til says that on the basis of God's counsel I can look for facts and find them without destroying them in advance. Why? Because God knows them in advance and makes them what they are, and then I discover them thinking God's thoughts after Him using rational, empirical, or pragmatic methods.

19. Van Til, *Why I Believe in God*, 14-15.

20. Cf. Psalm 36:9.

21. Genesis 1:1; Ephesians 1:11.

Looking about me I see both order and disorder[22] in every dimension of life. But I look at both of them in the light of the Great Orderer who is back of them[23].... I see the strong men of logic and scientific methodology search deep into the transcendental for a validity that will not be swept away by the ever-changing tide of the wholly new, only to return and say that they can find no bridge from logic to reality, or from reality to logic. And yet I find all these, though standing on their heads, reporting much that is true.[24] I need only to turn their reports right side up, making God instead of man the center of it all, and I have a marvelous display of the facts as God has intended me to see them.[25]

And if my unity is comprehensive enough to include the efforts of those who reject it, it is large enough even to include that which those who have been set upright by regeneration cannot see[26].... No human being can explain in the sense of seeing through all things, but only he who

22. Bahnsen: I don't think Van Til should have put it that way. What he meant is newness or particularity—that which is not already organized.

23. Bahnsen: Van Til says that "back" of the world there is a God who has ordered everything. I therefore don't have to deny either unity or particularity.

24. Bahnsen: Van Til is saying that these men are all messed up philosophically. They can't bring order and newness, particularity and unity into their experience and make it intelligible. They always have logic over here and they have particularity over there and the two are fighting each other.

25. Bahnsen: Van Til says that if we take man away from being the center, then we won't be reduced to subjectivism and skepticism at every point. We rather have to think God's thoughts after Him. We turn it inside out or right side up.

26. Bahnsen: Van Til is saying that he is offering a unity to my reasoning which is big enough to account even for the unbeliever's thinking. My unity is comprehensive enough to include the efforts of those who reject it. A child is able to slap his father in his face only because his father is holding him on his lap to do so. Unbelievers can slap God's face, they can argue against God; but only because, intellectually, they're sitting on His lap to begin with.

believes in God has the right to hold that there is an explanation at all.[27]

So you see when I was young I was conditioned on every side; I could not help believing in God. Now that I am older I still cannot help believing in God. I believe in God now because unless I have Him as the All-Conditioner, life is chaos.[28]

A Checkpoint Illustration

If you're arguing with somebody who, in essence, says that their view of the world is chance—there is no intelligence behind the world that governs the world, the things that happen, any connection between thoughts and truths, between events and so forth—they have lost the ability to give explanations. In a chance universe there are no explanations. *Ultimately, what appears to explain what happens can't really be an explanation because an explanation relies on principles of unity that relate individual events or individual truths to one another.*

So, then, if someone with this view approaches you, Van Til says that they cannot give explanations or reasons at all. There is no order in their experience, except, of course, the order that you impose on your experience by your own mind. But the problem with that is: 1. Even if you call that order, it would be imposed by your mind, thus making it subjective, not objective, in which case you would be reduced to skepticism; 2. How can the mind impose order on a chaotic universe? You've essentially cut yourself off from understanding anything. Even if it's ordered, it's all internal to you.[29]

---

27. Bahnsen: Only Christianity is in the explanation game. Nobody else can play it. Everybody is trying, of course. But as Van Til says, they're on their heads.

28. Van Til, *Why I Believe in God*, 15-16. Bahnsen breaks here, but a few sentences later Van Til pens one of his most famous lines which sums up his transcendental program (and his discussion with his unbeliever): "I hold...that unless you believe in God you can logically believe in nothing else."

29. To apply this view philosophically, Aristotle's theory of Forms runs into the

Why does Van Til then say he believes in God? Because without God you can't explain anything. All explanation itself assumes a view of the universe that is contrary to anything that doesn't endorse the Christian worldview.

---

same problem. How exactly is the mind capable of "abstracting" from particulars their corresponding Forms unless it were for the triune God's existence? His "god of the spheres" fails to explain this orderly, cognitive process (let alone an unbelieving philosophy which disregards entirely the existence of a deity). And so even the great Aristotle was, as Van Til puts it, on his head.

CHAPTER 4

A Survey of Christian Epistemology: Readings and Analysis

Method of Implication[1]

Let us look now at what Van Til says about the term *transcendental*:[2]

> One more point should be noted on the question of method, namely, that from a certain point of view, the method of implication may also be called a transcendental method.[3]

We have to back up in order to understand this sentence. Van Til has been talking about how we know what we know—the question of method. And he has identified the Christian method of knowing as what he calls the method of implication. That will not communicate to many people, and those to whom it does communicate will probably have the wrong idea because the word *implication* is being used by Van Til here in a very technical, narrow sense.

The term *implication* was used in idealist philosophy for any knowledge-gaining procedure. And the reason it was called implication is because from an idealist standpoint, to know something

---

1. Though a continuation of the same tape in the seminar, Bahnsen continues expositing the transcendental program of Van Til but in a more philosophical light than his pamphlet which takes place in the context of an every-day dialogue.

2. The edition of this work, since it is hard to come by today, is taken instead from an online PDF (https://bit.ly/46pvOow). All page citations will thus be based on the PDF version.

3. Van Til, *A Survey of Christian Epistemology*, 18.

is true is to know it in terms of a coherent theory. Things are never known in isolation. You cannot know just one truth; you have to know the truth in connection with other truths within a coherent system.[4] Therefore, to the degree that we know anything, any method by which we learn things or we draw deductions or inductions is called implication because we are moving out from a proposition to its broader context, thus *implicating* ourselves into the system.

What Van Til, then, is saying in this opening sentence is that he's talked about this method of implication and now calls it a transcendental method. Continuing:

> We have already indicated that the Christian method uses neither the inductive nor the deductive method as understood by the opponents of Christianity, but that it has elements of both induction and of deduction in it, if these terms are understood in a Christian sense.[5]

Van Til says that the Christian transcendental method rejects both deduction and induction if they are understood within the autonomous worldview of the unbeliever. If principles are abstract and stand by themselves (like principles of causation, logic, and mathematics), then we don't have anything to do with them. But, says Van Til, if you think within the Christian worldview, we affirm both deduction and induction. They are necessary for the Christian because the Christian's picture of knowing is that of thinking God's thoughts after Him.

The Picture of Knowing

Let me take another step back and take a look at this "picture of knowing." A good deal of the history of epistemology revolves

---

4. Bahnsen: The coherence theory of truth says that a proposition is true if it's found within a coherent context. The Idealists said that there is only one coherent theory that encompasses everything.

5. Van Til, *A Survey of Christian Epistemology*, 18.

around how we should picture ourselves as knowers. When we know something, what picture do you have given your theory of knowledge? I will give three examples by way of illustration:

1. For Plato, the picture is that of recollection. Plato doesn't just talk about abstract principles of epistemology. He says that when we know something we know its form or its general idea. And the way we know it is because we were familiar with it in a previous life. We've come into this world with a soul encased in a body[6] and the body has a sensation—an experience of the changing world around and about. In all of that, the mind is stimulated to remember duckness, triangularity, justice, etc. **So Plato's picture of knowing is a picture of recollection**.

2. Aristotle comes along and doesn't like Plato's picture. All of his objections against Plato are in the service of a different picture of us as knowers. For Aristotle, we are not being reminded of something that exists separate from us and which we knew in a previous life when we encounter the world. Rather, when I encounter things in the world, my mind is working on them to abstract from them their form. **Aristotle, thus, has an abstractive picture of the knowing process.** When I look and see ducks on the pond, my mind doesn't recollect the form of "duckness" from a previous existence, but rather abstracts from the particular ducks on the pond the form.

Let's jump ahead in the history of philosophy and think about Locke and Kant and their pictures of knowing.

3. What is the picture we have of ourselves as knowers according to Locke? For Locke, the mind is a *tabula rasa*, Latin for "blank tablet" or "blank slate". **The mind is passive and blank and then the senses impinge on that blank tablet.** From this we then combine our sensations into ideas.

---

6. Bahnsen: A pagan doctrine of incarnation.

4. Kant's picture was the complete opposite. Whereas Locke had a passive view of the mind, Kant is more like Aristotle in saying that the mind is active. **The mind actively imposes things on experience to make them intelligible.**[7]

So when we know things, are we recollecting, abstracting, being impinged upon passively, or are we actively forming? What is the Christian view? *Van Til says that we should see ourselves as thinking God's thoughts after Him.* Here is the picture he proposes: God is the original knower; God knows everything, first of all, in and of Himself, and He is the one who planned, created, and controls the universe by His thoughts; when we know things, we therefore need to know the mind of God.

Now, we can do this either by Him directly revealing Himself (God can actually give us in human words what we should think of Him) or directly through the world around and about us.[8] The mind of God is revealed in conceptual order, logical order, causal order, in ethical evaluations and aesthetic judgments. When we go out and experience the world empirically, Van Til says that we are learning about the mind of God. The world *reflects* how God has ordered things. I can learn about "duckness" because God knows the universal for ducks. He knows all of the properties and how they are to be applied. But God also knows particular ducks because He created the particular ducks. So he knows all the particular details and the universals, and when I learn either details or universals by generalization, I am reflecting God's mind. When I make causal

---

7. Bahnsen analogizes the view of the mind in Kant's philosophy to an ice cube tray. Water, in its liquid state, is unordered and unshaped in any substantive sense. However, when put in an ice cube tray (and under certain conditions), the water becomes solidified and compartmentalized; that is, it becomes ordered.

8. There is a third kind of revelation impinged upon man by God and that is man's being made in His image. Everything man does quite literally "images" his Maker in terms of being a moral and self-conscious creature. Man cannot efface this knowledge no matter how hard he tries.

judgments (back to quinine relieving malaria), if what I say about that is true then I am learning what the mind of God has done in ordering the universe.

Now, if we think God's thoughts after Him, *we must think deductively.*[9] Why is that? Because in God's mind there is perfect coherence. Thus, not only is logic permissible to the Christian, but Van Til says that logic is required for the Christian. It is not a virtue for a Christian to be illogical. To review what has been said before, Van Til believes in the use of empirical methods and in logic. He says that it's not only permissible but required because we have to think God's thoughts after Him. We can't create reality in our own image, so we have to study and research. And you don't have the right to arbitrarily draw conclusions either; you have to think in a coherent way as God thinks coherently.[10]

> Now when these two elements are combined, we have what is meant by a truly transcendental argument. A truly transcendental argument takes any fact of experience which it wishes to investigate, and tries to determine what the presuppositions of such a fact must be, in order to make it what it is.[11]

---

9. Bahnsen: Deductive reasoning draws conclusions from premises with certainty because there are laws of logic or binding laws which tell us how to use the words 'all', 'some', 'not', 'if', 'then', 'or', and 'and'. However, this is simply first-order predicate logic; there are other kinds of logics.

10. Bahnsen doesn't elucidate enough that this is not a rejection of inductive or abductive reasoning, only that all reasoning must be deductive in the sense that all knowledge or truths draw back *with certainty* to God's creative decree. There is no aspect of ignorance or impersonalism in the universe and the edifice of knowledge itself. All truths are certainly tethered to the Truth.

11. Van Til, *A Survey of Christian Epistemology*, 18.

> A truly transcendental argument takes any fact of experience which it wishes to investigate, and tries to determine what the presuppositions of such a fact must be, in order to make it what it is.

Van Til says that our argument does not depend on special kinds of information. He says, "I don't have to look at a fact that is a miracle fact; I can take any fact, whatever you want to talk about. You want to talk about electricity? Medicine? The Opera? That's fine."

If I talk about electricity, for instance, and I give someone certain facts about electricity, you can't understand what electricity is without knowing some other things besides electricity. You can't understand it (or anything for that matter) in a vacuum.[12] Van Til asks how it is possible to make a judgment concerning any particular fact. What presuppositions are necessary in order to make sense out of that judgment? What else would have to be true in order to make sense of what you are saying? And that, simply, is the transcendental method.[13]

An exclusively deductive argument would take an axiom such as that every cause must have an effect, and reason in

---

12. Bahnsen: No one can believe just one thing without believing anything else as the context. Try to believe just one thing and don't believe anything about the context or the language that's used to express that fact—just try to believe that one thing. Of course, that's impossible. *All of our beliefs come in clusters.* You can't have one belief by itself.

13. Though this will be expanded later on, there are two types of transcendental arguments the apologist can use: a conceptual transcendental argument and a metaphysical transcendental argument. In *asking what presuppositions are necessary* in order to make sense out of anything is to make a conceptual or epistemological transcendental argument. Here we are simply asking what we must believe conceptually in order to make intelligible our knowledge of any fact. However, the metaphysical version *asks what must be objectively true outside of us in order to make facts intelligible in the first place,* this latter one being more powerful in nature. The two preceding questions before this footnote were asked by Bahnsen in the same order.

a straight line from such an axiom, drawing all manner of conclusions about God and man. A purely inductive argument would begin with any fact and seek in a straight line for a cause of such an effect, and thus perhaps conclude that this universe must have had a cause. Both of these methods have been used, as we shall see, for the defense of Christianity. Yet neither of them could be thoroughly Christian unless they already presupposed God. Any method, as was pointed out above, that does not maintain that not a single fact can be known unless it be that God gives that fact meaning, is an anti-Christian method.[14]

What does this expression mean? To give a "fact meaning?" To put it bluntly, it means to give any particular sensation a context in terms of which it's connected to other things. Right now I am sensing Mike Butler's shoe. But in order for that sensation to make sense I had to understand that there was a shoe connected to a foot, I have to understand what shoes are for, I have to understand what the English word 'shoe' means, and so forth. Van Til says that we don't just have brute sensations; they are, rather, interpreted and therefore meaningful. Particulars are connected to other particulars and therefore there is a pattern of meaning.

On the other hand, if God is recognized as the only and the final explanation of any and every fact, neither the inductive nor the deductive method can any longer be used to the exclusion of the other. That this is the case can best be realized if we keep in mind that the God we contemplate is an absolute God.[15] Now the only argument for an absolute God that holds water is a transcendental argument. A deductive

---

14. Van Til, *A Survey of Christian Epistemology*, 18-19.

15. Bahnsen: "Absolute" means unqualified; without restriction. God is unrestrictedly God. Nothing keeps Him from exercising His sovereign prerogative.

argument as such leads only from one spot in the universe to another spot in the universe.[16] So also an inductive argument as such can never lead beyond the universe. In either case there is no more than an infinite regression. In both cases it is possible for the smart little girl to ask, "If God made the universe, who made God?" and no answer is forthcoming… But if it be said to such opponents of Christianity that, *unless there were an absolute God their own questions and doubts would have no meaning at all, there is no argument in return.* There lie the issues.[17] (emphasis, Bahnsen)

People may have, what seems to be on the surface, strong considerations against God. But Van Til's apologetic doesn't say, "Well, give us enough time and we'll work out an answer to everything that comes down the pipe." We can do that, too, to be sure. However, Van Til says that you couldn't even make sense of your argument if the God you are arguing against didn't exist.[18] I would like to give an illustration with ethics of this point to help since the realm of ethics is what is most known to people (over against epistemology and metaphysics).

Let's say somebody comes to me and says, "Dr. Bahnsen, how could you possibly believe in a God who allows all of these evil, wicked things to happen in the world?" Maybe I could come up with

---

16. Bahnsen: This is Van Til's metaphorical way of saying what Kant did—that deductive arguments for God are only dealing with the way our mind works with our phenomenal experience of the natural world. It never leads to another spot (or conclusion) outside of the universe.

17. *A Survey of Christian Epistemology*, 19.

18. This is a crucial point. Notice how in a matter of a few short sentences Van Til goes from arguing about what presuppositions must be held to (a conceptual transcendental argument), to arguing over an existence claim (a metaphysical/ontological transcendental argument). There is no either-or situation here, and the interchanging of these transcendental versions is wholly dependent upon the context of the discussion with the non-Christian.

an answer to every single thing that the unbeliever is unsatisfied with. But Van Til asks, "Why even get started going down that line when the best thing to say is that their very objection presupposes the thing they're objecting to?" How is that? Assuming a person approached me and argued that since evil things happen in this world, God can't exist. I say back to him, "That argument presupposes that God exists because if God didn't exist you couldn't call anything evil and wicked, ultimately." No matter what direction that argument goes, *as an argument* it presupposes the existence of God, and that is why no argument can ever disprove God because as an argument it assumes the Thing it's trying to disprove.

Now, there are psychological problems with the Problem of Evil, no doubt about it. If I tell someone that God has a morally sufficient reason for what He does, but you can't call anything good or evil if you don't have God to begin with, that doesn't automatically mean that you feel easy about the evil that you see in this world. I understand there are problems. But there can't be a logical or intellectual problem with the Christian worldview if someone is going to assume an absolute distinction between good and evil and then try to argue against God because God is the presupposition[19] for an *absolute* distinction between good and evil.

It is the firm conviction of every epistemologically self-conscious Christian[20] that no human being can utter a single syllable, whether in negation or in affirmation, unless it were for God's existence.[21]

---

19. Or "transcendental."

20. Bahnsen: Meaning we're not being arbitrary by just following our emotions and feelings, but rather that we are being reflective and thinking about ourselves and being consistent in our theory of knowledge.

21. Van Til, *A Survey of Christian Epistemology*, 19.

Another way of putting it is that the only way you can argue with me is by talking to me, but you couldn't utter a syllable, you couldn't make sense out of language, without the Christian worldview. Therefore, if you talk at all, you're assuming the worldview that you're arguing against.[22]

> Thus the transcendental argument seeks to discover what sort of foundations the house of human knowledge must have, in order to be what it is.[23] It does not seek to find whether the house has a foundation, but it presupposes that it has one. We hold that the anti-Christian method, whether deductive or inductive, may be compared to a man who would first insist that the statue of William Penn on the city hall of Philadelphia can be intelligently conceived of without the foundation on which it stands, in order afterwards to investigate whether or not this statue really has a foundation.[24] It should be particularly noted, therefore,

---

22. The use of language assumes a continuation in meaning of terms, a continuation in the use of their consistent applicability, the existence of non-atomic entities (letters, numbers, punctuation marks, subjects, predicates, nouns, direct objects, etc.) and a coherent, metaphysical connection between these immaterial entities and the material world (specifically, the brain (and mind)), a self-conscious knower who can apply this meaning, an ability to interrelate letters, numbers, words, and sentences, the law of identity, a principle of individuation between experiences, etc., all of which can only be accounted for on the Christian worldview. The exclusivity of the Christian worldview to account for these preconditions will be explained later.

23. Bahnsen: We're not arguing about what the house of knowledge is. We're taking it for what it claims to be.

24. Bahnsen: This was not a well-chosen illustration by Van Til because if you're not familiar with Philadelphia and its landmarks, you won't know what he is talking about. The statue of William Penn is on a pinnacle at the City Hall. [You can't conceive of the statue being there without first presupposing that it has a foundation.] Likewise, when we argue with people, we are taking for granted that this life we live is intelligible, that there is meaning in this world, that explanation is possible, that you can give reasons for things. Van Til says that we must ask what the foundation for this is. What allows us to give reasons? To make sense out of our experience?

that only a system of philosophy that takes the concept of an absolute God seriously can really be said to be employing a transcendental method. A truly transcendent God and a transcendental method go hand in hand.[25]

You can't use this argument for the limited God of Arminianism. Van Til is pointing out that if you don't have a sovereign, creator God, this argument isn't going to work. The sort of God we are talking about is crucial—He has to be an absolute God, not One who is limited by external conditions. Arminians are our Christian brothers and sisters, but we have to point out that their theology doesn't enable them to have the strongest type of apologetic.

---

25. Van Til, *A Survey of Christian Epistemology*, 19.

CHAPTER 5

Kant in Context

"Kant in Context" is a history of what transcendental argumentation is all about and what Van Til is hooking onto. Clearly, Van Til was not a Kantian. In fact, he has spent his scholarly career refuting Kant and post-Kantian ways of thinking, especially as they came in the expression of Neo-Orthodoxy and other theological apparitions. Nevertheless, Kant's project becomes the heart of Van Til's way of defending the faith. As such, it would be valuable for us to have an appreciation for the historical setting and what Kant himself said. It will also give a background for what Michael Butler does in the next couple of chapters.

To put Kant in context we are going to talk about his precursors:

1. Continental Rationalism as was seen in the philosophies of Descartes, Spinoza, and Leibniz. This school of thought was called "continental" because it took place on continental Europe.

2. British Empiricism as was seen in Locke (English), Berkeley (Irish), and Hume (Scottish).

After these two major schools of thought, Kant comes along and offers the transcendental approach, also known as **critical philosophy.** It is "critical" because he is looking for the foundations of both rationalism and empiricism—the transcendental which makes it possible to reason both logically and empirically.

Both rationalism and empiricism accepted the autonomous point of reference that is found in Descartes's intellectual method. Recall Chapter 2 where Descartes tried to doubt everything he could. "Is there any way that I could know something beyond doubt?" He concluded that his existence was beyond doubt: "I think, therefore I am." The point, though, is that Descartes assumed the self-sufficiency of man, that man could be his own starting point. There are a lot of things that are questionable about life, things outside my mind, etc., but the one thing that is not questionable is my own existence, he said. Everything would ultimately have to pass the standard of him being the final reference point. My point being that both the rationalists and empiricists assumed the centrality of man. *But what did we say happens when you begin with man? It reduces to subjectivism and then skepticism. Since everything pivots around man—his thinking, his authority, etc., since he is the point of reference—it shouldn't surprise you that when we start criticizing their philosophy, it reduces down to man himself and his subjective point of view. And since that isn't absolute and beyond doubt, it reduces to skepticism.*

Continental Rationalism

The Continental Rationalists all agreed on two things: 1. There are self-evident truths from which we can deduce substantial conclusions about reality; 2. We should search for certainty in our knowledge where mathematics is the ideal of knowledge. We have, of course, already criticized the rationalists (and empiricists) in Chapter 2. If these are self-evident truths, why did the three of them arrive at radically different conclusions about reality? One was a dualist, one was a monist, and one was an atomist!

If the indubitability of these self-evident ideas is their clearness and distinctness to me, notice that indubitability is tied to an internal and subjectivistic reference point.

The rationalists had a supreme confidence in the intellect's ability to solve human problems and to know reality as something that is rational.[1] However, if the indubitability of these self-evident ideas is their clearness and distinctness to me, *notice that indubitability is tied to an internal and subjectivistic reference point.* It's something in me, not outside of me, thus being something *subjective.* But there are other problems to consider.

If I look at an apple and I observe its "redness", whenever we encounter a property of an object there is an unperceived substance present. If any object of thought is multi-propertied, then there must be a substance that "holds" the properties together. Apples aren't just red, but also spherical, crisp, sweet, etc. Why aren't all of these things just loose and disjointed? Because the apple is a *substance* that has the properties red, sphere, crisp, etc. Thus, for Descartes, there must be an unperceived substance that is present. The key here is that the substance is unperceived. Have you ever seen what binds the redness, crispness, sweetness, etc. together? Of course not.

So in order to think clearly, I must assume that there is a substance. But I don't see a substance; I only see the properties of the alleged substance: mind and body substance. Some substances are not extended in space like souls or minds. Others, like apples and giraffes, are extended in space.

Now, Spinoza also wants to deduce the nature of reality from clear and distinct ideas. By definition, Spinoza says, a substance must be independent of other things.[2] But if substances are independent of properties, then he concluded that there must only be one substance. There can only be one independent thing since, if there are two things, then they're conditioned by each other. When you

---

1. Bahnsen: And since they believed reality is rational, you can see how they believed that education was the key to enlightenment. In order to solve man's problems we must be educated.

2. Bahnsen: Because a substance is what binds the properties together and makes one apple different from another apple.

think about it, this is a brilliant argument.[3] Therefore, says Spinoza, all is one, and what we call this one substance of reality is "nature" (or "god" if you're religious). So for him, physics and psychology are deductive sciences. They are not sciences where you go out and observe empirically and learn about the world, but rather that you can deduce the nature of the world, knowing that it's one substance.

Leibniz used Spinoza's starting point of saying that substance is wholly independent and drew an opposite conclusion. Since substance is independent, then there must be a plurality of independent things that don't have any relationship to one another. That is what makes them independent. *To put it another way, for Spinoza the independence of substance is gained by everything depending on it. For Leibniz, the independence is gained by nothing interacting with anything. Thus, Leibniz said that reality is made up of a number of "windowless monads."* They're windowless because they cannot have any interaction with other monads.

Both Spinoza and Leibniz were eventually dismissed as "dream philosophers" who had gained coherence in experience in an artificial way. By their artificial conceptions of unity or independent pluralities they had coherence, but it was all a "dream philosophy." You can understand, then, why the British Empiricists wanted to get away from all the abstruse speculations of the Continental philosophers.[4]

British Empiricism

The British Empiricists all said that there are no innate ideas (contra the Continental Rationalists), that only particulars exist, and third, that we should seek commonsense in observation and practicality.

---

3. A reminder from Bahnsen's compliment here that presuppositionalism does not endorse the position that non-Christians can't or don't know anything.

4. Being a country which originated from Great Britain, the American mindset (especially in today's day and age) is sympathetic to the empirical mindset of "seeing is believing" as our British forefathers had. American readers of this literature will almost invariably come to the same conclusion of the British Empiricists in wanting to get away from all of this "armchair" speculation of the Continental Rationalists.

Alright, so there are no innate ideas. Do we know that empirically? Uh-oh. The Empiricists said that everything we know we know based off of sensation. But there are no sensations one can have that will justify that there are no innate ideas.[5] Is empiricism presupposition-less and neutral, then? No. Empiricism is a dogma as Quine put it. Empiricism is prejudiced: it begins with a philosophical assumption and then after that says, "Alright, no more philosophical assumptions."

I am not kidding you when I say that there are no more sophisticated empiricists today. There are many people who defend empirical methods as the model of rationality, but the idea that there are no innate ideas? No, there are none. People account for innate ideas differently such as conventionalists, linguistic conventionalists, behaviorists, and so forth. But you couldn't know anything if there wasn't cognitive background to your experience. All observations are theory-dependent.

Secondly, empiricism says that only particulars exist. Well, if only particulars exist, notice that there can be no unity among the particulars because this thing we call "unity" is not itself a particular. There can't be *kinds* of things because a kind of thing like "duckness" is not particular, but universal.[6] And if there are no connecting principles between things, then you can't even say that an apple is an apple. To say that something is an apple is to assume this thing called

---

5. See Chap. 2, footnote 10.

6. An easier illustration concerning discussions of universals and particulars would center around concepts such as "kindness", which is a "-ness" more linguistically-familiar than talk of "duck-ness" or "car-ness", etc. In order for someone to be able to identify *particular* instances of a person/people being kind, one must first be acquainted with the *universal* or concept of "kindness" by which all particular instances are made intelligible under that umbrella. Moreover, the material-immaterial nature between particulars and universals can be illustrated by observing that only material agents (persons) can be kind and live suspended in material reality. But whereas I could accidentally hit a *particular*, material, kind person with my bike whilst not paying attention, I could never hit (accidentally or otherwise) the *universal* or concept of "kindness". It makes no sense telling someone that you accidentally hit "kindness" the last time you rode your bike.

substance—that the properties are united or indexed together as an apple. But you don't see the indexing of properties. Further, if only particulars exist, then there can be no causality because you can have a particular event and another particular event, but you can never say that there is a necessary connection between those two events.[7]

John Locke said that the substance that we think about that indexes properties and individuates particulars is a substratum for qualities. It is something that underlies the qualities like a pin cushion underlies the pins that are in it. But when pushed on what exactly this substance was, Locke openly said, "I know not what." (In passing, Locke said there were no innate ideas, but when it came to political theory he argued for inalienable rights. How do you bring those two things together in a worldview? How can it be inalienable if it's not innate?)

While Locke admitted that he knew "not what" what substance is, Berkeley argued that to be is to be perceived, and therefore there are no abstract ideas. Nothing exists in abstraction. Everything that exists is concrete and it must be perceived in order to exist. However, matter is an unperceived, abstract idea. Has anyone ever perceived matter?[8] No. Material substance is unperceived and therefore doesn't exist. Thus, Berkeley argued that there is no material reality. Okay, well what about materiality? Even sensations of materiality are mind-dependent, and so all reality is ultimately mental.[9]

Hume comes along and basically says, "Well, I can do you an even greater favor, Berkeley. You've gotten rid of Descartes's material

---

7. Because a "necessary connection" is not something that is *particular*ly material or observable. As with the previous footnote, you can't accidentally drive over or lick or befriend an (immaterial) necessary connection.

8. Bahnsen: I'm not talking about things that are material. The property of materiality may be there concretely in something, but the *idea* of matter is abstract.

9. Bahnsen: That is why you have this odd combination in Berkeley of a man who was an empiricist, but an idealist. He takes empirical presuppositions and pushes them to idealistic conclusions about the nature of reality.

substance, but if we're going to be really honest empiricists then we're going to have to get rid of mental substance, too." Why? Because earlier we talked about how there is nothing that gives unity to my perceptions if only particulars exist. I'm only a bundle of perceptions, and even then it's cheating to say that. For Hume, in order for something to exist it has to be traced back to a sensation, and we never have sensations of any connecting principles between our experiences. We don't have any psychological connecting principles and therefore there is no "me", there is no continuing personal identity. We don't have any perception of physical, connecting principles either and therefore there is no causation in the world. There is just one event followed by another random event and so on. Every experience is a separate isolated unit of consciousness. There is no necessity in the world of thought or experience, and there is no necessity in the world that is outside the mind which leads to there being no basis of a knowledge of the external world of enduring objects, no basis for a knowledge of causality among objects, nor is there a continuing self that could know the causation between objects.

If you wanted to just choose a term out of philosophy of this view, what would it be called? How about 'skepticism'? This is radical! How did Hume deal with this skepticism? He said that when these problem got him down, he went and played backgammon with his friends. That is such an honest admission, I'm glad he said that. Hume admitted that we do think causally, but that there is no rational basis for it. That is why he is a skeptic.

Checkpoint

To appreciate Kant, you can see how the "Age of Reason" ended in subjectivism and skepticism whether you were a rationalist or an empiricist, and that led to a collapse in confidence in man's intellectual ability and the objectivity of knowledge. Particularly, the objectivity of knowledge of a real, orderly world. Neither the rationalist nor the empiricist were able to find a reliable method of knowing. It turns out that there were major disagreements over this instrument called 'reason' and what reason is supposed to be.

It's one thing for the unbelieving world to say that they exalt reason. But if you were an analytic philosopher, you would have to ask, "What are you talking about when you speak of reason? Are you talking about reason as Spinoza understood it? Leibniz? Berkely? Locke? Hume? Who? What is 'reason' in the 'Age of Reason?'" It means a million different things, *and Kant was scandalized by that*.[10]

Immanuel Kant

The rationalists and the empiricists both reduced themselves to subjectivism and skepticism. Kant, in particular, wrote that he was "awakened from his dogmatic slumbers" by Hume, and thus Kant was led to alter the view of reason which he had previously held. That is why the title of his best-known and most important book is titled *Critique of Pure Reason* (1781). It is considered to be very obscure and prolix, but is nevertheless considered to be his masterpiece. The *Critique of Practical Reason* (1788) and the *Critique of Judgment* (1790) were two of his other famous books. We can see again why his philosophy is considered to be *critical*.

Kant came to such a new view of reason that he said it amounted to a Copernican Revolution in philosophy. As such, Kant said that Locke was wrong to think the mind is passive; rather, it is active. In order to make sense of our thoughts, the mind has to make them sensible, and not only sensible, but also intelligible. How, then, does the mind make these thoughts sensible? It always attributes to those

---

10. Recall the material in Chapter 3, footnote 15 concerning the narrow, scrupulous nature of analytic philosophy: "How exactly are we to define knowledge?" as opposed to a transcendental philosophy of, "What needs to be the case in order for knowledge to even be possible?" To be sure, "knowledge" requires a definition, but to wed oneself to an analytic viewpoint, you must answer that question only in a narrow and therefore tentative sense, this tentativeness underscored by, for instance, the recent Gettier Problem in epistemology.

sensations coming in time-and-space predicates. The mind actively imposes order on the chaos of the world that we encounter. Of course, that is assuming that there is a world out there.[11] We don't know things the way they are; we only know things by the way we experience them. But as we experience them, we impose temporal and spatial characteristics—we impose order on our sensations.

However, we not only make our sensations sensible (part of time and space), but we also make them intelligible because we have to categorize them. Our sensations have to be formed as things that are understood causally, substantially, numerically, and so forth. So Kant goes through his *Critique of Pure Reason* all of these categories in terms of which we must think.[12]

Hume had destroyed the notion of causation and therefore inductive reasoning since we never observe it empirically. If our minds are passive and we only know what impinges on our minds, causation is never impinged on our mind because nothing necessary can be particular and we only sense particular things. Hume's final word on why we think causally in the first place is because it's just a habit of the mind.

Kant comes along and says that he can save science, causation, and substance. How did he do it? He said that it's just a habit of the mind. Do you get it? *Kant just took Hume's despairing conclusion and made it the answer to Hume's skepticism.*[13]

Kant also had a portion of his *Critique* that he reserves for the categories of God, the world, and the self. On these he said that

----

11. Kant's view of the unknowability of the external world is, as Alvin Plantinga pointed out, self-refuting. If we cannot know anything of an external, noumenal world, then Kant wouldn't even postulate it and therefore his phenomenal-noumenal divide in the first place.

12. The 12 categories Kant said the mind imposes on the sensations coming to us are unity, plurality, totality, reality, negation, limitation, substance and accident, cause and effect, community, possibility, existence, and necessity.

13. Bahnsen points out that there is obviously more behind Kant's argument, but at base Kant just took Hume's conclusion and made it the answer.

though we have to think in terms of these other categories like substance and cause, we can't draw conclusions from them about god, the world, and the self—they are only limiting notions. The only god that could be intelligible to us would have to be a god that has a cause, but we know better than to say that. So that is just a way of thinking by which we limit all of our causal reasoning. We eventually stop and call that god, but we don't really intelligibly know god.

For Kant, god was part of the noumenal realm; that is, god exists as a thing in itself (German, *ding an sich*) and thus we cannot really know this god. We only know him (or it) as he or it appears to us, and god would have to appear to us in categories amenable to our way of thinking. Our thinking is causal; therefore, god can't appear to us in a miraculous way, because for us to think rationally about anything is to reject miracles.

What does all of this rest on? It rests on the assumption that we do not know the objective world; we only know the internal, phenomenal world—the world as it is experienced by us. And since *that* world is itself formed or made intelligible by the activity of the mind, then naturally what we think (in terms of the categories) is necessary. What is it necessary by? Psychological habit: "It's a habit of the mind."

Concepts without percepts are empty;
percepts without concepts are blind.

So, then, where does Kant's philosophy end up on the spectrum between his rational and empirical predecessors?

- Against Rationalism, Kant said that there are no innate ideas. According to him nothing can be known rationally apart from experience. The mind, though it makes experience intelligible to us by the use of its 12 categories, does not in itself have ideas embedded in it inherently. So here he is against the rationalists and favors the empiricists.

- But against Empiricism, Kant said that the mind is not a *tabula rasa*. The mind is not passive, but is rather a constructive, active agent, so that what we know is to be attributed not just to the world outside us, but also to the activity of the mind constructing a world that is intelligible to us.[14]

To use the famous line for which Kant is known: concepts without percepts are empty; percepts without concepts are blind. That is, if you only have perceptions and they are not made intelligible by concepts, then they are blind. But if you only have concepts (like causation, substance, limitation, etc.) without perceptions, then they would be empty.

Kant claimed to save science and make room for faith in his philosophy. How did he save science? He resurrected the causal principle, the principle of unity between perceptions, substance, and so forth. However, he saved science by claiming that the objects of knowledge must conform to the knowing process. *Essentially, Kant saved science by subjectivizing it.* Science becomes a necessity of our subjective thinking process.

Do we find natural laws? Sure we do. But that is because our understanding/mind *imposes* those laws; it doesn't find them out in the ether somewhere as if they exist objectively external to us. Kant was, accordingly, a metaphysical agnostic. He didn't know reality, and yet he held to the certainty of the knowing process by subjectivizing it. *Now what did we say earlier when philosophies are reduced to subjectivism? They end in skepticism.*

———————————

14. It is crucial to understand how Kant's program is a constructive program. It is constructive in that it is the mind which "constructs" the intelligibility of human experience through the use of 12 categories. Footnote 13 in Chapter 4 referenced the two types of transcendental arguments the apologist can use: conceptual and ontological. Kant's transcendental program is a third type of transcendental argumentation (though it is a cousin of a conceptual transcendental argument), but it has no legitimacy in presuppositional apologetics because of its endorsements of both autonomy and Idealism.

For all of what Kant was trying to do in his transcendental thought, Kant himself succumbs to skepticism as well. If nothing else, Kant never gets beyond the egocentric predicament because if Kant is right about how his mind must think in a certain way, *Kant doesn't show us that all minds must think in that way.* He thought he did, but he didn't really. Much more, he did not show that if all minds must think this way that the objects of the mind must be like that.

Kant called his position **transcendental idealism.** The reason he used that language is that he said that a transcendental is what is presupposed by experience in order for it to be experienced. I believe it is easier to say that it is what is presupposed to make experience intelligible. Experience is automatically intelligible for Kant because he argued that experience is formed by the mind. But outside of/ setting aside Kant's philosophy, we would say that a certain experience (or experience as a whole) is only made intelligible to us by certain presuppositions. Those presuppositions are the transcendentals.[15]

Transcendental analysis asks what the preconditions for the intelligibility of human experience are.

Transcendental analysis, thus, asks what the preconditions for the intelligibility of human experience are. Or another way of putting it is asking under what conditions is it possible to make sense of the world or to rationally experience it. Why don't we just stop our Christian apologetical search with Kant, then? As I've already

---

15. Conceptual transcendentals, or what must be cognitively held as opposed to the existence-aspect of those transcendentals. Pertinant to apologetics, for the unbeliever to say that he just presupposes that his senses work properly, or that nature is uniform, or that there are laws of logic is not an avenue out of subjectivism and skepticism. You can presuppose anything you want, but if you cannot *metaphysically* justify or tether the explanation or origin of those presuppositions themselves, and if you cannot exhaustively achieve cohesion between *all* of your presuppositions in a worldview-fashion, then you just end up in the same skepticism-ridden boat as Kant.

indicated, Kant's transcendental analysis is subjective. It doesn't give us any metaphysical information. Additionally, his transcendental analysis is *psychological* and assumes without any warrant the universal psychological operations of men (that is, taking for granted that all people's minds work the same way).[16]

According to Kant, reality could not be understood by a single, unified, common set of principles. To understand nature you have to use causal principles. But to understand morality and human personality (which I have not mentioned) you have to use principles of freedom. So even on his own approach, there are two wonders—"the starry heavens about and the moral within"—and he can't bring these two things together. He basically said that the way you understand the physical cosmos will not help you understand the moral law and vice versa: the physical cosmos is governed by causation and determinism, but morality presupposes freedom and indeterminism. *Kant admitted that and just left it out there.*

So does he have a unified worldview? No. I therefore do not believe that his transcendental arguments save science as he thought because they really succumb to subjectivism, and he doesn't save philosophy in general because he doesn't have a common principle by which you can account for things and to give explanations.

There is one final comment about Kant I would like to make just to understand why Van Tillians like what he was trying to do but not the way he did it. Did Kant save human personality? The unity of a person? Hume said that we are only bundles of perceptions, and twice now I've indicated that he doesn't have the right to say

---

16. Bahnsen: Kant himself thought that in the nature of the case [thinking proceeds by way of the 12 categories]. He thought he was analyzing thinking, per se, and so if you want to talk about reason, Kant said, then we have to talk about what he is talking about. But how do you interpret that reply? Is Kant saying that if we're not using terms in the same way then we are not using the same conceptual scheme? Is he a cultural relativist? Probably not. But on the other hand he wasn't trying to make some empirical psychological observation for which you can have sufficient evidence. Kant left some things unexamined (or, at best, ambiguous).

"bundle." He argued that there is no unity between perceptions so there couldn't be any person to have the experience. Kant realizes that that is devastating so he argued that there must be a unity of thinking—a subject who thinks. But according to him, that subject cannot be known observationally.[17] The subject of thinking can only be known through its thinking. That is, we only know ourselves in the act of knowing. In that case, in knowing myself, Kant says that I only know a place marker. The human person is diaphanous: when I look at myself as a knower, I am really looking through me because the only "me" there is is this place marker for all of these experiences that are coming in.

Apologetical Assessment of Kant's Transcendental Approach

We obviously do not find this to be adequate in apologetics. Again, God cannot be known because He is in the noumenal realm, and any god that you could rationally know would have to be subject to scientific determinism (no miracles, etc.). The only god you could know would be one which stands behind the moral law as a limiting notion that there will be a day of judgment if we don't live up to the rational, moral law within us. But that moral law can't be related to the world that we know rationally about us either. And finally, we don't even know ourselves except as a philosophical necessity or place holder for some *thing* to unify a perception.

---

17. Bahnsen: Having mirrors doesn't help this problem because you may observe a physical body in the mirror, but you're not observing *the mind* that *experiences* and *unites* all of those experiences.

CHAPTER 6

Non-Transcendental Attempts to Answer Skepticism

Having introduced Kant in his context, I would like to talk briefly about transcendental arguments in the context of modern philosophical argument.

In the case of Kant, we see that the transcendental approach is distinct because he is not looking for observations to justify his philosophy; he is not an empiricist. But he isn't trying to look for clear and distinct ideas from which he can deduce the nature of reality either, so he isn't a rationalist. Rather, he is asking what must be true in order to make sense of my thinking of the sciences, as a logician, as an ordinary individual, etc. He is asking for the presuppositions of the intelligibility of any experience.

Now, in modern epistemology you can think of their strategies as being various responses to skepticism. The reason why we need a theory of knowledge is, to put it bluntly, because there are skeptics. It is possible to ask skeptical questions about what we know. When we answer questions on how we know what we know, we get pushed back to assumptions that we have been using, and then the skeptic is going to keep pressing how we know about those assumptions. But eventually, we reach what we call **fundamental assumptions**. Can your fundamental assumptions be rationally justified (or can rationality be justified)? The answer of the skeptic is no. Fundamental assumptions cannot be rationally justified, and therefore all belief systems are ultimately arbitrary. Why? Because the standards of justification also need justification if you're going to be rational—you'll either have an infinite regress of justifications or you'll reach some level of commitments that is not rational.[1] These are the horns of the dilemma.

If the skeptic cannot be answered, then we have given way to intellectual anarchy or dogmatism.[2] We're left, then, with skepticism needing an answer if we are going to save rationality. The attempts to meet the skeptical challenge can be divided into three parts.

The Foundationalist Attempt

Foundationalism unites various epistemologies which want to eliminate arbitrariness, prejudice, unwarranted conjecture, and relativism in our thinking, and attempts to attain cognitive certainty that isn't just a cognitive psychological assurance. And the way in which we attain cognitive certainty, according to the foundationalists, is to anchor our beliefs in some kind of foundation—a foundation of propositions which are themselves unassailable. From that foundation we can conduct intellectual inquiries according to some strict rules of reliable method for reasoning, and we don't admit into our belief system any proposition that hasn't been certified by its connection to the foundation or other foundationally certified beliefs. In this way we can guarantee ourselves an accurate depiction of the world.

So first, we have foundations, then we have a reliable method by which to relate all our other beliefs to the foundation (inductive

---

1. Bahnsen here is referring to the Münchhausen trilemma: one will either be committed to an infinite number of regressions in trying to justify any belief, or he will be committed to arbitrary or defective axiomatic foundations, justified either through circularity or dogmatism. All three of these outcomes are philosophically unsatisfactory.

2. Bahnsen: Anarchy says that everything is relative, and no one can know anything for sure. Therefore, everyone has the right to believe what they want to believe and do what they want to do. Dogmatism is the view where we come down to power plays. There are institutional restraints on what can be said or believed since it is the institution (or State) that dictates what should and shouldn't be followed.

method, deductive, abductive, perceptual, commonsensical, etc.), and by this means we can be assured that the skeptic is wrong. There are three types of foundationalism that you should be familiar with: conceptual/logical foundationalism, perceptual foundationalism, and commonsense foundationalism.

A logical foundationalist holds that the standards by which we judge everything are the rules of logic. Unfortunately for this view, the rules of logic are purely formal. So, if that is the only foundation you have, then the only knowledge you can get is knowledge which is going to be formalized. It will be consistent, but it won't have any details from experience, anything that we know about the world.

Perceptual foundationalism holds in one form or another that ultimately everything we know needs to be traced back to some kind of perception with the perception thought to be infallible. This obviously is not accurate since our perceptions are fallible and at best incorrigible. Maybe I can't deny the way I see things, but I can't argue that the way I see things is the way they are. And so perceptual foundationalism hits the rocks hard. This naïve empirical approach to epistemology hasn't fared well, and its modern advocates like the logical positivists[3] have reduced themselves to self-contradiction and the inability to talk about their own philosophy.

Commonsense foundationalism can itself be divided into two ways of "seeing" common sense:

1. It makes no sense to question the rationality of our standards of rationality. Since we accept these as the standards of rationality by commonsense, it makes no sense to now question them.

2. The more popular version of commonsense foundationalism has been **conventionalism** which says that the standards

---

3. Logical positivism holds that the only things meaningful for conveying truths are those things which are either empirically observed or statements which are analytically true (by definition) (i.e., all bachelors are unmarried). The positivists aimed at holding no metaphysical assumptions at the outset, wanting to get away from all the speculation around it.

we call commonsensical are part of a form of life in terms of which we have grown up within our society. This version of foundationalism doesn't hold up either, since one man's commonsense could be another's absurdity. And when you run into people that don't accept what you call commonsense, all you can do is yell, "Heretic!" At that point there is no reasoning between these two viewpoints. *Commonsense foundationalism can only work if the things we all have senses of are common.*

Foundationalism, thus, does not fare well. There are still some people who defend it today, but not many.[4]

The Pragmatist Attempt

The next way of trying to counter the skeptic is pragmatism. In my way of cutting the cake—though it might not be the best way, but it helps me—there are two ways of answering the skeptic.

The first way answers skepticism by referring in some normative way to the model of science. The logic of scientific inquiry becomes the paradigm of rationality. And the reason why the skeptic ought to concede to this model is that it is the most potentially-true and potentially-successful way to organize our lives intellectually. After all, look at all the scientific advancements made in the 20th century. But the difficulty with this is that, regardless of what you think of science and its accomplishments, *the presuppositions of science must first be defended before science itself can be a rational answer to the skeptic.* And the general organizing principles of experience are not themselves appraised by experience itself. And so, science resting on experience and observation is itself assuming some organizing principles that cannot be scientifically verified or made sense of. Moreover, when

---

4. At least during the time of this seminar in 1995.

you start talking about the "model of science" you're going to be embarrassed by two things:

1. There have been plenty of cultures, both simultaneous to our own and before our own, that do not follow what we call scientific procedures, and yet we still would call them rational people. To say that what we do today is the *model* of science assumes that everybody who did things differently was/is irrational. That's nothing more than cultural prejudice talking at that point.

2. There is no "model of science" to begin with! There is no agreement within any narrow field of science. If there were, you wouldn't have the O. J. Simpson trial with all the experts competing with each other. And you know what the judge must do there? This is fascinating: he must decide who is scientifically credible. But did Judge Ito have the standards of rationality to decide who is really doing genuine science and who is engaged in quackery? That's a scary thing, isn't it? Whose model of science? But it's worse than this. It's not just that you have different, competing schools of science within a narrow domain, you don't have any one scientific procedure that is used by all the sciences. As Gilbert Ryle once said: "There is no one science; there are many sciences."

The other pragmatic approach of answering the skeptic is the appeal to the success or fruitfulness of science. We can't answer the skeptic ultimately, but we can point to the fruitfulness of science as attaining its goals. Now the question that must be asked if you're a skeptic or honest philosopher is, "Are the goals of science rational?" The problem didn't go away; it just got rephrased. Are the ultimate assumptions of science rational? Can rationality itself be justified? The pragmatists said that it's certainly fruitful. Okay, but is such fruitfulness rational? The response from the pragmatist might be to say that it achieves its ends. But as was brought up before, how do we know which goals or ends to seek? Is preserving the species what makes us rational? Social egalitarianism? It's ultimately arbitrary because different people will choose which consequences to achieve. There is no one justification for which end to choose.

What Are We Left With?

What, then, are we going to do if the foundationalists and the pragmatists are not able to answer the skeptic? There is one more form of reasoning one can utilize to answer the skeptic and that is a transcendental argument. A transcendental argument takes the form of saying that we know something is true from the impossibility of the contrary. Another way of putting it is that we are looking for the precondition(s) for the intelligibility of experience.

A transcendental argument takes the form of saying that we know something is true from the impossibility of the contrary.

We say that there are certain things we know to be true because those things are the preconditions or presuppositions for intelligibility.[5] So now the skeptic can keep blabbering all he wants, but our point is that if you, the skeptic, want to argue, you're presupposing the intelligibility of what you're saying. Ultimately, the skeptic can't pursue his skeptical argument without this metaphysic or worldview in terms of which their language and argument can make sense.

---

5. Another allusion to the conceptual-ontological transcendental distinction. To say that something is a *precondition* typically refers to a metaphysical entity or aspect. To say that something must be a *presupposition* refers to a conceptual or epistemic necessity.

Summary of Chapters 1-6

To summarize the material covered thus far before proceeding to the heart of transcendental arguments, I began by saying that there is an objective proof for God's existence. Necessarily, we had to talk about the notion of proof itself. When I say that the existence of God is objectively provable, what am I getting at? We talked about proof and persuasion, and the differences between the two.

After discussing the notion of proof, we began to look at the kinds of proofs that are available and took the cosmological argument as being an example of an exceptionally bad one. There is something, however, to the notion of causation. If we go back and do a transcendental analysis of it, the cosmological argument does turn out to be a very strong proof for the existence of God. We talked about rational proofs, empirical proofs, and pragmatic proofs, but now after reassessing the cosmological argument in a transcendental fashion, we now have the notion of transcendental proof.

We then introduced Van Til's works—both the easy illustration of *Why I Believe in God* and the more technically precise, philosophical description of transcendental arguments in *A Survey of Christian Epistemology*—and afterwards looked at the history of philosophy to assess Immanuel Kant and to put him in the context of the situation. The reason for doing so is that Kant is the one person in the modern world who brought attention to the idea of transcendental analysis or argumentation. This entailed studying the Continental Rationalists and the British Empiricists where we saw that they, for all their differences, end up with the same problem. Kant was scandalized by that and suggested a program for answering the problem. I do not believe Kant solved the problem, but I do believe that the program— what he tried to do—was the right strategy.

Finally, I put modern epistemological approaches into context for you. I said that epistemology is stimulated by the skeptic's challenge. There are all sorts of differences among epistemologists, but the way in which you respond to skepticism is going to fall into one of three schools of thought: First, you can be a foundationalist where you will argue that there are some things which are indubitable, be they logical, perceptual, or commonsensical. Or you will skirt this whole thing, try not to argue in this fashion, and rather be pragmatic about everything. That is, you will talk about what is fruitful or what will bring success or what the model of science is that becomes the most rational way to approach things. And finally, you can be transcendental in your analysis or response to skepticism. And the heart of the transcendental method is showing that the skeptic can't even formulate his argument without denying what he is trying to say.[6]

---

6. There is a fourth major type of justification known as Coherentism which says that our beliefs are not justified in a *linear* regression as Foundationalism assumes, but rather in a web-like fashion where every belief is justified via some sort of logical relation, be it deductive or inductive. This view of justification likewise succumbs to its own problems, the most prominent being that it reduces to relativism—whose webs of beliefs is the correct one? Relational consistency within a web of beliefs is purely internal, and someone else can have web which is likewise analytically and synthetically consistent. It's unclear why Bahnsen did not mention this fourth major type of justification, perhaps because its problems are akin to Kant's, which he sufficiently scrutinized. Thus, it, too, is ultimately defective in countering skepticism.

SECTION 2
CONTEMPORARY TRANSCENDENTAL ARGUMENTS

(Michael Butler)

CHAPTER 7

Contemporary Transcendental Arguments

The assessment of contemporary transcendental arguments will be somewhat difficult for those not philosophically well-read, but I will attempt to make it as simple as possible for the reader. The goal here is to be able to pick up something from the contemporary debate over transcendental arguments and apply it to Van Tillian transcendental arguments to see how this debate affects them. That is, we are going to see whether the criticisms leveled against contemporary transcendental arguments apply to Van Tillian transcendental arguments.

When I refer to "contemporary transcendental arguments," I am referring to those relevant in the literature from around the 1950s. Since then, there has been a resurgence, which is why it is important for us as Van Tillians to look at them.

As Dr. Bahnsen has already alluded to, most philosophers today do not believe that transcendental arguments are good. Most philosophers are analytical in that they try to break down a field into narrower and narrower portions and forget the whole "picture" of things. The "majority view" in both American and British philosophy is that transcendental arguments are somewhat spurious in one way or another. But, again, there have been some proponents who have tried to make a resurgence of them in order to rebut the skeptic, as Dr. Bahnsen also has gone over. This is an important insight to grasp to understand the contemporary debate.

Most contemporary transcendental arguments are used to rebut the skeptical challenge to *certain types of issues*, and I will give some contemporary philosophers who believe transcendental arguments *do* work while also going over others who think that they aren't good arguments at all.

Conceptual Schemes

In order to understand modern transcendental arguments, we first must understand that a **conceptual scheme** is *a system through which we interpret our experience, bringing to bear on our experience our conceptual resources*. Here are some examples.

If we imagine a box that was made of wood with a glass pane in the front, with silver knobs, and a black wire coming from the back and plugged into a wall, what would we think of that box? If someone walked into a room and saw what I described, he or she would know that it was a television.[1] Why? Because we live in the modern world in which we interact with modern technology, and thus we bring certain concepts to bear on our experience. We have ways of understanding and interpreting the world around us.

What would happen if we brought in an aborigine from Australia who has never had contact with any part of the modern Western World and saw the same object? Would he reach the same conclusion that we would have of it being a television? No. Is he seeing the same thing we are? Yes and no. He would have the same phenomenological experience in the sense that he would see the same parts of the object, however, contrary to his own phenomenological experience, conceptually speaking, he is not seeing the same thing we are.

The point here is that we both see the same phenomenon (or object), and yet we see the object differently. We see the object as

---

1. Televisions are, of course, different today in size and form, but 1995 was a different time!

a television and all of its functionality; he sees the object as a who-knows-what.[2] This distinction of "seeing" versus "seeing as" is a crucial part of being able to understand the contemporary debate of transcendental arguments.[3]

Conceptual Centeredness

There are three levels in our conceptual schemes of conceptual centeredness with centeredness equating to conceptual importance. In terms of outer-level considerations, most everyone will have the concept of the game of billiards. It is easy for us to sit back and think about the concept of the game. If we were to lose that concept, our outlook on the world, our conceptual scheme, would not be greatly impoverished. That is, we could all get on in life very well without the concept of billiards (unless, of course, you were a professional billiards player).

Going inward to the middle level we can consider the concept of a game in general. The concept of a game is much more central to our conceptual scheme than the concepts to the game of billiards is. Why? *Because it is much more general.* If we lose the concept of a game in our conceptual scheme, our lives would be somewhat impoverished—all the types of activities we enjoy and engage in wouldn't make any sense to us.[4]

----

2. Bahnsen: Beyond artifacts and going to the natural world by way of illustration, if I go out into a field and I look at a portion of a field alongside a Native American, I may see the very same thing—I see dead grass, he sees dead grass. But on the other hand, because of his experience in the wilderness, he sees a deer's footprint, whereas I see only dead grass. So, if you're asking whether we see the same thing, the answer is both yes and no: we see the same things sensibly, but because his conceptual scheme is richer, he can see something that I don't.

3. Butler gives one more illustration from a calculus textbook. Students of calculus will see the same formulas and equations and so forth that the teacher sees in the book, but because he or she is already proficient with calculus, they see and fully understand each formula and equation, whereas students, while looking at the exact same material, would not be able to do so.

4. In addition to rendering all of the activities we do and watch on TV

Finally, there are things in our conceptual scheme which are fundamentally more central than the concept of, say, a game. One example is the concept of causation—the concept that certain events happen for certain reasons or causes antecedent to them. If, somehow, our conceptual scheme lost the concept of causation, what would be the ramifications? What would our conceptual scheme be like if we didn't have the concept of causation? For starters, we wouldn't have the ability to play games because all games presuppose the concept of causation, cause and effect. We couldn't play games, do science, go to work, you couldn't do theology, and so on.[5] In fact, the Bible says that God created the world, so that *without the concept of causation, you can't have a concept of creation either.*

Loosely speaking, the concept of causation is what is called *a transcendental.* For the present purposes, the term 'transcendental,' used as a noun, is a condition of experience. Something transcendental is the condition[6] for some kind of experience. Speaking of causation, we would refer to it as a transcendental for all our experience. Similarly (going outward in the conceptual scheme), the concept of 'game' is a 'transcendental' to the game of billiards. The point here is that there are different types of transcendentals.[7]

---

unintelligible to us should we lose the concept of a game (or "gameness"), with it we would also potentially lose tangential concepts such as teams, opponents, competition, points, scoring, penalizing, rounds, quarters, etc. Such losses are indeed more central to our daily lives than not having a concept of one game (billiards).

5. Butler: Some philosophers do believe that there could be a causeless conceptual scheme. Whether that is true or not it certainly is correct to say that it would be so different that it would have no similarities to our conceptual scheme. Bahnsen: If I could piggyback on that, it seems like there are some modern philosophers who would say that you can have a causeless conceptual scheme. But they can't say that without assuming causation.

6. Or "precondition."

7. For our present purposes, the concept of causation would be considered a general or conceptual transcendental. It is general in that such a concept must be employed in absolutely every facet of experience, and conceptual in that it is

Comparison with Deductive and Inductive Arguments

A deductive argument is one in which if the premises are true then the conclusion follows as being true also. (Simply stated, "If A and B are true, then C must also be true.") In inductive arguments, the conclusion follows only with probability. For example:

Fact: I see fireflies in my backyard every summer.

Assumption: This summer, I will probably see fireflies in my backyard.

Both arguments refer to the form of argumentation. Transcendental arguments, although they do refer to a form of argumentation (which we will get to), *include the type of conclusion that is drawn in the argument itself.*

Put another way, when we talk about deductive arguments, we are not referring to the type of conclusion that is being drawn, except that it follows from the premises. But what becomes a conclusion in a deductive argument can be any number of things. I could give two deductive arguments which draw conclusions that have nothing to do with one another. There is no necessary correlation in the conclusions of deductive (or inductive) arguments. And so, again, inductive and deductive arguments make no reference to the *type* of conclusions drawn. Transcendental arguments do refer to the type of conclusion that is being drawn; conclusions of transcendental arguments are purported or aimed to be transcendentals.[8]

---

something we must think in terms of. The concept of billiards would be considered a narrow, conceptual transcendental in that such a concept is not as necessary as causation which is required for every experience whatsoever. It is thus "narrow" (or at least "narrower"). Butler will talk about this shortly.

8. That is, the argument is aimed at making its conclusion a particular thing: a transcendental. Deductive, inductive, and abductive arguments only aim at making their conclusions follow from their premises (which transcendental arguments obviously do as well).

Why am I bringing this up? In the debate on transcendental arguments there are some who say that when you compare a transcendental argument with a deductive argument all you're doing is comparing two different forms of argumentation. There is something to that, but that is not all that is happening between the two. Based on what we have discussed above, it is a mistake to say that deductive, inductive, and transcendental arguments are all the same just with different forms used. It is a category error in that you are categorizing all three of the arguments under the same rubric without giving further qualifications.[9]

The Form of a Transcendental Argument

Turning now to the more formal aspects, what is the form of a transcendental argument? We can put it this way:

Premise 1: For x to be the case, y must be the case because y is a precondition of x.

Premise 2: x is the case.

Conclusion: Therefore, y is the case.

The "because" clause is what we want to consider because it is the crux of proving what is a transcendental for x. It is usually proved by a *reductio ad absurdum* argument. The aim is to show that if you didn't have y, then you couldn't have x either, the x being a given—something both parties agree on. So, you assume *not-y* and show that starting without y, you couldn't even have x.

---

9. In other words, transcendental arguments belong in their own category apart from deductive and inductive arguments for the fact that their aim is intended to conclude with a specific something—a transcendental (a necessary precondition for x). Thus, transcendental arguments belong to the category of concluding with a transcendental; deductive and inductive arguments belong to the category of concluding only with a corresponding conclusion to the premises and nothing more.

Examples of Transcendental Arguments

Here is a down-to-earth example of a transcendental argument:

P1. In order for there to be carpet in this room there must be a floor underneath it because having a floor (or foundation) is a necessary precondition for there being carpeting.

P2. There is carpet in this room.

Conclusion: Therefore, there is a floor under the carpet.

How do we prove that there must be a floor underneath the carpet for there to be one? We show that if that (y) was not the case, then it would be an absurd reality—a foundationless carpeting.

Here is another:

P1: For the concept of creation to be intelligible to us (x) we must possess a concept of causation (y) because the concept of causation (y) is a necessary precondition for the concept of creation (x).

P2: We do have a concept of creation (x).

C: Therefore, we have a concept of causation (y).

How do we prove the y-clause? Creation is God's acting to bring about a state that previously wasn't in existence. ithout y we couldn't have x. Without a concept of causation, we could not have a concept of creation in the first place.

There is a distinction between the two transcendental arguments I just gave: The first one I gave is ontological[10] and narrow in scope—we were only talking about carpeting in a particular room. The second argument is conceptual and general. Why? Because the second transcendental argument made no existential claim to any "thing" existing in the world (except if you want to call the concept

---

10. Butler: Having to do with what exists (in this case a floor). In other words, it is making an existence claim.

of causation in our minds as something that exists, but this doesn't exactly amount to an ontological claim). The argument is aimed at showing that we must have a certain type of concept in order to understand creation. In this way, it is a conceptual transcendental argument, but it is also more general in scope than only arguing about some carpeting in one room on the entire planet.

We can also mix and match these categories: we can have a conceptual argument that is narrow in scope and an ontological argument that is general in scope. *Van Til's transcendental argument is an ontological argument of large or general scope.* It makes an existence claim by claiming that God exists and that without Him existing, we could not make sense of experience.

It's important to note that in the contemporary climate, most transcendental arguments are not of that form. They are usually general in scope, but they are conceptual in nature. They say that we must have certain types of concepts for us to get along in the world or to have the experiences that we do. This is a crucial distinction that must be understood in order to understand where Van Til's transcendental program lies.[11]

---

11. Butler interjects here and gives a brief example of a narrow conceptual transcendental argument in response to a question. We've already touched on a narrow, conceptual TA, but here is another one by Butler and embellished: Another narrow conceptual argument would be showing that in order to have a concept of something being real you must have a concept of the polar opposite term in order to make sense of it. You can't know terms like 'real' or 'small' etc. without already having a concept of 'fake' and 'large', etc. This is a narrow conceptual example in that such concepts do not have wide sweeping consequences unlike the concept of causation which is required for any experience at all to be intelligible to us as well as Van Til's argument for God's existence.

Are Contemporary Transcendental Arguments Really Transcendental Arguments?

The contemporary debate has always made references to what Kant was doing in his *Critique of Pure Reason*. The reason I bring this up is that some philosophers argue that what is going on under the name "transcendental arguments" is something very different from what Kant was doing in his *Critique of Pure Reason*. Because of this, we should not call our arguments "transcendental" arguments. They're not Kantian and therefore not transcendental.

The following is from my thesis "The Transcendental Argument for God's Existence."[12]

> Before analyzing and evaluating contemporary transcendental arguments it is obligatory to say a few words about Kant.... [A] number of philosophers have accused contemporary advocates of TAs ... of denuding Kant's TAs of their distinctiveness ... [so much so] that the contemporary reformulations do not deserve the title of "transcendental argument" at all. Before one is tempted to cast aside this whole debate as a petty etymological squabble, it should be realized that more than nomenclature or lexical proprietorship is at stake, although some of the debate is indeed trivial. For although Kant made the term a technical one and, thus, must be conceded a certain propriety over it, philosophers should be more concerned with the success and

---

12. Michael R. Butler, "The Transcendental Argument for God's Existence" in *The Standard Bearer: A Festschrift for Greg L. Bahnsen*, ed. Steven Schlissel (Nacogdoches, TX.: Covenant Media Press, 2002). When not skipping over unnecessary sentences, Butler sometimes reads something different from what is now published. This is either due to the fact that Butler had not at the time graduated with his Master's degree and thus his thesis was still being edited, or he reworded parts for the sake of speaking publicly in a classroom setting and not formally. I have either marked such parts in brackets or ignored his paraphrasing and kept the published version of the sentences in for the sake of simplicity.

failures of the arguments at hand rather than lexicographical particularities.[13]

It is more interesting, therefore, to take the modern versions of transcendental arguments on their own terms and evaluate them rather than trying meticulously to object and ask whether or not these contemporary arguments really deserve the name "transcendental."

Before one is tempted to cast aside this whole debate as a petty etymological squabble, it should be realized that more than nomenclature or lexical by proprietorship is at stake. Kant is, among other things, the father of TAs.[14] Thus it would be a rather odd conclusion to state that his arguments were not TAs. Indeed, one is tempted to say that whatever Kant is doing in the first Critique, he is arguing transcendentally.[15]

This is perhaps what Jaakko Hintikka is getting at when he states that "the first order of business in any discussion of such arguments is to try to see what Kant understood by the term." Ross Harrison is even more explicit: "Since Kant invented the label, anything properly called a 'transcendental' argument must have some analogy to the arguments which Kant used."[16]

---

13. Butler, "The Transcendental Argument for God's Existence." 94-95 and footnote 53.

14. Butler: In Aristotle's *Metaphysics*, Aristotle argues transcendentally for the Law of Non-Contradiction, so transcendental reasoning goes much farther back to the beginnings of Western philosophy. But Kant is certainly the father of modern transcendental arguments.

15. Butler: Just definitionally, whatever Kant is doing in his first *Critique* he is arguing transcendentally. Or putting it another way, whatever Kant says a transcendental argument is, that is what he is doing.

16. Butler, "The Transcendental Argument for God's Existence." The names and backgrounds of these philosophers are irrelevant for our present purposes.

My conclusion is that what Kant was doing in using transcendental arguments is not what contemporary proponents of transcendental arguments are doing. They are different types of arguments altogether. In Kant's *Critique of Pure Reason*, however, there is an argument-form that is analogous to contemporary transcendental arguments.

> Before we acquiesce to [the] claim that contemporary TAs are "unKantian" because they do not make appeals to constructive knowledge,[17] it is important to point out the obvious. Kant did use an argument analogous to contemporary TAs in the Refutation and the Second Analogy.... So in another sense it is not correct to call contemporary TAs "unKantian." They are indeed Kantian arguments, but they are not Kantian *transcendental* arguments. What then of the charge that they are spurious? At this point the question has become a mere linguistic matter. Nothing of philosophical import hangs on the answer at all. Since it has been the practice to call contemporary TAs "TAs" and since ... Kant did not take out a copyright on the term, there seems to be no pressing need for a change in nomenclature. It is little more than schoolmarmism ... to insist that all TAs must comply with tight Kantian strictures in order to warrant the honorific title "Transcendental Argument." Thus, it is legitimate to continue the practice of calling contemporary TAs "TAs" bearing in mind that not all TAs are Kantian in nature.[18]

What is this all about? Most modern philosophers who use transcendental arguments use them in a certain form that is not used with Kant. They are different types of transcendental arguments. Within Kant, however, there is a form of argument that is analogous

17. Remember that Kant's use of transcendental arguments was a constructive one in that the mind constructs or imposes order on the chaos coming to us from the noumenal, external world.

18. Butler, "The Transcendental Argument for God's Existence," 100-101.

to the modern debate, and this is how some modern philosophers have been confused. They thought that this form was a Kantian transcendental argument and thus rehabilitated it and called it a transcendental argument, but it really wasn't what Kant thought was one at all. My conclusion is that Kant doesn't have a copyright on the term "transcendental." And if what we are discussing aren't exactly Kantian transcendental arguments, it doesn't mean that they aren't transcendental arguments at all.

After this discussion it makes more sense to talk about the divisions *in* transcendental arguments. There is a conceptual transcendental argument, an ontological transcendental argument, and now a Kantian, constructive transcendental argument, which is neither conceptual nor ontological (though it sides more with a conceptual TA).

CHAPTER 8

The Contemporary Debate

Strawson's Argument

Remembering that contemporary transcendental arguments are always aimed at defeating the skeptic, we turn now to contemporary illustrations, the most famous is found in Sir Peter Strawson's book Individuals: An Essay in Descriptive Metaphysics.[1] The following is from page 35 of his work where his most famous argument is found:

> There is no doubt that we have the idea of a single spatiotemporal system of material things.[2]

What Strawson is getting at is that when we view the world, we have a picture of the world in which our experiences in the present have some relationship to our experiences in the past. This is a fundamental part of all our conceptual schemes. I assume that the objects I saw at church on Sunday are in some spatial relationship to the objects I see now. I see all of the material objects in the world as residing in

---

1. Peter F. Strawson, *Individuals: An Essay in Descriptive Metaphysics* (Oxfordshire, England, UK: Routledge, 1959). Butler begins reading on page 35 of the work, but it is unclear whether he is reading from the original 1959 edition or a newer edition. For the sake of accuracy, references to quotations will only consist of the title without page numbers.

2. Strawson, *Individuals: An Essay in Descriptive Metaphysics*. Here is Strawson's set-up to give his argument.

single spaces. If I sat in a particular chair in a classroom yesterday and I return to the classroom today and see the same chair, I would assume that that chair is the same one as the one I sat in yesterday.

What if someone comes along and asks, "Well, how do you know it's the same chair? Were you continually observing it?" This brings us to the question of identity in philosophy. How do we know something to be the same throughout time? Strawson then turns to the hub of his argument:

> Now I say that a [necessary] condition of our having this conceptual scheme is the unquestioning acceptance of particular identity in at least some cases of non-continuous observation.[3]

Strawson is laying out that if we have this conceptual scheme, x (believing that all objects are in the same space-time continuum), then, Strawson claims, the necessary precondition is "the unquestioning acceptance of particular identity in at least some cases of non-continuous observation," y.[4] Simply put, in order to have the conceptual scheme of believing all objects are in the same space-time continuum, we have to draw the conclusion that we are seeing the same chair we sat in yesterday, to use a previous example. When we stop observing something and come back to observe it later, we always assume that it is the same object as we saw it in the past.[5]

---

3. Strawson, *Individuals: An Essay in Descriptive Metaphysics*.

4. Formally laid out, Strawson's first premise (and subsequent argument) would run as follows:
P1: For us to believe (or have an idea) that all objects are in the same space-time continuum (x), we must have an unquestioning acceptance of particular identity in at least some cases of non-continuous observation (y), since having an unquestioning acceptance of particular identity in at least some cases of non-continuous observation (y) is a necessary precondition for believing that all objects are in the same space-time continuum (x).
P2: x is the case.
C: Therefore, y is the case.

5. Butler uses many analogies, the easiest to understand being that when you

Strawson says that we have x, and as we have already stated, x is the given; no one doubts x. This is just how we view the world. However, y is more controversial. In order to prove that y must be the case, Strawson employs a reductio of assuming *not-y* in order to show that if y is indeed not the case, then x is not the case either.

What, then, is Strawson's use of the reductio? Supposing once more that a skeptic objects to you believing that you are seeing the same chair that you sat in the day before, Strawson says that the whole objection or challenge can't even get off the ground because the skeptic posing the challenge is assuming y, that there is an unquestioning acceptance of particular identity in at least some cases of non-continuous observation. Let me lay it out in simpler terms.

x is that we must believe there is a single spatiotemporal continuum. y says that for x to be the case, we have to, in some cases, assume that objects continue to exist even though we don't perceive them.[6] Strawson's comeback against the skeptic who challenges the notion that we perceive the same objects throughout time is that the skeptic can't even formulate his skeptical challenge because in order to formulate it he has to assume y to begin with. In even asking, "How do you know that objects continue to exist unperceived?" the skeptic has to assume that objects continue to exist unperceived.[7] Strawson

---

set the alarm on your alarm clock before falling asleep, upon waking up to the alarm clock you never assume that, lo and behold, it is an identically-looking but completely different alarm clock than the one you had before you fell asleep.

6. Notice the conceptuality of this transcendental argument in the terms "believe" and "assume"—a testament to the conceptual nature of contemporary, secular transcendental arguments contra Van Til's ontological program. Strawson's argument is *not* that particulars do continue to exist unperceived; Strawson, rather, is attacking the rationality of *believing* objects don't continue to exist unperceived. But since the skeptic implicitly believes this, Strawson's point is that he is being inconsistent with his skeptical challenge of y.

7. Bahnsen: I want to interject and clarify here that there are two types of skeptics we can talk about. The skeptic might come in and say, "How do you know that particular chair is the same one that was there yesterday?" That is, how do you

never argues that objects do continue to exist unperceived. His transcendental argument is purely conceptual: he is saying that we view the world in a certain way, not that the world is in fact a certain way. His point is we have no basis for doubting that objects continue to exist unperceived, but he hasn't proven that objects in the external world do continue to exist even when we don't observe them.[8]

Stroud's Criticism of Strawson

The most famous criticism of Strawson's argument came from Barry Stroud (1935-2019), a professor at the University of California, Berkeley. Though he misunderstood Strawson, he wrote an article against his argument some years later.[9] What Stroud tried to show is that transcendental arguments are really nothing special and are ultimately dependent upon a verification principle.[10] Stroud takes Strawson's argument to have three

---

know that there wasn't some clever guy who went to the furniture store last night while you were asleep and substituted one chair for another? This is a *particular* challenge: it assumes a particular furniture store, particular people coming at night to replace the chair, and so forth. That is not what Strawson is refuting. What Strawson is talking about (and considering absurd) is what we might call "general" skepticism wherein the skeptic asks general questions such as how do we generally know that objects continue to exist unperceived? *Strawson is saying that you have to assume that to even raise the argument.* Strawson knows that we can be deceived, but he says we have to have reasons for knowing we are being deceived; you can't just have a general skepticism without reasons for it.

8. Butler: It should be noted that Strawson believes it is possible for the skeptic to deny x (even though x is what is supposed to be agreed on by both parties). If, after the argument, the skeptic wants to be nasty, he could just say that he doesn't accept x. Well, give me an alternative, then. How else should I view the world? Rejecting x is just a desperate ploy. If the skeptic just wants to deny x, then you really just respond by saying, "Very well. Have a nice day." For the skeptic to say "Well x just isn't true" is an absurd claim.

9. Barry Stroud, "Transcendental Arguments," *The Journal of Philosophy*, 65:9 (1968), 241-256.

10. Simply put, a verification principle is that principle which "verifies" how the external world actually is or which propositions are verifiably-true. Perhaps the

premises and a conclusion. His conclusion (for Strawson's argument) is that objects continue to exist unperceived. Now, we should see that the problem here is Stroud takes Strawson's argument to have ontological ramifications. Stroud is not giving a right interpretation of Strawson. He conceives of Strawson making an ontological transcendental argument. Here is how he lays out the argument:

P1: We think of the world as containing objective particulars in a single spatiotemporal system.

P2: If we think of the world as containing objective particulars in a single spatiotemporal system, then we are able to identify and reidentify particulars.

P3: If we reidentify particulars, then we have a satisfiable criteria on the basis of which we can make a reidentification.

C: Therefore, objects continue to exist unperceived.[11]

Quite rightly, Stroud says that this does not follow whatsoever. From those three premises you can't get to a conclusion that says objects do continue to exist unperceived. He thus tries to help Strawson by adding two additional premises to the argument:

P4: If we have the best criteria for reidentification of particulars and this criteria has been satisfied, then we know that objects continue to exist unperceived.

P5: We sometimes know that the best criteria we have for the reidentification of particulars has been satisfied.

most commonly-known verification principles are those of the logical positivists mentioned in Chapter six, footnote 3, which asserts that the only propositions that have meaning are those which are either a) analytically true (by definition, i.e.. all bachelors are unmarried males), or b) are empirically verifiable (going out to the world to verify a truth claim). However, once again, one should immediately notice how this thesis itself is neither analytically-true nor empirically-observable.

11. Butler: For somebody to blow Strawson's argument this bad is incredible to me. This is *not* Strawson's argument.

What is wrong with premise-5? It is a factual premise, to be sure. But remember that Strawson is attempting to defeat the skeptic in giving a transcendental argument. So is the skeptic ever going to allow this premise? No. The skeptic will rightfully come back by saying that this is precisely what he is arguing against. Stroud's additional premises of Strawson's argument here amount to a begging of the question.[12]

Well, what if we just drop P5 and keep P4? In doing this, Stroud is giving us a verification principle of Strawson's argument. Stroud thinks that in order for Strawson's (what he thinks to be ontological) argument to work, there needs to be a verification principle incorporated into it. That is, there must be something empirically verifiable about the world. And since Stroud thinks that Strawson's argument depends upon a verification principle in order to work (again, because he thinks it is an ontological argument) that it is therefore useless. But more than that, Stroud said that if a verification principle is needed, then a transcendental argument is unnecessary because a verification principle would directly refute the skeptic.[13]

---

12. A "general" skeptic will question anything and everything. Therefore, Stroud's fifth premise does not give credence or aid to Strawson's anti-skeptical argument.

13. To restate this all another way, Stroud thinks that Strawson gave an ontological transcendental argument—that objects do continue to exist unperceived. On this false assumption Stroud does, however, rightfully draw the conclusion that in order to reach such an ontological conclusion requires the arguer to utilize some sort of verification principle. That is, the arguer must use some principle which shows that our concepts of the world do in fact marry up with the world outside of us (i.e., our belief that objects continue to exist unperceived is, in fact, the case outside of us—objects do continue to exist unperceived). However, if one could procure such a potent principle, that principle alone would be enough to refute the skeptic without the need for a transcendental argument in the first place. Herein lies Stroud's dilemma toward those utilizing transcendental reasoning from an ontological perspective, despite misinterpreting Strawson's argument.

CHAPTER 9

Analysis and Overview of the Contemporary Climate

A. C. Grayling's Analysis

Next is A. C. Grayling's article found in the *Companion to Epistemology*.[1] Grayling is a British philosopher who defends a version of Strawson's transcendental argument.

> [Transcendental arguments] were brought into philosophical prominence by the work of Kant, who used them to establish the role of certain fundamental a priori concepts in our knowledge of the external world. The role which transcendental arguments show these concepts to play is ... that they make experience possible, and that therefore sceptical doubts about our possession of them are empty. It is the scepticism-refuting promise of transcendental arguments that has provoked most interest among subsequent philosophers.[2]

Kant did not formulate his transcendental program merely as a skepticism-refuting argument. Though he believed it refuted skepticism, he also believed that it put something in its place.[3]

---

1. A. C. Grayling, *Blackwell Companions to Philosophy: A Companion to Epistemology*, eds. Jonathan Dancy, Ernest Sosa, Matthias Steup, 2nd ed. (West Sussex, U.K.: Blackwell Publishing Ltd, 2010), 768-771.

2. A. C. Grayling, *Blackwell Companions to Philosophy: A Companion to Epistemology*, 768-769.

3. Contra contemporary transcendental arguments which seek to refute the

Kant's central question concerns the possibility of synthetic a priori knowledge. An answer to it presupposes an answer to the more general question, what are the necessarily presupposed grounds of experience in general? In arguing for the categories, and for space and time as pure forms of sensibility, Kant is arguing that there can be experience only under certain conditions, and this strategy displays the characteristic form of a transcendental argument. Simply in respect of its form, the argument is that there must be something Y if there is something X of which Y is a necessary condition. In crude outline, therefore, the transcendental strategy consists in the search for key necessary conditions of some given region of discourse or experience. Reasoning of this character is not unique to Kant, nor do all the varieties of it found in the philosophical literature model themselves exactly on Kant's procedure. Wittgenstein in the *Philosophical Investigations* and *On Certainty* argues transcendentally about the impossibility of private language and the possibility of knowledge respectively.[4]

J. L. Austin argues transcendentally in formulating a theory of truth by distinguishing between demonstrative and descriptive conventions in language, his point being that some such distinction is required for a certain other concept— that of truth as correspondence—to have application. A

---

skeptic only in certain philosophical areas. Strawson's argument refuted *a* skeptical challenge, but it was not postulated as a proof by which to refute skepticism holistically.

4. Butler: In his later works, Wittgenstein showed transcendentally that a private language is impossible, and the reason he did this was for the purpose of refuting solipsism. Now, if it is the case that we can't have a private language then we must have a public language which presupposes the existence of other people. Thus, the skepticism of the existence of other minds and people is refuted by the argument. It is a very difficult argument with about twenty different interpretations of it. However, it generally takes the form of a transcendental argument. It should also be noted that Strawson likewise argued transcendentally that we shouldn't even question the existence of other minds. He is not saying that there are in fact other minds, but that it makes no sense to bring it into question.

different example is supplied by Gilbert Ryle in his use of "polar concept" arguments. The sceptical suggestion that we might undetectably be in error on any given occasion is refuted, Ryle claims, by the fact that just as we cannot have counterfeit coins unless there are genuine ones, so we cannot have a concept of error unless we have the concept of being right, and therefore we must sometimes know we are right. Once again, the strategy is to argue that X cannot be the case unless Y is the case; and since X is indeed the case, Y must be the case also.

These examples show that transcendental-style arguments are commonplace in philosophy. But there is a marked difference between reasonings of these familiar sorts and the weightier, more ambitious transcendental arguments found in Kant and others. One way to mark the distinction is to say that the familiar kinds of argument just sketched share their methodology with transcendental arguments proper, but not their scope; for the latter are not concerned merely with local conceptual polarities like "illusory-veridical," but with the conditions under which highly general concepts—the concept of other minds, or the concept of an independently existing reality—have application, given that such concepts play a key role in entire discourses and are central to our experience as a whole.[5, 6, 7] So put, the aim of transcendental

---

5. Transcendental arguments usually have a larger scope than some of the preceding examples, but it is not entirely inaccurate to refer to these arguments still as transcendental arguments. (see footnote 3)

6. Butler: In the example of Gilbert Ryle concerning real from counterfeit coins, the concept of realness is important to our conceptual scheme, but it is not absolutely central, whereas the concept of other minds (Wittgenstein) or causation (as we have discussed earlier) is much more central.

7. Bahnsen: If we look at Descartes's *cogito* argument, it is a type of transcendental argument, but Van Til would say that this is like a rock falling in a bottomless ocean. By itself it's not going to do anything to make knowledge

arguments is to establish the conditions necessary for experience, or experience of a certain kind, in general; and, at their most controversial, to establish conclusions about the nature and existence of an external world, or other minds, derived from paying attention to what has to be the case for there to be experience, or for experience to be as it is.

Classic contemporary examples of transcendental arguments are to be found in P. F. Strawson's Individuals. One of them is aimed at establishing the vacuity of sceptical doubt about the existence of other minds, and proceeds as follows. One can ascribe states of consciousness to oneself only if one is able to ascribe them to others, Strawson argues, because to doubt the existence of other minds one must employ the concept of other minds itself, and this can only be done if one can distinguish between "my states of consciousness" and "others' states of consciousness." But this can only be done, in turn, if others exist, because the identification of conscious states can only be effected by reference to particulars of a certain kind, namely, persons; the concept of which—in turn again—demands that there be criteria for distinguishing one person from another, for otherwise the identification of states of consciousness would be impossible. So one can talk of "my experiences" only if one can talk of "others' experiences"; this is possible only if there are criteria for distinguishing between persons; and since one can indeed talk significantly of one's own experiences, such criteria must exist. But if they exist they constitute logically adequate grounds for ascription of states of consciousness to others. Hence sceptical doubts about the existence of other minds are vacuous, because the sceptic cannot so much as formulate them without employing the discourse whose

---

possible. And so in the end Van Til will say that all of these individual arguments must push out to a worldview-level which they cannot do on their own.

very conditions of employment legitimize what he wishes to question.[8]

Strawson is first and foremost saying that we can ascribe states of affairs to ourselves. He then argues that the precondition of this is that we have the ability to ascribe them to others. But if you deny this then you wouldn't even be able to ascribe states of affairs to yourself. Therefore, it makes no sense to question the existence of other minds.

Another transcendental argument in Strawson's *Individuals* concerns the perception-independent existence of material particulars, and it has been much discussed as a result of Barry Stroud's criticisms of it. The subsequent debate can be said to turn on the following points.

One of the crucial questions about transcendental arguments concerns what they might hope to establish. The options, simply put, are that either they establish the existence of something (an external world, other minds), or they establish that certain concepts are necessary to our conceptual scheme. Clearly these are quite different results, and the latter involves the further problem of whether our conceptual scheme is the only possible one, for if not the terminus of a transcendental argument is strictly relative.[9]

Grayling is saying that there are two types of transcendental arguments: ontological and conceptual.[10] Obviously, the ontological transcendental argument has more force since it claims that the world really is such-and-such. But the conceptual transcendental argument has a difficulty, according to Grayling. Specifically, he points out that even if we must presuppose certain types of concepts in order to make

8. Grayling, *Blackwell Companions to Philosophy*, 769-770.

9. Grayling, *Blackwell Companions to Philosophy*, 770.

10. In the context of his discussion, apart from the other two types of TAs discussed—Kantian and Van Tillian/"Worldview."

sense of certain experiences, there is the further question of whether this conceptual scheme we possess now is the only possible one.

If we recall the example of the television in the case of the aborigine, he has the same phenomenological experience that I have, but he has a different conceptual scheme and thus views the world differently. This illustration shows that there are at least two different conceptual schemes in a certain context. But what if our "general" conceptual scheme which includes causation (and other generalities) isn't the only possible one? What if there is an aboriginal conceptual scheme that is completely different from our own but can still make perfectly make our experience of reality intelligible? How can we know that our conceptual scheme is the only possible one? Grayling wants to say that just because Strawson's argument works, it doesn't mean that the skeptic can't say that there could be another conceptual scheme out there.

Now the transcendentalist has a further burden of showing that the conceptual scheme he is arguing for is the only possible one (whether on a local issue like Strawson's argument or on a general issue such as the concept of causation). The ultimate question now is how do we go about showing that our conceptual scheme is not merely sufficient, but necessary and therefore exclusive? As Grayling will go on to say, only an "option A" ontological transcendental argument will work. To grasp the difference between these options it is useful to consider them as responses to sceptical challenges over our belief in the existence of an external world. On the first option, call it option A, the aim is to establish the existence of the external world. On the second, call it option B, the aim is to show that we must believe in the existence of an external world as a condition of the coherence of experience. To settle the sceptic's doubts outright under B one might have further to show that our conceptual scheme is the only conceivable one.

The chief difficulty faced by option A is that even if one could show that it is a necessary condition of our having coherent experience that we possess and apply a concept of an independently existing world, it still needs to be shown that something "out there" answers to that concept; in other words, that it is a necessary condition of our having the concept of an external world that an external world exists. It is one thing to argue that we must have and employ concepts of space, time, causality and particulars conditioned by them, and another to show that there exist things corresponding to these concepts and existentially prior to their use.

The difficulty here is that it does not look possible to argue from the fact that there is experience, or from some richer premise characterising that experience, to talk about the way things are independently of experience, without either supplementing the argument with additional factual premisses, or arguing that it is somehow constitutive of the concept-introducing terms employed that they have empirical conditions of application under which, and only under which, they can be known to be truly applied.[11]

Grayling is dealing with verification principles. In order for Option B conceptual transcendental arguments to prove there is an independently-existing external world, one must either import a factual premise—which wouldn't work since the skeptic is calling into question factual premises in the first place—or you need a verification principle, in which case, as we've already belabored, a transcendental argument is therefore unnecessary.[12] Option B transcendental arguments look, by comparison, like relatively mundane affairs.

---

11. Grayling, *Blackwell Companions to Philosophy*, 770.

12. The seemingly ubiquitous acceptance of transcendental philosophers to argue that the skeptic can only be refuted via a verification principle but not additional, factual premises seems to simply beg the question. If the skeptical challenge negates the use of factual premises to refute skepticism, then a verification principle is needed. But what's to stop a skeptic from calling the verification principle into question? Could it also not be seen as a "factual premise" despite holding the status of "principle"? A militant skeptic will question anything and everything, even if it leads to self-defeat.

There is no special difficulty in exploring the necessary conditions of the experience we enjoy; we are, at very least, entitled to claim attention for investigations into the role of our concepts of objects, space, time and causality, given that it at least seems to us that ours is a world of causally interactive spatiotemporal things. If we have a concept of objects, we must have a concept of the continued unperceived existence of objects, because this is necessary to the concept of a single spatio-temporal world; and it is precisely a belief in the continued unperceived existence of objects that the sceptic asks us to justify. Showing that we must have such a belief as a condition of experience is not the same as proving that such objects exist. One is stating what we must believe, not how things are; but since the sceptic wishes us to justify the belief, doing so—the argument goes—is enough to put an end to scepticism.

The sceptic, however, can in response shift his attack to a more general level, by arguing that there might be a certain parochial interest in pointing out what a given form of experience requires as its fundamental concepts, but that this does not settle doubts about the general validity of those concepts.[13]

That is, in order to talk about experience you must have certain concepts in your conceptual scheme. However, the skeptic can comeback by granting this point. But, asks the skeptic, how do we know our concepts really apply to what is out there in the external world?

What if there are forms of experience which are non-spatial, or non-causal, or in which there is no need to distinguish experience from its objects? To counter scepticism at this more general level B-type transcendental arguments require

---

13. Grayling, *Blackwell Companions to Philosophy*, 771.

supplementation by antirelativist arguments, themselves a form of transcendental argument designed to show that the concepts required for our experience are the concepts required for any experience. That, clearly, is in its different way as ambitious a project as option A transcendental arguments themselves.[14]

Grayling is making reference to another philosopher by the name of Donald Davidson in which he tries to show that there is only one possible conceptual scheme. If he shows that our conceptual scheme (contra the skeptic's) is the only conceptual scheme, then he has completely defeated skepticism, and I will give a thumbnail sketch of how Davidson tries to do this.

Davidson's Attempt to Defeat Skepticism

In his article "On the Very Idea of a Conceptual Scheme,"[15] Davidson takes issue with the fact that many philosophers discuss this idea of a conceptual scheme without actually knowing what they're talking about. The conclusion that Davidson ultimately draws is that there is no such thing as a conceptual scheme. However, what he really means is that there is only one conceptual scheme, and so to talk about conceptual *schemes* is meaningless since we have to view the world in a certain way.[16]

Barring issues of translation between different peoples, Davidson says that we still have to translate a person in a way that is appropriate

---

14. Grayling, *Blackwell Companions to Philosophy*, 771.

15. Donald Davidson "On the Very Idea of a Conceptual Scheme," in *Inquiries into Truth and Interpretation* (Oxford: Clarendon Press, 1984), 183-198.

16. For those knowledgeable of Davidson's philosophy, Butler then delves here into how Davidson was a student of Quine who argued that "translation between any persons is indeterminate" and that "meaning has no objective value," but this is not directly pertinent to the subject of TAs.

with our way of looking at the world. In order to recognize a language at all we must translate it into terms which are intelligible to us. From this point, Davidson concludes that there is no such thing as a conceptual scheme[17] simply because I cannot translate another language into a different conceptual scheme than my own. I wouldn't be able to understand it. That is, if someone really had a different conceptual scheme than I did, I wouldn't be able to recognize that person as a speaker of another language. If I were ever to recognize someone as speaking a language, I must presuppose that he is operating within the same conceptual scheme as I am. Otherwise, I would never recognize what he was doing speaking a language.

This is a quick overview, to be sure, but the bottom line here is that according to Davidson there is no such thing as a conceptual scheme given the fact that it makes no sense to even talk about it (i.e., the aborigine conceptual scheme versus my own conceptual scheme).

Grayling picks up on this insight and claims that this is exactly what one needs in order to put forth an "Option B," conceptual transcendental argument. At base such an argument would, again, only show that certain types of concepts are necessary for our experiences, and the skeptic can come along and say that there are perhaps other types of experiences and conceptual schemes. But to this we could therefore use Davidson's argument to show that the conceptual scheme we are arguing for is the only one.

Analysis of Davidson's Argument

How much does Davidson's argument really cut away at the skeptic? If it is true that we can only conceive of (or say that there is only) one conceptual scheme in the sense that we can only recognize speakers of other languages by presuming that they share our conceptual scheme, that doesn't mean that they really do, right? If people do have different conceptual schemes, then we would never be able

---

17. As if they're just flavors of ice cream where you can pick and choose.

to recognize them. But this has nothing to do with the fact that they actually do have another conceptual scheme. *Davidson's point is strictly epistemological. He is saying that we could never know about another conceptual scheme. But his argument says nothing about whether or not there really are other conceptual schemes.* There *could* be other conceptual schemes.[18] The way Grayling utilizes Davidson's argument is to show we could never recognize a different conceptual scheme (although there could, in fact, be others beyond our knowledge and comprehension).

How should we look at Davidson's argument under theological considerations? What does the Bible say about this? Are God's thoughts our thoughts and vice versa? To a certain degree our thoughts are reflective of His thoughts when we are thinking properly. But are the limits of our conceptual schemes also limits in God's conceptual scheme? Absolutely not. Davidson is begging the question in giving his argument since we can recognize Somebody with a different conceptual scheme than ours—God.[19] We share a

---

18. We see here a parallel distinction between a conceptual transcendental argument and the more powerful ontological transcendental argument, Davidson's argument falling under the rubric of the former. It should also be noted that the nature of people recognizing others as speaking a language (despite not understanding it) does not necessitate the conclusion that we only know of or can be one conceptual scheme. For all we know, there are a plethora of conceptual schemes with an underlying commonality, namely, the recognition of language-speakers. The enterprise of arguing that there is only one shared conceptual scheme amongst mankind requires delicate and meticulous use of defining terms, conditions, parameters, etc. That we all recognize other people as speaking a language is not, in isolation, enough to definitively prove that there is therefore one conceptual scheme. Whose parameters of conceptual schemes should we follow?

19. This is one of the crucial issues to remember. In starting with himself, Davidson has, at the outset, not started with God. His argument thus rests upon a naturalistic and egocentric picture of man. Davidson has implicitly believed in the non-existence of God in stipulating his argument and therefore begged the question metaphysically. Here again we see the impossibility of neutrality; everyone has their own taken-for-granted assumptions. The ultimate question is how you justify those very assumptions (or presuppositions).

certain amount of His conceptual outlook, but other parts of God's conceptual outlook are unknowable to us. But this doesn't mean that God can't have a different conceptual scheme. We know that He does since He has told us within our own conceptual scheme that He has a larger scheme than we do.

Finishing Grayling's Article and Final Conclusion

Grayling finishes his article with this final paragraph:

> The primary importance of transcendental arguments resides in the fact that we have to reflect on our concepts and beliefs from the internal perspective of having to use them even as we investigate them. There is no external point from which we can view our conceptual scheme; like Neurath's sailors we have to rebuild our ship at sea.[20] Transcendental arguments offer ways of reflecting on our concepts which at least promise to tell us much about their nature and interrelations, and about the degree of strength possessed by sceptical challenges to our use of them.[21]

There is something right and something wrong with this. Transcendental arguments as we have been primarily discussing them in the conceptual option B form do show us (and can be helpful in showing us) that types of things like causation are necessary for our experiences. But then he says that we are all in this position like Neurath's sailors,[22] and that we can only piecemeal build our

---

20. Butler: The analogy here basically goes that we have this conceptual scheme like a ship that we are sailing on. If we want to change anything in it, we can't drydock the epistemological ship. It's not an option since we are out in the middle of the sea. We could only change things plank-by-plank as it were; we couldn't do a complete overhaul of the hull otherwise we would sink.

21. Grayling, *Blackwell Companions to Philosophy*, 771.

22. "We are like sailors who on the open sea must reconstruct their ship but

epistemological ship together. This is something that is fundamentally opposed by worldview transcendental-type arguments. Grayling believes that transcendental arguments are to be done in a piecemeal way. Van Til says that this is not the way to do it. The way to do it is to drydock it and to determine what the necessary preconditions for experience as a whole are. And the only way to do this, Van Til says, is by evaluating worldviews.

Contemporary transcendental arguments are *fundamentally* different from Van Til's worldview-transcendental arguments. Formally, the two share some aspects (in trying to show transcendentals, utilizing reductio arguments, etc.), but they are different altogether in scope and the manner in how they are argued. Van Til says that worldview-level considerations are the only way transcendental arguments work.[23] Interestingly enough, Grayling doesn't consider this type of argument a possibility. He says that our shared predicament is like Neurath's sailors without consideration to worldview-level transcendental arguments. Why? Because he acts like an autonomous man.[24]

---

are never able to start afresh from the bottom. Where a beam is taken away a new one must at once be put there, and for this the rest of the ship is used as support. In this way, by using the old beams and driftwood the ship can be shaped entirely anew, but only by gradual reconstruction."

23. That is, work meaningfully. If you can't argue for an entire worldview, a holistic unit that takes every precondition for human experience into account, then any other argument you try to give is ultimately meaningless and useless as Bahnsen mentioned earlier in footnote 7.

24. A worldview which pivots around the autonomy of man can never furnish a proof or principle by which man can "verify" reality outside of himself, hence Grayling's allusion to Neurath's sailors. Since we cannot escape the sea of subjectivism and solipsism by which we can *externally* view our ship to observe its current state, we can only deal with one issue at a time, repairing the ship only at particular points that never see the whole, "real" picture. Using Butler's vocabulary, the Christian *can* drydock his boat to observe it in the sense of possessing God's revelation to mankind which comes to man as objective, absolute truth—the "blueprint" of our ship.

SECTION 3

VAN TIL'S TRANSCENDENTAL PROGRAM

(Dr. Greg Bahnsen)

CHAPTER 10

Summary of Transcendental Argumentation

Revisiting Skepticism

Having gone over of the contemporary climate of transcendental arguments with Michael Butler, it will be good to reflect once more about the skeptic because, as has been belabored, all of these types of epistemologies and arguments have been aimed at eventually answering the skeptic.[1] I want to analyze a particular sentence that has become a famous specimen in 20th-Century philosophy and has led to many different discussions: "This sentence is false."

What do we make of this? What if someone came up to you and said, "What I'm saying right now is false?" How would you reply? Doesn't it first have to be true in order to be asserted false? In which case it couldn't be false, right? Is this not self-refuting? What if that person says he hasn't refuted himself? At that point it comes down to not being able to make sense of what he is asserting because he has either refuted himself or this is nonsense.

In contemporary epistemology and philosophy of language this specimen is used to show that sometimes when we are engaged in self-reference, we must iterate our beliefs (go to a different level of linguistic analysis) so that we have an object language and a language in terms of which we evaluate the object language. So, "This sentence is false" can only be meaningful in another language, in a language

---

1. See chapters 6-9 for how all of the arguments being discussed have been aimed at skepticism.

reflecting on this language.[2] While we aren't going to get into this specifically, I would like to use this discussion as an analogy on talking with the skeptic.

The problem with the skeptic is that
he doesn't really want to be a skeptic.

What if the skeptic asserts, "My challenge to any rational justification is not rationally justified?" The skeptic says that he doesn't think there is any rational justification. Ultimately, rationality cannot be justified. Well, *is what he is saying when he asserts that rationally justified?* The skeptic would have to say no. But when he says no, hasn't he ended up saying something like "This sentence is false"? If somebody says, "You can't justify rationality and what I'm saying is not rationally justified," then we have the right to say, "Oh, well then we can ignore you." He's basically proclaiming, "Here's what I'm saying and I mean it with all my heart, and it's false!" Well, if we take what you're saying on your word as being false, then let's just move on to the next candidate. You're wasting our time. The problem with the skeptic is that he doesn't really want to be a skeptic.

The skeptic will not like being ignored. He will say, "You can't ignore me! I'm going to keep asserting this because you haven't answered me yet!" To this you respond, "You don't need an answer because what you're saying is not rationally justified." The reason I'm playing out this skit is because in apologetics we're saying that if you want to play the reason-giving game you have to be a Christian. But I

---

2. What would be called a "meta" language, meaning a language which transcends the normative language of English by which seeming paradoxes can be understood fully. This observation parallels the seeming paradoxical problems and understandings of Christian theology as well, pertaining to things such as the Trinity, decretive determinism yet volitional responsibility for sin, etc. Human finitude necessitates the existence of meta language and understanding to transcend the plain of mere apprehension to that of full comprehension.

can't force you to play that game. Nor can I force you to keep coming in and out of the game. That is, I can't prevent you from stepping into the arena, then stepping out, then stepping in again, etc. Given the skeptic's challenge, he is not in the reason-giving game. Every time he wants to assert his position, he has to deny his position, and thus by denying his own position we just tell him, "Then get out of here. We want to talk to people who will argue and use reason and so forth."

Now, some people might look at that and say, "Well if your apologetic comes down to that, you haven't answered this guy because he keeps coming in the door objecting that you haven't answered him." To this we must point out that in apologetics, apologetics by definition is only interested in people who play the reason-giving game.[3] If the skeptic doesn't want to play that game, then we can't do apologetics with him. Now, is this a defect in my system of apologetics that I can't make everyone play? No. That is like saying Michael Jordan was not a very good basketball player because there are some people who refuse to get on the court with him. That shows he can't defeat them, right? That's absurd. Our point is that we can beat anyone who comes on the court to play. But if you don't want to get on the court, then don't get on the court!

Two Pictures of Ourselves as Knowers[4]

Now, imagine two different ways of picturing ourselves as knowers.

If you begin with an egocentric picture, don't be surprised when you end with an egocentric predicament!

---

3. See 1 Peter 3:15. We give an apologetic to anyone who asks us for a "reason" for the hope that is in us. This kind of skeptic nullifies the possibility of any notion of reason altogether; there is no use or point in engaging with him.

4. This is a crucial section in explaining and summarizing how Van Til's transcendental program falls under an "option A" *ontological* transcendental argument (using Grayling's terminology from the previous chapter).

1. One says that God created us and our minds, and God also created the world that we know with our minds. This is the Christian view of things. As a diagram, we can put God above the mind of man and the world, and since He is the Creator, we can put arrows going from Him to both the mind and the world. He is the cause of the human mind and the way it operates, and the cause of the world (the world including the human mind) and the objects of knowledge. God made the mind and the objects that the mind knows. Therefore, our conceptual scheme is automatically in touch/automatically corresponds to the objects of experience on this presupposition. If this is your beginning outlook or perspective, then you already begin with the idea that our conceptual scheme (or the human mind and the way it works) is in connection with the objects of knowledge. And what is the connecting link? God. Now, I realize that some philosophers will just say to this that we are doing theology.[5] Okay, fine, but if you won't do theology with me, then let's see what happens to your philosophy.

2. Another approach says that we can't know anything about God at the outset. All we can know is that we have a human mind, we assume its sufficiency, and we are pretty sure that there are objects out there that the mind can know. Everything here is loose and disjointed. The objects of knowledge are not connected to one another by God's creative, sovereign, foreordaining work. Nor are the objects automatically connected to the mind of man in his conceptual scheme. In fact, all minds are loose and separate as well. God is not brought into the picture here because we don't want to do theology in the place of philosophy after all, right? We'll just do philosophy autonomously. We begin with man and

---

5. Of course, it is an erroneous assumption to believe that theology and philosophy are two mutually exclusive and distinct subjects. The theology just laid out has *numerous* philosophical implications in it.

then work out from man, and this mind also operates on a conceptual scheme. The skeptic comes along and asks, "How do you know there is a connection between your conceptual scheme and the objects in the world?" This worldview by definition cannot answer the skeptic *because it begins with a separation between minds and the objects in the world.* There's no connecting link. And any attempt to bridge the dividing link is going to be easily criticizable by the skeptic. If you begin with an egocentric picture, don't be surprised when you end with an egocentric predicament! If you start your philosophy with man, you end up with man separated from everything in the universe. How do you know there's any connection between your thinking and what's outside the mind? The skeptic can push even harder and ask how we know there is anything at all outside of our minds. Autonomous philosophy—which says we don't want to bring God into the picture—if pushed hard enough becomes solipsistic.[6] If you leave God out of the picture, you leave man separated from everything. Not only can you not know if there are other objects outside of your mind, if that's the case, then you couldn't even know that there are other minds outside of your own mind.

When the skeptic raises the question, "How can you be sure your conceptual scheme corresponds to the world outside of us?," our answer as Christians is that this is our presupposition; that is the picture we begin with. We don't face the problem that you're raising. But your problem is a really good one for those who start with man without God in the picture.[7] For those people who want to

6. "Solipsism (from the Latin 'solus' (alone), and 'ipse' (self)) is the philosophical idea that only one's mind is sure to exist."

7. It is rather humorous when presuppositional opponents accuse it of erroneously starting with the existence of God and all the metaphysical truths of Christianity therein. Why shouldn't we begin our metaphysical picture that way as the "default" position? Has the non-Christian opponent not likewise begun his metaphysical

do Godless philosophy, the skeptic is on very good grounds to push them. But then again, as we have just seen, given that you're a skeptic, you have to say there is no rational justification for rationality, so we can dismiss you, too. We thus have three possibilities to choose from:[8]

Skepticism: You can be a skeptic, in which case you can be dismissed if you want to argue rationally.

Autonomy: You can have this autonomous picture of the knower as self-sufficient. He is in this world and now he has to work out from himself to other minds, objects, and so forth. But he has no assurance that his conceptual scheme ever has any contact with the objects outside the mind.

The Christian Worldview: If someone asks, "How do you know that the mind is in contact with objects? That the conceptual scheme corresponds with objects and other minds?" You respond, "That, definitionally, is my worldview. That is what I start with." I realize people will say, "Oh, you're begging the question!," but I'm not begging the question; that's my worldview.[9] "Now," we respond,

---

picture as if it was the "default" position unless or until proven otherwise? What's sauce for the goose is sauce for the gander. The non-Christian, presuppositionalist opponent hasn't so much proven that his agnostic metaphysical scheme is the default position as he has taken it for granted. He thus has no legitimate philosophical reasons to vilify the presuppositionalist for beginning his philosophy with his Christian metaphysic and thus has no basis for wielding Hitchens' Razor against him, especially since objective proofs are impossible on non-Christian grounds. *Everyone* begins their philosophy with certain metaphysical presuppositions.

8. Bahnsen: Though I'm not altogether happy with this scheme, but to make my point…

9. This illustrates the difference between an assumption and an argument. To assume the metaphysical scheme of the Christian worldview and starting with God is not an *argument* for it and is thus not a fallacy since stated assumption are, in most cases (and here), nothing more than psychological states (which are then uttered to an interlocutor). This is what Bahnsen is referring to here—you can't beg the question when *simply expositing* the metaphysical aspects (or any aspects) of your worldview. Any course in logic teaches the differences between

"do you want to play on the court, or do you want to get off the court?"

What I'm getting at here is that anyone who wants to challenge us is going to be reduced to skepticism. We've already indicated that the skeptic has to get off the court, and even if someone says, "Believing we are in touch with the external world is necessary to our conceptual scheme" in an autonomous framework, we say, "Well, yeah, but that doesn't show that it's true. That doesn't show that it corresponds to the objects in the world, that reality really is that way." This is, as Van Til puts it, nothing more than a rock in a bottomless ocean—you haven't done anything to help us get in contact with reality.

There is no egocentric predicament if you're a creationist.

However, within the Christian framework of thought we can say that is our presupposition. Not only can we show that rationality is justified in terms of God's existence and man being made in His image, but if you take that picture, you've already overcome the egocentric predicament because there is no egocentric predicament if you're a creationist.[10]

---

explanations and arguments, here truncated, it is the difference between mere psychological states and utterances and inferential premises to a conclusion. Fallacies pertain to arguments and their explicit or implicit assumptions, not *mere* explanations or psychological states per se (though there are some fallacies aimed at psychological pertainments apart from arguments such as complex questions or certain ad hominem accusations and explanatory-reifications).

10. Bahnsen here is not using this term as would be used in the debate between old-earth and young-earth creationism; only that all Christians, disagreements notwithstanding, are creationists regardless.

Summary of Transcendental Arguments

Keeping in mind that we are dealing with the skeptical challenge, let me quote for you something Hume wrote, one of the best sentences in all of his writings: "If reason be considered in an abstract view, it furnishes invincible arguments against itself."[11]

Now, what is reasoning for an empiricist? John Locke said to use the "Historical, Plain Method"[12] of reasoning. That is reasoning if you're an empiricist—no innate ideas; it's just particular experiences and everything that is true must be built up from particular observations of the world.

Hume comes along and says that if reasoning be considered in the abstract—that is, if you generalize that to know anything, to reason at all, you must trace it to its particular observational components— then reasoning furnishes invincible arguments against itself. Hume is saying that empiricism refutes itself because the empiricist cannot give observational components of genetic, psychological, historical tracings of observational components for the claims being made about continuing substance, causality, and so forth in this world. We can't say that there is a knower, we can't say that there are objects in the world that continue to be known, nor that there is any causal relationship between them.

Kant is scandalized by this situation and gives his transcendental program. To quote him: "It still remains a scandal to philosophy and to human reasoning in general that the existence of things outside us … must be accepted merely on faith, and that if anyone thinks good to doubt their existence, we are unable to counter his doubts by any satisfactory proof."[13] Kant, thus, proposes transcendental reasoning:

----

11. David Hume, "Essays and Treatises on Several Subjects" (Leadenhall St.: London), 461.

12. Bahnsen: Meaning we trace the historical method of our ideas; he does typologies and cognitive psychology. And for something to be true all of its component parts must be able to be analyzed simply to some kind of observation.

13. Immanuel Kant, *Critique of Pure Reason*, trans. Norman Kemp Smith

"I entitle *transcendental* all knowledge which is occupied not so much with objects as with the mode of our knowledge of objects in so far as this mode of knowledge is to be possible a priori. A system of such concepts might be entitled transcendental philosophy."[14]

Transcendental knowledge is knowledge of the mode of knowing, that is, the mode of our knowledge of objects. If thinking in this way is possible, we must ask how that is. Kant says we come to the objects of knowledge imposing these categories on them (i.e., I'm going to think causally; in fact, I *must* think causally. Anything that goes through my mind goes through the filter of causal reasoning). This is Kant's notion of transcendental argumentation.

Does Kant, then, bridge the gap between conceptual schemes and objects outside of the mind? No. In fact, he just poured cement around his feet. *He can't get out of that!* His whole point is that given the way the mind is, you can't know anything outside of the mind; there is no *ding an sich*, thing in itself. There is no reality outside of the mind that I can rationally know because to understand anything rationally is to have my mind inform it. So Kant has a transcendental program, but it's a program that is going to be caught in that same autonomous web. His worldview, his presuppositions will destroy him.

Another important thing he said about transcendental argumentation is that the conclusion of a transcendental argument "should be entitled a *principle*, not a *theorem*, because it has the peculiar character that it makes possible the very experience which is its own ground of proof, and that in this experience it must always itself be presupposed."[15] We learn a couple of things from this quotation:

1. Kant did not think you could use transcendental arguments to prove specific points of information about the world or experience.

(New York, 1965), 34, B xl/a.

14. Kant, *Critique of Pure Reason*, 59, A12.

15. Kant, *Critique of Pure Reason*, 592, A 737/B 765.

For example, if you want to know whether Aspirin or Advil works better for pain relief, a transcendental argument can't tell you that. It can't tell you a point of history, it can't give you any specific scientific theorem and so on. *It's not intended to do that.* Rather, *the transcendental argument provides a principle in terms of which any answer that is offered to those questions can make sense.*

2. The conclusion of a transcendental argument (the experience itself) already presupposes the transcendental.

    So when we are talking about transcendentals, we are assuming the transcendentals when we talk about them. At the end of Grayling's article he reflects on that when he says that if a conceptual scheme is transcendentally necessary, then you need to use it even when you talk about it.[16]

I can't talk about Christianity without assuming it, and you can't talk against it without assuming it!

At this point you can appreciate the naïveté of Van Til's critics. Many critics of Van Til say that when he calls presuppositional argumentation circular, he is begging the question. Well, would anyone suggest that Dr. Grayling is somehow a philosophical dunce? "How silly can you be, Dr. Grayling!? If you say we have to assume this conceptual scheme even when we talk about this conceptual scheme, you're reasoning in a circle! That's vicious and a logical fallacy so we can dismiss you!" No, Grayling is saying something very profound. It's not a schoolboy mistake in logic and nor was it for Van Til. What Van Til said is, "If what I am arguing is true about Christianity being

---

16. "The primary importance of transcendental arguments resides in the fact that we have to reflect on our concepts and beliefs from the internal perspective of having to use them even as we investigate them," (Grayling, 771).

the presupposition of all intelligibility, then you have to presuppose Christianity even when you argue about Christianity." And that, you see, is the strength of the proof. *I can't talk about Christianity without assuming it, and you can't talk against it without assuming it!*[17]

Apologetical Context

When someone asks what you are getting at when you're talking about a transcendental argument, there are two lines we should give them that tell you what the argument looks like in its broadest form:

1. Take *p* and show that *q* is the precondition of *p*.

2. Take *p*, show that it implies *q*, *and* that the denial of *p* implies *q* as well.

This is the argument, this is how simple it is. Take anything, *p*, and show that *q* is the precondition of *p*. I am not arguing to take *p* and then deductively conclude *q*. Nor am I saying to take *p* and a lot of things analogous to *p* and inductively say very generally that *q*. This is not a deductive argument, and this is not an inductive argument.

---

17. As a localized illustration, imagine a deranged skeptic demanding that you prove language exists. Laughable as this may be, you proceed to give some sort of an argument. But upon doing so the skeptic calls foul seeing as you are using a language in order to prove that there is a language. The skeptic will predictably exclaim that you cannot assume the very thing you are arguing for (in your argument) as this is textbook circularity. Well, what's the problem with this comeback? *The problem is that you must use a language in order to argue for it; it is impossible to do so otherwise.* Why? Because the "status" of language is a transcendental, a necessary precondition for proving that there is language (or anything else for that matter). This is what Dr. Grayling refers to with regard to transcendental circularity: we cannot help but presuppose necessary preconditions for the intelligibility of our experience— we must presuppose or assume the laws of logic in order to argue for them, we must assume our existence (whatever that may entail) when arguing for it, etc. These certain preconditions (transcendentals) must always be presupposed at the outset in a circular fashion, and even Kant himself—the Father of transcendental reasoning—acknowledged this. Contrary to the erroneous, dogmatic mindset of modern analytic philosophers, not every circle is a *petitio pincipii* fallacy, and thus not every circle is fallacious per se.

This is an argument that simply asks what has to be true? What is the precondition for *p*?

In more detail, when I say "take *p*," I am referring to some general principle.[18] Or, if you don't like that approach, take any operational feature of experience or thinking.[19] Notice how wide and general the scope of a transcendental argument is. A transcendental argument must be involved with something that is so situated or central in our conceptual schemes that it has a wide-ranging impact. Put philosophically, this means that it must be systematically fundamental or applicable. Because it is so central to our web of beliefs, it touches just about everything else we do. The principle of causation, the laws of logic, and the notion of personal identity would be such principles.

By way of example, if somebody says, "If the milk man is going to know not to bring eggs, then tonight I have to leave him a note," that doesn't seem very profound, right? But that operation within the realm of experience itself would make no sense. Why would you leave the milkman a note if you didn't assume that there are some causal connections in the world? That minds could communicate with each other? That the words on the page provide meaning for an English speaker to communicate to him and so forth?

Start with a note for the milkman if you want. Start with science trying to show what the cause of cancer is. Start with the laws of logic. Start with anything you want and what we want to show is if you didn't have the Christian worldview, you wouldn't be able to show that p is possible.

---

18. Bahnsen: A general principle would something like every event has a cause, or no proposition can be true if its opposite is true.

19. Bahnsen: When people argue with each other they are going through certain acts. That is, they're operating in a certain way (using language, reasoning from one premise to another, etc.). These are examples of operational features.

So the first step in a transcendental argument is to take p— whether it's a general principle or an operational feature of your experience or thinking—and now show that q is the precondition of p. That is, q is necessary to explain the possibility of p. Another way of putting all of this is to show that q is presupposed by p, not that it is deduced from p or induced from p and analogous to it, but that *it is the presupposition* of p. In our case, q is the Christian worldview, which means we don't have to start with miracles or angels or death or anything of that sort. Start with a note for the milkman if you want. Start with science trying to show what the cause of cancer is. Start with the laws of logic. Start with anything you want and what we want to show is if you didn't have the Christian worldview (q), you wouldn't be able to show that p is possible.

How do we show that q is presupposed by p? I will give two methods: the *indirect* method and the *dilemma* method:[20]

The *Indirect Method*: *not-q* (rejecting the Christian worldview) implies an absurdity or renders the operational feature impossible. If you deny the Christian worldview (q), you will be led to an absurdity or you will be led to a contradiction of p which is undoubted.[21] The p cannot be something wobbly. It, rather, needs to be something your opponent takes for granted. So whatever your opponent asserts, you show him that if he denies the Christian worldview, that operational feature is either impossible or the p he has taken for granted is in fact false. This is the indirect method; it's proven "indirectly" because you take the opposite position and show that it creates intellectual difficulty.

---

20. Bahnsen: The sharper logicians reading this will point out that they're one in the same and that they are just different versions of the same thing, but I think you'll like the "variety" approach, so I'll give it in two ways.

21. See Butler's remark on pg. 96, footnote 8. Remember that the p—whether it be causality, logic, uniformity—is usually agreed-upon by both parties. The point in question is q and whether it is a precondition for p. If the skeptic wants to deny any and all options for p like causality, uniformity, etc., then we just ask him to walk off the court or tell him, as Butler quipped, to have a nice day.

The *Dilemma* Method: This method is a little more sophisticated but says to take *p* and show that it implies *q*, *and* that the denial of *p* implies *q* as well. What if someone says that adding insulation to your attic will lower your electricity bill? Okay, if that's true, then that implies God exists.[22] But here is the interesting thing about a transcendental argument. What did Kant say? He said the conclusion of a transcendental argument is not a particular theorem; it's a *principle* for understanding all theorems. So now I can take the opposite of *p* and show that it proves God exists, too. If it is true that adding insulation to your attic will *not* lower your fuel bill, that is because God exists. For you to know or assert that, you once again have to have causation, induction, observation, and so forth which can only be explained on the Christian worldview.[23] I'm not trying to argue about electricity bills and insulation in your attic. I'm saying that *any* argument, whichever way you go, is going to imply the existence of God.

So *p* implies *q* and *not-p* implies *q*. But it must be that *p* or *not-p*. Therefore, *q* must be true. All of this is just a long, quasi-fancy way of saying that you have to believe in God in order to prove anything.

Van Til has said that any statement or any fact
can be used to prove the existence of God.
That is precisely his program.

What if someone says that *p* is "God exists" and *not-p* is "God does not exist"? The easy part is that if God exists, then God exists. However, if you argue *not-p*, that God does not exist, that

---

22. Bahnsen: Obviously the argument is not just the assertion I gave; it'll be a long set of considerations, but basically if we don't live in an orderly universe where what we've experienced in the past is the basis for predictions about the future, then you couldn't make this kind of claim predicting the future of your bill.

23. The exclusivity of the truth of the Christian worldview will be embellished later.

also implies that God exists. This is getting at what Van Til said: antitheism presupposes theism.[24] Saying God doesn't exist wouldn't even be intelligible unless God existed.[25]

Do you see now how this is such a strong approach to apologetics? You don't have to worry about *anything* a person out there may have. Take any experience about anything whatsoever, take any point you want to argue—*even the atheistic point of view*—and the transcendental argument says that to argue that point you have to presuppose God. Van Til has said that any statement or any fact can be used to prove the existence of God. *That is precisely his program.*

Conceptual versus Ontological Interpretation

I would finally like to point out that the transcendental method is useful on either interpretation of transcendental arguments, either the conceptual or the existential/ontological interpretation of the argument.

The conceptual transcendental approach is what has just been discussed. What we say here is, "If you wish to argue at all—to use predication, reason, make use of experience—then *you must presuppose* the existence of the Christian worldview or God to make sense of your own argument or communicating it." Here, the word "must" is interpreted *psychologically*. If you want to reason, you must psychologically presuppose the Christian worldview. Now, granted, this is not the strongest form of a transcendental argument. But if that is all we have of what Van Til has given us, we have enough. Why? Because what I am saying to the person who argues with me is, "If you want to argue with me, you have to assume that you're

---

24. Van Til, *Survey of Christian Epistemology*, 8.

25. "It is the firm conviction of every epistemologically self-conscious Christian that no human being can utter a single syllable, whether in negation or in affirmation, unless it were for God's existence." (*Survey of Christian Epistemology*, 19)

wrong." Obviously not right at the outset, but through our discussion I'm going to point out to him that he is assuming the very thing he is arguing against.

The stronger, existential interpretation says that if you wish to give an account *of our ability to know anything or argue or predicate, etc.*, then your explanation must presuppose the *existence* of the Christian worldview/God. Here, the "must" is not the psychological "must" (viz. "You can't escape thinking about the Christian God when you argue the way you do."). Now we are saying your explanation of our *ability* to argue necessarily includes a reference to the Christian worldview. There is no way to explain or materially account for our ability to know things unless you make a reference to the Christian worldview, in fact, many references to the Christian worldview.[26]

So we have two interpretations and what I am getting at is that while the existential interpretation is stronger *and legitimate*, even if someone were to say that we're only showing that we have to think as Christians, I'll take it. After all, it's pretty good to tell people that if they want to think at all they have to think as a Christian.[27]

---

26. Specifically, the metaphysical/existential truths of Christianity.

27. This is considered to be a somewhat controversial statement by Bahnsen among the more philosophical presuppositionalists today. Van Til certainly intended and argued for his program to draw a metaphysical conclusion; thus, it seems *inadequate* and insufficient to conclude only modestly with a conceptual necessity (option B TA) apart from a "concrete" proof (option A TA). But, as Bahnsen says earlier in this paragraph, he still does believe the metaphysical aspect of TAG is "legitimate" and thus Van Til's apologetic proves absolutely that the Christian God *exists*, not only that we must think that He does.

CHAPTER 11

Commendations of Van Til's Transcendental Method

Before delving into Van Til's apologetic specifically, I would like to point out a few things. When it comes to analyzing Van Til and his works, I don't believe he said everything exactly right, nor do I want to suggest that he thought through in as much detail the contemporary issues in transcendental arguments that arose in the 1960s and 1970s. After all, he was developing these things all the way back in the 1930s, 1940s, and 1950s *and doing it from a tradition that is not like the analytic tradition of today.*[1] However, I do *not* believe that he has made the major mistakes that people think he did and that what he has given us is the most powerful apologetical tool that is available.

To take Van Til's works as a whole, why does he say that the transcendental approach to reasoning commends itself to us? There are five commendations I would like to give.

1. The transcendental method is the most penetrating means by which the Holy Spirit presses the claims of God upon man.

Van Til says in his book *The Defense of the Faith*:

> Man's own interpretative activity, whether of the more or less extended type, whether in ratiocination or intuition, is no

---

1. Bahnsen recapitulates here his opening material from Chapter 1: "Modern philosophy is almost allergic to worldview considerations; it is really out of touch and out of style. Many philosophers would consider it amateurish or gush in some sense to even think about the big questions in philosophy anymore. Philosophy has taken such an analytical turn in the 20th Century."

doubt the most penetrating means by which the Holy Spirit presses the claims of God upon man.[2]

If you're going to use an apologetical strategy, Van Til says the method that shows the greatest promise for the Holy Spirit driving home to the heart of man the *absolute demand of God to turn and embrace Him* is one that focuses on man's reasoning or thinking, that is, his interpretive activity as a whole. That is what the Holy Spirit is going to make the best use of in driving home God's claims on men's hearts, Van Til says. Continuing:

> The transcendental argument amounts to nothing less than a call to conversion.... Calvin argues that as created in God's image every man, of necessity, has a knowledge of God. This "innate knowledge" is correlative to God's revelation in man's environment.[3]

So it is that we know God innately as well as through man's environment.

> And try as he may, the sinner cannot efface this knowledge. He can only seek to suppress it. Without first knowing God, he could not seek to deny it. He must be originally in contact with the truth in order to love and propagate the lie. Meanwhile God calls men to conversion. His natural gifts to them are calculated to make them return to God.[4]

When we challenge people intellectually, we are not interested in playing academic chess. Van Til is not saying, "Well, here's an issue. I wonder how we can find an answer to that problem epistemologically." This argument, he says, amounts to a call to conversion! This is a life-and-death situation we're dealing with; his apologetic is *passioned*.

---

2. Cornelius Van Til, *The Defense of the Faith*, ed. K. Scott Oliphint, 4th ed. (Phillipsburg, NJ: Presbyterian & Reformed, 2008), 255-256.

3. Van Til, *The Defense of the Faith*, 281.

4. Van Til, *The Defense of the Faith*, 281.

2. The transcendental argument is objectively valid regardless of the attitude of the man to whom it comes.

Van Til writes: "The transcendental argument is objectively valid regardless of the attitude of the man to whom it comes."[5] He continues:

> It is an insult to the living God to say that His revelation of Himself so lacks in clarity that man himself through and through a revelation of God does justice by it when he says that God probably exists…. The argument for the existence of God and the truth of Christianity is objectively valid. We should not tone down the validity of this argument to the probability level. The argument may be poorly stated and may never be adequately stated, but in itself the argument is absolutely sound. Christianity is the only reasonable position to hold.[6,7]

This quotation shows up in a number of places among Van Til's critics. "What kind of argument is it that is never stated?," they'll ask. However, this can simply be likened to when my students give me papers that are on the right track but need to be cleaned up a little bit. There may be ambiguities, wanderings, etc., and yet I know underneath that the student has a grasp of the conceptual issue.

Now, when I see this type of thing in a student's writings do I have the right to say that he doesn't have a good argument? Or rather that

---

5. Van Til, *The Defense of the Faith.*

6. Cornelius Van Til, *Common Grace and the Gospel*, ed. K. Scott Oliphint, 2nd ed. (Phillipsburg, NJ: Presbyterian and Reformed, 2015), 77.

7. While Van Til's critics are not addressed until the final chapter, it is important to note in the second-to-last sentence that Van Til is arguing that his transcendental program is objectively valid and "absolutely sound" *"in itself."* The understandable inability for a lay apologist to philosophically articulate transcendental reasoning to the last jot and tittle does not detract from the objectivity of TAG "in itself" as Bahnsen now elaborates.

he has an argument that is poorly-stated but it's a good argument? In all charity I would say that he does have a good argument but it needs to be cleaned up a little bit, so to speak, and I believe this is what Van Til is saying.

Some people may be confused by the argument and need further illustrations. And maybe, Van Til says, it will never be adequately stated for every type of audience, but he maintains that it is an objectively valid argument regardless of the attitude of the person to whom it comes. It's not one of those types of arguments that is only beneficial to those who are already believers. No, Van Til says this is a good argument regardless of your attitude.

Moreover, not only is this argument objectively valid, he also maintains that this argument is not affected adversely by the subjective elements in disputes over the canon of Scripture, the translation of Scripture, and the interpretation of Scripture.

What about the attitude of a textual critic? Some people think that presuppositionalism gets "rocked" when people raise questions about canonicity, translation, or interpretation. Our argument is that if you begin with the Bible—God's revelation—then you can make human experience intelligible. If you don't begin with Scripture, then you cannot do so. But what if someone comes along and says, "Well that's great as a general, abstract claim. But what is the Bible?" Appealing to the book on the shelf won't do it because we have to argue about canon, and then how the Bible should be translated if it should even be translated at all, and then after these issues, how do we interpret the Bible? So people will come back around and say that what Van Til has put forward sounds good formally, but until you actually have a concrete interpretation of the Bible that has been verified in terms of translation and have some argument about the canon, those subjective elements get in the way of this great objective argument that he has.

Well, Van Til addresses this directly in *A Survey of Christian Epistemology*. Speaking of two critics who level this criticism he says:

Turning to Taylor or Bowne's argumentation, we say that their argument against the idea of an absolute Scripture was that man must always at some point or other introduce a subjective element.[8] It makes no difference whether that subjective element comes in when there is interpretation, or translation, or canonization, or even when there is reception of revelation; it must come in at one or at several places.[9] Now this argument, we have pointed out, rests upon the *antitheistic assumption* that the human consciousness can function independently of God to begin with.[10] (emphasis added)

As a word of advice to budding apologists, when someone raises an objection, even though it looks like it's internal to your claims about an absolute Bible, Van Til says, "What foundation are they standing on when they raise that objection?" *Van Til was not trying to beg any questions about canon, translation, or interpretation. He admits that we have to do all of these things in this very quote.* But when someone says, "You can't really be sure what the Bible is until all of those things are made objective and absolutely certain," Van Til's response is to ask what foundation the critic is standing on when he says that. You see, the point is in a transcendental argument that you can't argue against Christianity without already assuming the Christian worldview in terms of which your argument can be stated, can make sense, can be intelligible.

Well, then, how do we know what the Bible is? Can you put Playboy magazine between the covers of the Bible, pull out other pages and just use the argument anyway? No. Van Til is not saying

8. Bahnsen: That is, when you're arguing for an absolute Scripture, the subjective element is that we have to accept what the canon of Scripture is, we have to do translation, and we have to do interpretation.

9. Bahnsen: Van Til clearly says that he recognizes this. As people, we are going to have some "fuzziness around the edges" if you will (e.g., we have to decide which books belong in the Bible, how they should be translated, and how they should be interpreted).

10. Van Til, *Survey of Christian Epistemology*, 190.

anything as absurd as that. We are talking about a concrete revelation about a very specific kind of God. But Van Til maintains that *we can know the essence or substance of that even if there are boundary conditions that have to be tacked down* (i.e., even if we have to talk about the extent of the canon or how to translate and interpret). The point is that because God made man and made him in His image, man couldn't even be thinking of this problem of making more precise the boundaries if he wasn't in touch with God. *It's a transcendental argument now used in defense of the Transcendental Argument for God.* There is no way to escape this.

In short, Van Til is willing to say that we can talk about getting more precise in our interpretation of the Bible, but the point is that if you didn't have the *substance* of the Biblical revelation, you couldn't even talk about making it more precise in the first place. The content of the Bible is there and when we understand that content, then we can use it as a foundation to go back and make more precise our understanding of the content.[11, 12]

---

11. Bahnsen: In other places this is called the "hermeneutical circle". Every time we go through the Bible we understand it better and better such that we are continuously correcting our understanding of it. But that doesn't eliminate everything we understood to begin with.

12. The critic may respond here by asking exactly how much of our interpretation of the Bible must be correct for this apologetic to ground itself in Scripture objectively. Hearkening back to Van Til's transcendental program ultimately being "concrete" or metaphysical in nature, quite naturally, then, it is ultimately the metaphysical propositions in the Bible pertaining to the nature of who God is, the nature of who man is, the nature of revelation (thus epistemological propositions as well), the nature of the universe, the nature of sin—noetic, epistemologically; death, metaphysically/ontologically; depraved, ethically—and the redeeming work of Christ "in whom are hid all the treasures of wisdom and knowledge." God certainly has made these metaphysical, epistemic, and ethical propositions known to man, and to dichotomize exegesis and God's personally endowing wisdom is erroneous. It should also be rather obvious that mistaken interpretations regarding things such as eschatology, the age of the earth, baptismal considerations, and the like are, while just as divinely inspired, are not as pertinent to Van Til's transcendental apologetic specifically. However, the

3. You do not have to worry about any future research changing or undermining it.

From his book *Common Grace*, Van Til says:

> Men ought, if only they reasoned rightly, to come to the conclusion that God exists. That is to say, if the theistic proof is constructed as it ought to be constructed,[13] it is objectively valid, whatever the attitude of those to whom it comes may be. To be constructed rightly, theistic proof ought to presuppose the ontological trinity and contend that, unless we may make this presupposition, all human predication is meaningless. The words "cause," "purpose," and "being," used as universals in the phenomenal world,[14] could not be so used with meaning unless we may presuppose the self-contained God. If the matter is put this way one argument is as sound as the other.[15] In fact, then, each argument involves the others. Nor is any one of the arguments then at any point vulnerable. And future research cannot change their validity.[16]

---

metaphysical substance in the Bible is already clearly understood (given the imago Dei), and it is the *broad* metaphysical doctrines in the Christian worldview that Bahnsen is referring to here as the "substance" of Scripture and TAG. Contrary to these broad considerations, *particular* doctrines such as eschatology, baptism, etc., on the other hand, are what are more subject to exegetical investigation but are not as immediately pertinent to Van Til's apologetic.

13. Transcendentally.

14. Our world of experience.

15. Bahnsen: What he is getting at here is that you can argue about purpose, cause, being and from these we have our version of a cosmological, teleological, and ontological argument. If you're reasoning transcendentally, it really doesn't make much difference.

16. Van Til, *Common Grace and the Gospel*. Notice here how Van Til is fixating around the conceptual aspect of his transcendental program (i.e., underscoring our *presupposition* of the "ontological trinity") while elsewhere in his writings he focuses on the metaphysical aspect for "God's existence" (pg. 129, footnote

Future research does *not* change the validity of transcendental reasoning.

By way of contrast let's look at the historic argument for Christ's resurrection.[17] Can future research change the validity of this argument? Of course. In the nature of the case, new information may weaken or strengthen the case that you are making. That is the logical structure of an inductive/historical/natural argument—it's all a matter of what the pool of relevant data is, and what you add to it or take from it affects the strength or weakness of the argument.

So if the argument Van Til is giving is not prone to changing given future research, would that not call for commendation? Wouldn't it be nice if we didn't have to keep up with all of the journals and sciences and historical insights being developed? I don't have to worry about who I run into. I don't care what stage they are in life or their academic preparation, I don't care whether they're trained in nuclear physics or historical research [or philosophy]. Why? Because given the transcendental approach you have to realize that when all is said and done, *they all have to face the same questions: they all have to come to the same bottleneck of logic, causation, reliability of sensation, etc.*[18] I can let them talk all they want and be fascinated by what they

---

25), thus reinforcing Bahnsen's analysis from the previous chapter that Van Til's TAG can be used either way, though as has been belabored already, it is ultimately metaphysical/ontological.

17. Bahnsen: This argument does have a place in apologetics; I am not doubting that at all.

18. The "etc." here should be underscored to the highest degree, for the number of philosophical questions that need absolute, objective justification is seemingly innumerable from an analytical perspective, and if there is inadequacy in justifying even one precondition of intelligibility (transcendental), then that worldview crumbles. *It's an all-or-nothing criterion.* That is, if an opposing worldview can account for every single transcendental but cannot account for the uniformity of nature, that problem alone singlehandedly undermines their entire worldview since uniformity is required/a transcendental to rationally explain anything and everything, including all of the other transcendentals posited.

say, but at the end of it all I will ask them, "What is the foundation you're standing on when you do this?"

4. The argument is a forceful all-or-nothing challenge.

The argument is all-or-nothing because, according to Van Til, the unbeliever cannot make any aspect of his experience intelligible. The argument covers every kind of experience. We therefore don't have to worry about what we are talking about, what the subject matter is, or what people will bring up—anything intelligible is subject to this type of analysis and can be used to prove God's existence. Van Til:

> Thus the Christian theistic position must be shown to be not *as defensible as* some other position; it must rather be shown to be *the position which alone does not annihilate intelligent human experience*...But all of this[19] is out of line with Calvin's *Institutes* which stress with the greatest possible force that the revelation of God's demand is so clear that it has absolute compelling force objectively.[20] (emphasis Van Til's)

Van Til says that in the transcendental argument there is no room for idolatry anywhere.

Later in the book, Van Til argues against Ridderbos[21] who says that Christianity can be shown to be the most probable or the best position available:

> But even if it is said that Christianity is more probably true than is the non-Christian position, this is still to allow that

19. Bahnsen: This "twilight zone" of neutrality between the believer and unbeliever where you don't have any kind of religious demands on you.

20. Van Til, *The Defense of the Faith*, 198.

21. S. J. Ridderbos (1909-2007) was a fellow Dutch Reformed theologian whom Van Til addresses in *The Defense of the Faith*.

objectively something can be said for the truth of the non-Christian position. Something objectively valid can be said for idol worship as well as for worship of the true God.[22]

Van Til says that in the transcendental argument there is no room for idolatry anywhere. *Nothing* can be said for the allowance of idolatry. Van Til again, responding to another critic:

> The philosophy of the non-Christian[23] cannot account for the intelligibility of human experience in any sense[.] Would counting, weighing, and measuring be possible in a universe that is run by chance? Is it not true that unless the world is controlled by God there could be no science?[24]

Many people who read this mock Van Til for what he is saying. Does he really mean to say that the unbeliever, given his chance philosophy can't make sense out of counting? Out of weighing and measuring? Van Til says explicitly that that is what he is saying.[25] Of

---

22. Van Til, *The Defense of the Faith*, 198.

23. By "non-Christian" here Van Til is primarily referring to atheism (or naturalism), pagans, and moralistic religions like Buddhism. One may grant (controversially) that Classical Theism broadly-speaking has a justification for the uniformity in nature and the relinquishing of chance. But even questionably-granting this point, since at one point or another their worldview cannot withstand philosophical scrutiny as pertains to the intelligibility of human experience (e.g., rectifying the problem of the One and the many, explaining the exhaustive relationships between all facts, harmonizing the relationship between the a priori concepts in the knower with a posteriori facts, etc.), they inevitably fall into the same boat as the atheistic worldviews which annihilate intelligible experience.

24. Van Til, *The Defense of the Faith*, 343.

25. Bahnsen: Let's digress a little bit. Why is it that counting is impossible in a chance universe? Because there is no order, obviously. Counting presupposes not only the laws of mathematics but also order in the universe. And order means that you can identify, reidentify, and distinguish (or individuate) between particulars. But if everything is ultimately random in a chance universe, I can't even count the number of times that I've seen a particular car, for instance. For all I know it

course the unbeliever can count, but given that his worldview were true he couldn't make sense out of that. So he must be using the Christian worldview while he does his counting. Van Til is saying that *in principle* the unbeliever couldn't count and do any of the other things mentioned. His entire point is that Christianity alone makes facts intelligible. Continuing, Van Til says:

> He must therefore present the facts of theism and of Christianity[26] as proving Christian theism because they are intelligible as facts in terms of it and in terms of it alone.[27]

Van Til is not saying that here we have a sufficient condition for the intelligibility of human experience, that is, Christianity. He is also saying that it is a *necessary* condition; it is the *only* condition that will make the facts intelligible.

So the fourth commendation of Van Til's approach is that we don't have to be concerned with some people not being interested or some people not being touchable by the argument or dealing only with special facts like miracles. It is an all-or-nothing, forceful challenge. The unbeliever is not given the privilege of saying that Christianity is good up to a certain point or that only some unbelievers are susceptible to this challenge. Again, it is all-or-nothing. We can talk about *any* fact and say that it is only Christianity that allows you to talk about it.

5. It justifies the rejection in advance of hypotheses which contradict Christianity.

If someone offers a theory to be explored and that theory contradicts the Bible, other approaches to apologetics will say that we have to get out there and do our research to hopefully keep up with the

---

is the same experience over and over again since I can't individuate anything in a random universe. Therefore, you can't have mathematics in a chance universe.

26. Bahnsen: That is, of Christian-theism.

27. Van Til, *The Defense of the Faith*, 261.

unbeliever and show that his theory which contradicts the Bible is not a good one. Van Til says that we don't even have to worry about going out there and doing battle that way. If his theory contradicts the Bible, it's wrong in advance. Van Til's apologetic allows us to have that *a priori* authority to say, for instance, if someone wants to go out on an expedition looking for the bones of Jesus that that is an irrelevant hypothesis. It can be repudiated without any further study.

Now, this really bothers people. "You can't determine what happened in history without research," they'll say. But I can. God reveals Himself in the Bible and if we don't think in biblical terms, we can't even think at all,[28] so it won't do you any good to go looking for the bones of Jesus. If we lived in a universe where the bones of Jesus would still be there, then the Bible wouldn't be true, the God of the Bible doesn't exist, and you couldn't go searching for the bones of Jesus because you can't make sense out of science and research anyway.

The Nature of Van Til's Challenge

According to Van Til, Christianity is not nearly just as reasonable or just as defensible as any other position. Nor is it a matter of it being more probably correct. We're not accepting ties, nor are we accepting that our opponent to score any points whatsoever. The score is always 100-0. If Christianity isn't true, then *nothing* is true. And so the nature of the challenge, according to Van Til, is:

> [T]he Christian-theistic position must be shown ... *to be the position which alone does not annihilate intelligent human experience.*[29] (emphasis Van Til)

28. That is, in terms of God existing and upholding the universe, in terms of God being three yet one, in terms of being made in His image so that we possess consciousness and have reliable faculties—in terms of the metaphysical preconditions laid out in Scripture.

29. Van Til, *The Defense of the Faith*, 198.

On unbelieving assumptions everything is
meaningless and everything is unknowable.

Without the Christian worldview, Van Til says:

> Our argument, then, is that those who come apparently ever
> so near the Christian position but stop short or maintaining
> the fundamental conceptions of an absolute Christ, an
> absolute Scripture, and regeneration, reduce experience to an
> absurdity.[30]

Here he is talking about people who come close to Christianity. He
is talking about those people who we think to be friendly – who give
credit to Jesus, who give a little credit to the Bible. Van Til says that it
makes no difference how close they come. Whatever their outlook on
life is outside of Christianity, it reduces to absurdity. On unbelieving
assumptions everything is meaningless and everything is unknowable.[31]
Van Til again:

> One makes no deal with [the unregenerate man]. One shows
> that on his assumptions all things are meaningless. Science
> would be impossible; knowledge of anything in any field
> would be impossible. No fact could be distinguished from
> any other fact. No law could be said to be a law with respect
> to facts. The whole manipulation of factual experience would
> be like the idling of a motor that is not in gear. Thus, every

---

30. Van Til, *A Survey of Christian Epistemology*, 189.

31. An appears-to-me-that outlook doesn't constitute knowledge in an
objective, public, and therefore meaningful sense. Moreover, from an ontological
perspective one has to justify in the first place how it is the human mind can
cogitate, to hold to these things we call beliefs, what this thing we call justification
is, and what truth is. The inability to do so precludes the possibility of objective or
meaningful knowledge.

fact—not *some* facts—clearly and not probably proves the truth of Christian theism. If Christian theism is not true, then nothing is true.[32]

This is exhilarating. Rising above the muck of all of the probabilism and all of the granting of points to the unbeliever, it's an all-or-nothing challenge. Van Til says that "Christianity is the only position which is philosophically justifiable…. It's the only rational, objectively valid position."[33]

----

32. Van Til, *The Defense of the Faith*, 264.

33. Van Til, *Common Grace*, 8, 82.

CHAPTER 12

The Uniqueness of the Presuppositional Use of Transcendental Reasoning

In order for the reader to understand that Van Til understood the uniqueness of his approach, I will give a few quotations from him as illustration.

The Impossibility of TAG in Idealist and Kantian Thought

First, Van Til says that we are using a transcendental method but in a way that the idealists and Kant could not:

> Without the presupposition of the truth of Christian theism no fact can be distinguished from any other fact.[1] To say this is but to apply the method of idealist logicians in a way that these idealist logicians, because of their own anti-Christian-theistic assumptions, cannot apply it.[2]

Van Til is making it explicitly clear that he is not arguing as the idealists ultimately argue, nor that he is arguing as Kant did, ultimately. He is taking their program and using it in a way that they could not. Why? Because of their anti-Christian assumptions. In *An Introduction to Systematic Theology* Van Til says the same thing:

---

1. Bahnsen: That is just one illustration of how you destroy intelligibility.

2. Van Til, *The Defense of the Faith*, 137.

[W]e may speak of our method as being transcendental. But if we do we should once more observe that our meaning of that word is different from the Kantian or modern meaning. Kantian thought does not really find its final reference point in God. Modern thought in general does not really interpret reality in eternal categories. It seeks to interpret reality by a combination of eternal and temporal categories. For all non-Christian thought, as we have observed before, eternity is nothing more than a correlative of time.[3] It is only the Christian who really interprets reality in exclusively eternal categories because only he believes God is self-sufficient and not dependent upon time reality.[4]

So we are using a transcendental argument but different from the way Kant would use it. Speaking of Valentine Hepp,[5] Van Til says:

Hepp does not point out adequately that on Kant's basis there can be no science at all, either for the things of this life or for those of the next. If he had shown that Kant's foundation of reasoning is wrong inasmuch as it is based

---

3. Bahnsen: Another way of putting it is that unbelieving thought (and also for Kant) has the ultimacy of the human mind with its categories (rationality) and then there is bruteness of facts "out there" (irrationality) and you can never bring the two together.

4. Cornelius Van Til, *An Introduction to Systematic Theology*, ed. William Edgar, 2nd ed. (Phillipsburg, NJ: Presbyterian and Reformed Publishing Co., 2007), 14.

5. Valentine Hepp (1879-1950) is a frequent subject of Van Til's reflections. He was a minister in the Reformed Churches in the Netherlands and a prolific theological writer who took a strong interest in the American churches. He disapproved of the founding of Westminster Theological Seminary, believing that the separation with Princeton was too hasty. Van Til appreciates Hepp and praises him for continuing Bavinck's good work. But he finds him less than radical in his critiques of Kant and the theistic proofs. (William Edgar, *An Introduction to Systematic Theology*, pg. 45, note 98).

upon the assumption of the ultimacy of the human mind, and inasmuch as it has assumed the existence of brute fact, he could never have said that Kant sought the solution of the question of certainty *in the same direction* in which a Christian should seek it.[6]

So here we have an individual who says that we should do what Kant was doing since Kant was seeking the problem of certainty in the right way, *and Van Til says that he never should have admitted that.* In general, you can say that we are going to do what Kant set out to do, but we can't do it the way Kant did it because time and eternity get mixed (see footnote 3). Thus, Kant doesn't save the intelligibility of human experience. In the same book Van Til says:

A non-Christian idealist might readily say what Bavinck said on this point. It is not enough for a Christian to point to the mere fact of the necessity of an *a priori* element in science. He must also show that unless that *a priori* be given the Christian theistic basis, it is no true *a priori*.[7]

Unbelievers criticize each other, philosophically. We criticize unbelievers, philosophically. But Van Til says that our criticism is something that no unbelieving philosopher could utter against another unbelieving philosopher. The point being that yes, we do use a transcendental program, but Van Til himself has already flagged in his writings that he is *not* arguing as Kant did, nor as an idealist. His critique, he says, *is one that no unbeliever could utter.*

---

6. Van Til, *An Introduction to Systematic Theology*, 109.

7. Van Til, *An Introduction to Systematic Theology*, 93.

The Distinguishing Factors in Van Til's TAG

With all of this in mind, what, then, is the difference? What makes the Christian presuppositional use different from what a Kant, a Descartes, an idealist, or a modern analytical philosopher would be doing with respect to reasoning transcendentally?

1. The first and most important difference is that we are not arguing about particular, isolated principles or operations. We are not just talking about causality or logic. Rather, the presuppositional argument is over *entire worldviews*. We are using a transcendental program to argue about an entire worldview, not about an element of a worldview.[8] Christianity must be defended as a *unit*, not in a blockhouse fashion. We do not take the elements of Christian theology as so many blocks where we have the creation doctrine, and over there we have the incarnation doctrine, and here is this doctrine and that doctrine, and block-by-block we build up the edifice of Christianity. Van Til says that we are not defending Christianity in such a manner; we are defending it as a unit.[9] Van Til:

> All men presuppose, whatever name they may use for it, a synoptic view of reality as a whole. We continue to call it metaphysics.[10] For convenience we speak of this total outlook on reality as a world and life view.[11] The fight between

---

8. Remember that while there is one broad transcendental argument in terms of defending the Christian worldview holistically, the discussion will most often diverge into particular subjects like causality, logic, etc. The point, however, is that the presuppositionalist's use of transcendental reasoning is to show that only his worldview can account for all of the "lesser" transcendentals.

9. Bahnsen: This doesn't deny that there is a distinction between the doctrine of creation, and the doctrine of incarnation, and so forth. The point is that it all hangs together.

10. Cornelius Van Til, *The Case for Calvinism* (Penna, PA: Presbyterian and Reformed Publishing Co., 1979), 115.

11. Cornelius Van Til, *The Protestant Doctrine of Scripture* (Phillipsburg, NJ:

Christianity and non-Christianity is, in modern times, no piece-meal affair. It is the life-and-death struggle between two mutually opposed life-and-world views.[12]

Christianity must be defended as a unit, not in a blockhouse fashion.

The Christian, perhaps thinking that his argument with the non-Christian is over the truth of some external matter such as creation versus evolution, may set out to prove from science that the alternative is implausible. But if you were to pursue that argument very long, you will find that the Christian and non-Christian also disagree over the genuine character of science, the nature of scientific theorizing.[13] A Christian may think that his argument with the non-Christian is simply over a fact like Christ's resurrection from the dead and may set out to prove from history that that event occurred. But soon, if you argue with a sophisticated, thoughtful unbeliever, you will see that the Christian and the non-Christian also disagree over the proper character of historical research, historical reasoning, and evaluation.[14]

Presbyterian and Reformed Publishing Co., 1967), 103.

12. Van Til, *An Introduction to Systematic Theology*, 23.

13. Is the venture of science ultimately a purposeless, cosmic accident where man approaches facts for the first time to try and figure out the origin of the universe and the meaning of various materialistic relationships? Is the venture of science a methodology by which we acquire facts of the nature of God's creation as He has already established the facts and thus a methodology used to glorify Him?

14. Historic disagreements between historians allow for the nature of contention and debate within the field. Contrary to popular belief, history is not a linear, ubiquitously-agreed-upon science; it is likewise subject to debates, and thus we must ask what "the proper character of historical research, historical reasoning, and evaluation" are. Should history be looked at within a naturalistic paradigm where every event is a result of cosmic determination that leaves out

We may think as Christians that we are only arguing with a non-Christian over philosophical matters having to do with coherence and practicality in what the Bible says. But if we deal with thoughtful unbelievers, we ultimately see that the two of them also disagree over the nature of meaning, the nature of utility, the nature of possibility, the nature of explanation, and so on. These are *worldview differences*.

Because both parties operate under the context of conflicting worldviews, the believer and the unbeliever will find, if they're consistent (and their dialogue pushes into deeper reasons for differing with each other), that their disagreement covers their theory of knowledge, as well as what they claim to know about God, the world, man, life, conduct, and values—their metaphysics, their ethics, as well as their epistemologies. Thus, Van Til taught:

> If man does not own the authority of Christ in the field of science, he assumes his own ultimate authority as back of his effort. The argument between the covenant-keeper and the covenant-breaker is never exclusively about any particular fact or about any number of facts. It is always, at the same time, about the nature of facts. And back of the argument about the nature of facts, there is the argument about the nature of man. However restricted the debate between the believer and the non-believer may be at any one time, there are always two world views ultimately at odds with one another.[15]

So, if I want to argue with the unbeliever about some particular fact, I also have to talk about the *nature* of facts. But it isn't enough to know just the nature of facts. I also have to know the nature of man who understands the facts and argues about them. Van Til says that

---

meaning, ultimately? Or should history be looked at as a continuous chain of events ordained by God from eternity past?

15. Van Til, *The Protestant Doctrine of Scripture*, 5.

ultimately every argument is going to be an argument that is at the presuppositional or worldview level. *This is completely different from what you find in people using transcendental programs.*

We know it is different with respect to Kant because he began by saying that we cannot know the nature of reality. He openly restricted himself to the way the mind works. If experience is going to be intelligible, then my mind has to make it intelligible. Idealist logicians don't start with worldviews; they begin with particular conceptual problems. Van Til says that he wants to argue transcendentally, but what he is going to do is bring two worldviews into conflict. And the way in which we are going to argue over the worldviews is by transcendental methods. He says the argument for Scripture is the same as the argument for God. How could he say that unless he meant that he was arguing for the whole enchilada? The whole worldview?

Since we are arguing for the whole worldview, then one aspect of the worldview is that we know about God (mainly) from the Bible. But then what does the Bible tell us about? God. So whether you're arguing about God or the Bible, you have to bring both of them onto the same platform at the same time when you're arguing—it is the whole worldview that we are talking about.

2. This form of transcendental reasoning is *concrete. It is not merely formal or abstract.* Van Til says that we must present to the unbeliever the fact that he must accept or reject the whole of the Christian system. We are not trying to go through and devise first a transcendental argument for God's omniscience and then a transcendental argument for creation, and so on. Van Til is convinced that one of the reasons philosophers run from God is that they want to take certain elements of God (like orderliness), but they never want to get personal about it; they never want to get *concrete.* They don't want to talk about God.

Van Til says in *The Defense of the Faith* that we are not answering skepticism with something formal or abstract:

Kuyper insists that the concept of faith that he here speaks of is without content. It is inherent in the subject, therefore, not because the subject is unavoidably confronted with God, but simply as such.[16] By means of this purely formal faith the human subject is first to become conscious of its own existence. Then by means of this formal faith a bridge is to be laid to the external world. The laws of thought by which the environment of man is to be manipulated also rest on this formal faith.[17]

By 'formal' faith Van Til means the generic idea of faith rather than the substance or content of faith. And by means of a purely formal faith you have first of all the human subject established (i.e., I think, therefore I am). I don't know what I am, but I must exist formally. And then by means of this formal faith a bridge is built to the external world. Here you have the philosopher who is trying to answer these abstract questions about "What is it for me to exist?," "How can I know objects outside myself?," and so on, and Van Til is upset with Kuyper for buying into that. Jumping a few sentences, Van Til goes on to say:

> To be sure, all men have faith. Unbelievers have faith as well as believers. But that is due to the fact that they too are creatures of God. Faith therefore always has content. It is against the content of faith as belief in God that man has become an unbeliever. As such he tries to suppress the content of his original faith.[18] He tries to reduce it to something formal.[19]

16. Bahnsen: The claim here is that all men operate on some kind of faith; everybody has faith in *something*. Here we are just talking about generic, abstract faith rather than faith with particular content or concrete character to it.

17. Van Til, *The Defense of the Faith*, 370.

18. The "original faith" of which Van Til speaks here is the knowledge of God implanted in all human beings by virtue of our being created in God's image. (K. Scott Oliphint, *The Defense of the Faith*, 370, footnote 37).

19. Van Til, *The Defense of the Faith*, 370. Unbelievers will take features of God (such as coherence/uniformity, causality, logicality, etc.), abstract them from that

To summarize this point again, Van Til's transcendental approach is not an abstract, formal kind of argument; it is concrete. We confront the unbeliever with an entire worldview, and the method is personal and in-your-face. "God is confronting you and if you do not submit to Him, then you will die intellectually!" And the way in which we demonstrate this is by a transcendental program: reducing the unbeliever's philosophy to absurdity, showing that *no* experience is intelligible apart from this very concrete kind of God and worldview.

> No experience is intelligible apart from
> this very concrete kind of God and worldview.

Van Til says we are not being speculative; we are not interested in trying to find the highest philosophical concept and calling it God. Elsewhere in *Common Grace* he says, "We are not positing an indeterminate god."[20] Van Til admits that most unbelievers are not all that averse to admitting that *a god* exists, which is why his argument is not over whether or not a god exists; it's over whether or not *the God* exists. This is why Van Til maintains that our apologetic must start with the "actuality" of the Bible:

> The Reformed faith has set the idea that we must begin with the actuality of the Book over against the rationalism and irrationalism of unbelieving thought. We must not pretend that we have established the possibility of the Book and the necessity of it in terms of a philosophy that we did not get from the Book. We have as Christians indeed learned with Calvin to interpret ourselves in terms of the Book and that

concrete reality that is God, and talk about them in general and impersonal terms. They formalize their faith and approach so that they don't have to deal with their Creator in their reasoning processes.

20. Bahnsen: An indeterminate God refers to a formal idea of a god "out there" (such as Aristotle's "God of the Spheres").

on the authority of the Book and then we look to the Book for the interpretation of the meaning of the facts.[21]

Van Til says that we are not going to come to the Bible with a philosophy outside of the Bible that has allowed me to say that this is possible or even necessary. Or another way of putting it is that I'm not going to begin with, say, Quine's philosophy and come to the unbeliever and say, "You know, if we're good Quinians, I can show you the necessity of the Bible." Van Til says that we don't work up to the possibility or even the necessity of the Bible from outside the Bible—a philosophy that now makes it credible or respectable to then turn to the Bible. He says that we begin with the *actuality* of the Bible.

In short, we can say that this apologetic is immediately in-your-face. "God has spoken!" I'm not going to talk about the general idea of revelation or the notion that maybe such a god would reveal himself. "Isn't it very probable?" No, I am going to say, "Here's a book. It claims to be from God, a very specific kind of God, and it says that you are in rebellion against Him and you need to repent." We begin right there with the *concrete* actuality of the Bible and the full details of the Christian worldview! *This is not what transcendental arguments look like when you follow Kant or Strawson or anybody else.* We take this concrete reality and say, "Without this worldview, you couldn't know or prove anything. This is the precondition for the intelligibility of human experience."[22]

---

21. Van Til, *The Defense of the Faith*.

22. Bahnsen: Where did Van Til get this? Van Til was a very Godly man, and if you asked him this question his response was, "I am merely standing on the shoulders of giants." Van Til said that Calvin and Kuyper and all of the rest of the great Reformed theologians taught him, and if he was able to just see a little bit further than them, he felt that he was being a little more consistent with what Kuyper believed from Calvin and so forth. If he was able to do that, it was only because, as he said, he was standing on their shoulders. That is what Van Til would say if he were alive today, and hopefully it would be that God gives us all such

3. The position that we are arguing about rests on authority. Ultimately, the unbeliever who is being refuted by our argument needs to see that he needs to throw away the authority by which he has been living, and now live a new kind of life, now come to live under a new Authority. How is it that we get the Christian worldview? Do we get the Christian worldview by building up block-by-block or element-by-element logic, self-consciousness, uniformity in nature, moral absolutes, the personality of God, and so on? Is that how we get this worldview and then go out to challenge the unbeliever? Not at all.

I've had many people ask why someone couldn't come along and just say, "Well my worldview is a god that is the foundation for logic and the uniformity in nature and moral absolutes." That is, just take as much of what you have been talking about with them as is convenient for their intellectual purposes and then get rid of all the other stuff like the Old Testament stories, miracles, and so forth. Wouldn't that kind of deistic worldview defeat us? Why couldn't we just have deism be the transcendental for the intelligibility of human experience? How do we answer that? Well, the answer is to ask them, "Where did you get your worldview?" Did they get their worldview by building it up block-by-block and element-by-element? If so, then the person who proposes this deism or this reduced version of Christianity must show every element to be necessary and coherent with every other element on its own. He cannot begin with the system and then decide to arbitrarily throw the parts out he doesn't like. Why? Because if you begin *concretely* with the Christian system, you are not allowed to throw any elements out.

Another way of looking at this is to ask what determines this off-brand Christian worldview? One answer is to say that they took the Bible and they edited it, getting rid of all the stuff they didn't need. Well if this is the case, then he didn't really start with the Bible

---

humility to recognize that we all have learned from others.

because the Bible says that every "jot and tittle" must be there. So we ask them again. They would have to say that maybe they didn't start with the Bible as their authority, but they got their ideas from the Bible.[23] But if this is the case, then each and every one of them has to be built up block-by-block individually which brings us right back to the rock in a bottomless ocean scenario. The unbeliever cannot take individual elements—logic, uniformity in nature, morality, a human mind—and bring them together.[24] And so as it turns out, anyone who wants to take Christianity and edit it down has an authority outside of the Bible (that person's mind) by which he is living. And by that authority he edits the Bible.

Summation of points

To sum up the distinguishing factors, Van Til says that we are first arguing over entire worldviews, second, that it is concrete and not formal and abstract, and third, we openly admit that our position rests on authority. The adherent of this off-brand Christianity used the authority of his finite mind. If this same person asked us where

---

23. Keep in mind that everyone must use their mind as the "proximate starting point" as Van Til says, so that we, too, as Christians also get our "ideas from the Bible." However, here the unbeliever is elevating the status of his *proximate* thinking to the *ultimate* level, determining ultimately what is and isn't credible in the Bible to formulate his off-brand Christianity. The Christian subordinates his mind to the authority of God's revelation, using it only as a proximate basis by which this, and all other types of knowledge, are acquired.

24. The finite unbeliever cannot conjure up an exhaustive system by which to save intelligibility since he himself is not "exhaustive", let alone infallible. He may argue transcendentally for the above preconditions, but he will never be able to bring them all together into a workable worldview. That is, he may argue transcendentally (from the impossibility of the contrary) that nature is uniform, that there are laws of logic, that we are conscious, but there is no meta-transcendental (namely, God) to unite and explain them all into a coherent system. As Bahnsen has already alluded to earlier, Van Til says it's like a rock falling in a bottomless ocean—you have a solid substance here (a transcendental/argument) but you have nowhere to "put it" in an all-encompassing system, so who cares?

our position came from, we say that God revealed it. "Why do we accept it?" We accept it on His authority. "You can't just accept it on His authority." Well, if the ultimate authority is speaking here, then I certainly can because if it is the ultimate authority who is speaking, *there is no authority outside of that by which I can establish His authority.* The Bible has to be accepted on its own say-so because of the nature of what it claims.[25] Van Til says:

> We accept this God upon Scriptural authority. In the Bible alone do we hear of such a God. Such a God, to be known at all, cannot be known otherwise than by virtue of his own voluntary revelation.[26] He must therefore be known for what He is, and known to the extent that He is known, by authority alone. We do not first set out without God to find the highest philosophical concept in terms of which we think we can interpret reality and then call this highest concept divine.[27]...Have we no philosophical justification for the Christian position? Or are we to find a measure of satisfaction in the fact that others too, non-Christian

---

25. Once more the charge of circularity arises. But now the question we can pit on our opponent is which type of circularity is it? Does he naively assume there is only one type of circularity? There are, in fact, many kinds: "direct", linear circularity (question-begging), epistemic circularity, transcendental/indirect circularity, and worldview circularity (internal coherence). Are they all fallacious? Are only some of them fallacious? On a non-Christian worldview who or what absolutely and objectively justifies which circularity is acceptable and which isn't without resulting in arbitrary delineation?

26. Bahnsen: If God is absolute, if He is the Creator, if He is transcendent and distinct from creation, if He is sovereign, if He is self-contained, if He is in need of nothing, this kind of God, Van Til says, could only be known by His own voluntary revelation.

27. Bahnsen: As I alluded to already, we don't start abstractly talking about generic philosophical problems, find the unifying concept, and say that that must be God. Van Til says we begin with a God who is personal, concrete, and He reveals Himself in terms of His own authority.

scientists and philosophers as well as ourselves, have in the end to allow for some mystery in their system?[28]

To all this we must humbly but confidently reply by saying that we have the best of philosophical justification for our position. It is not as though we are in a bad way and that we must seek for some comfort from others who are also in a bad way. We as Christians alone have a position that is philosophically defensible. The frank acceptance of our position on authority, which at first blush, because of our inveterate tendency to think along non-Christian lines, seems to involve the immediate and total rejection of all philosophy—*this frank acceptance of authority is, philosophically, our very salvation.*[29] (emphasis mine)

To analogize all of this, say you are engaged in transcendental, presuppositional apologetics and someone asks you, "Well where do you get your worldview?" We say that we accept it on the authority of God speaking in the Bible. Van Til says that we do blush, why? "Because of our inveterate tendency to think" like unbelievers. Isn't that true? Why does it bother us to say we accept the Bible on the authority of God to unbelievers? Because they will make fun of us, right? So we want to think like unbelievers think. But they do not think on the authority of God, so now there is a real tension here. Van Til says that at first blush the acceptance of this authority "seems to involve the immediate and total rejection of all philosophy."[30]

---

28. Bahnsen: Van Til asks: "Are we to just be satisfied that everybody has mystery in their systems, we don't have philosophical justification, so we just accept our position on authority?" J. W. Montgomery, *decades later*, portrays Van Til as saying this very same thing, yet Van Til anticipated this criticism in his first major apologetical discussion!

29. Van Til, *The Defense of the Faith*, 14.

30. The contents from footnote 25 can also be tied in here. Since we are told that circularity is fallacious (the critic disingenuously not defining the diversity of

---

If you don't start with authority—this authority, this God,
this worldview—you will destroy all philosophy.

A more literate unbeliever may respond to the fact that we accept
the Bible on its own authority by saying, "Then you're not doing
philosophy because philosophy can't be done on authority!" How does
Van Til reply? "This frank acceptance of authority is, philosophically,
our very salvation." So my reply to the person who says I'm not doing
philosophy anymore is to point out that what I am doing is the
very salvation of philosophy! If you don't start with authority—*this*
authority, *this* God, *this* worldview—you will destroy all philosophy.[31]

I begin with authority and the unbeliever begins with authority.
But since the unbeliever begins with a subjective authority, it
therefore reduces to skepticism. The authority I begin with is
God's authority, therefore I do not fall prey to subjectivism of the
unbeliever's worldview. So we all begin with authority, the non-
Christian's destroys reason, mine saves reason, so if he wants to
continue reasoning he better confess his sins and give thanks to
God, for it is *only* because of God that he can reason at all. This is
nothing short of a heavy-duty apologetic.

Van Til says that the issue is not what the unbeliever can do
intellectually. He is not talking about the intellectual accomplishments
of unbelievers. *He would be the first to say that unbelievers are brilliant*

---

circles), philosophical Christians "know better" than to start with the Bible since,
after all, to do so is to engage in fallacious reasoning. Thus, they resort to neutral
thinking, beginning autonomously, resulting in having an "inveterate tendency to
think along non-Christian lines."

31. It should also be noted, as Bahnsen will now go on to explain, that
everyone argues on some sort of authority; a professor's insights, a textbook or
holy book, an ideology, all pass through the *authority of your mind* and what *you*
deem as sound and unsound, and thus the objection that we ought not reason
from authority is self-refuting.

in many areas. The issue is whether or not the unbeliever can give an *account* of what he has done. Van Til would always use a particular aphorism to illustrate this point: he is not questioning whether unbelievers can count, but rather that they cannot give an account of their counting; they can't give a worldview in terms of which counting makes sense.[32]

Van Til says that what we must do is find within a worldview an answer to the basic epistemological questions:

> The ontological Trinity will be our interpretive concept everywhere. God is our concrete universal;[33] in Him thought and being are coterminous, in Him the problem of knowledge is solved.[34]

The key issue is what worldview will enable you to settle the problems of epistemology? Van Til says it's the worldview of the triune God. Another way of putting it is who first gives order to the particulars? Is it the mind of God or does the mind of man running side-by-side with God give order to the particulars first? Who first rationalizes the facts? Van Til:

---

32. To this point, many unbelievers (depending on their view of reality) will argue that it *must* be the case that there are, metaphysically speaking, numbers and laws of mathematics in order for reality to even be possible (note the transcendental line of reasoning here). But this does not even come close to giving an account for counting, and the unbeliever here has not understood the full force of the challenge. He has, rather, simply put himself back in the "rock in a bottomless ocean" predicament. He has one transcendental here (mathematics), but he has to relate mathematics to laws of logic, to the uniformity in nature and the inductive principle, to the contingent human mind and how it can comprehend necessary abstract entities, to identity through change, to unity and diversity, to contingency and necessity, to causality, and so on.

33. Bahnsen: This is jargon for saying that God is the One who has universal knowledge, but also all the details as a concrete person. God doesn't gain universality in His understanding by becoming abstract. He is the "concrete universal."

34. Van Til, *The Defense of the Faith*, 79.

On a non-Christian basis, facts are "rationalized" for the first time when interpreted by man.[35] But for one who holds that the facts are already part of an ultimately rational system by virtue of the plan of God, it is clear that such hypotheses as presuppose the nonexistence of such a plan must, even from the outset of his investigation, be considered irrelevant.[36]

Who first rationalizes the facts? Is God's mind that which gives coherence, intelligibility, meaning, and order to the facts, or does man first do it? Over and over again Van Til says that you have to choose between one of those two worldviews.[37] And if you choose to say that man does it first, what does it reduce to? Subjectivism and therefore skepticism![38] Start with man, you will end with man, and you will not be able to have public, objective knowledge. You must begin with the Christian worldview where the order that is given to the facts is there because of the mind of God. He is the one who plans and creates all things.

In *The Reformed Pastor and Modern Thought* Van Til says:

The consistently Christian conception of the *a priori*[39] is that which presupposes the Creator-creature distinction and makes the covenant inclusive of all the activities of man. Thus there is involved in every act of interpretation a two-fold

---

35. Bahnsen: You have all of these brute facts—this random world out there—and man brings order to the facts when he interprets them. He gathers them together and then he gives a system of interpretation.

36. Van Til, *The Defense of the Faith*, 121.

37. Generic or Classical Theism can likewise posit that their god first ordered the facts, but so long as there is no Creator-creature distinction, so long as this god and man simultaneously look at the facts together, there can be no absolute knowledge of any facts since both god and man approach them from the same linear perspective.

38. See all of Chapter 2.

39. That which we know apart from observation or experience.

activity, an activity of God and an activity of man. The two are not opposed to one another, nor do they work at different times or in different dimensions. No facts can be interpreted without reference to the activity of the human mind. But if skepticism and subjectivism are to be avoided there must be back of the activity of man the activity of God.[40], [41]

Van Til says that our minds are active, and we are trying to interpret things, but if you don't have a worldview that says that back of all my interpretive efforts is God's original interpretation, then you will be reduced to subjectivism and skepticism. The facts will never be brought together, there will be no coherence, no order, no intelligibility.

40. Cornelius Van Til, *The Reformed Pastor and Modern Thought* (Phillipsburg, NJ: Presbyterian and Reformed Publishing Co., 1971), 89.

41. For critics of presuppositionalism who attack it for confusing the proximate with the ultimate starting point, Van Til directly deals with it here. And so, as with Dr. John Warwick Montgomery, inadequate research is the embarrassing and telling Achilles' Heel for any critic.

CHAPTER 13

Back to Basics: Readings from Van Til

If you want to boil Van Til down to the apologetical bones of his argument and the structure itself, it is nowhere more prominent than in *A Survey of Christian Epistemology*. It is to the following readings of Van Til that we shall see that his transcendental program was right in front of us all along.

A Survey of Christian Epistemology

In this respect the process of knowledge is a growth into the truth. For this reason we have spoken of the Christian theistic method as the method of implication into the truth of God. It is reasoning in a spiral fashion rather than in a linear fashion. Accordingly, we have said that we can use the old terms deduction and induction if only we remember that they must be thought of as elements in this one process of implication into the truth of God.[1] If we begin the course of spiral reasoning at any point in the finite universe, as we must because that is the proximate starting point of all reasoning, we can call the method of implication into the truth of God a transcendental method. That is, we must seek to determine what presuppositions are necessary to any object of knowledge in order that it may be intelligible to

---

1. Bahnsen: Think of it as spiraling down, implicating yourself deeper and deeper into the truth of God using deductive and inductive reasoning as you go.

us. It is not as though we already know some facts and laws to begin with, irrespective of the existence of God, in order then to reason from such a beginning to further conclusions. It is certainly true that if God has any significance for any object of knowledge at all, the relation of God to that object of knowledge must be taken into consideration from the outset. It is this fact that the transcendental method seeks to recognize.[2]

The transcendental method is trying to exhibit something, namely that if what you are trying to talk about is significant, you must immediately have God as part of your worldview (or you must immediately acknowledge or incorporate the Christian worldview). It doesn't reason deductively or inductively outside of the Christian worldview *to* the Christian worldview. It, rather, says that all of your deductive and inductive reasoning already presupposes the Christian worldview if you claim that it has validity, meaning, or significance.

> The charges made against this type of reasoning we must turn upon those who made them. It will be said of this type of reasoning that it introduces the subjective element of belief in God, which all men do not share. Of this we can only say that all men should share that belief, and before the fall of man into sin man did have that belief. Belief in God is the most human attitude conceivable. It is abnormal not to believe in God. We must therefore hold that only the Christian theist has real objectivity, while the others are introducing false prejudices, or subjectivity.[3]

This is a nuclear-strength paragraph if I may put it that way. Van Til says that in order for your argument to have significance you

---

2. Van Til, *A Survey of Christian Epistemology*, 173-174.

3. Van Til, *A Survey of Christian Epistemology*, 174.

must incorporate belief in God.[4] The comeback to that is, "Oh, well you're saying coherence, logical validity, and significance all depends on a subjective element – whether you believe in God or not!" Van Til says that to this he must turn the criticism back on the critic. He says that *they* are the ones who are introducing subjectivity. Sound familiar? All of the arguments stipulated by autonomous men end in subjectivism and skepticism.[5] He says that because of the way the unbeliever approaches matters, he is the one who makes everything subjective. Van Til says that he is the only one who is introducing objectivity because the God of our point of view can make sense out of or give intelligibility to the way you're reasoning in the first place.

> The charge is made that we engage in circular reasoning. Now if it be called circular reasoning when we hold it necessary to presuppose the existence of God, we are not ashamed of it because we are firmly convinced that all forms of reasoning that leave God out of account will end in ruin.[6]

The critic will say, "You're engaging in circular reasoning," and Van Til says that there are two ways of responding to that.[7] First, if you remember that anybody who doesn't reason the way we are ends in ruin, then who cares what you call it? Call it circular reasoning, big deal. The point is that our circular reasoning saves intelligibility, and the opponent's reasoning—deductive, inductive, linear reasoning—destroys the intelligibility of thinking. Here comes the second response:

---

4. The conceptual aspect of the transcendental program at this point as opposed to the existential or ontological aspect. In Van Til's program, both are wedded to one another but can be spoken of independently.

5. See Chapter 2.

6. Van Til, *A Survey of Christian Epistemology*, 174.

7. There are more ways one can respond to it as I have illustrated in the previous chapter, but for present purposes Van Til says two.

Yet we hold that our reasoning cannot fairly be called circular reasoning, because we are not reasoning about and seeking to explain facts by assuming the existence and meaning of certain other facts on the same level of being with the facts we are investigating, and then explaining these facts in turn by the facts with which we began. We are presupposing God, not merely another fact of the universe.[8]

God has a special status because God is a transcendental! He is not just one more object among many.

Van Til says that if we are arguing about some creaturely element of thought or experience and we try to introduce something on the same level and the two were "paying each other's debt" in the argument, then yeah, we would be (fallaciously) reasoning in a circle. But we're not reasoning about another fact of the universe. We are arguing about God; we are not arguing on the same level with the facts of the universe. We are arguing about Something which is the "Framework" that makes intelligible all the other reasoning that we engage in. And about that kind of thing *all you can do is reason in a circle.* When people argue about logic, they have to assume logic while they argue about it. So "circular reasoning?" No, "spiral reasoning" because we are assuming something on a different level, a transcendental level, from that which we deal with when talking about the facts of history or science or anything else that we reason about. God has a special status because God is a transcendental! He is not just one more object among many. He exists in such a way that nothing else could exist without Him.[9]

---

8. Van Til, *A Survey of Christian Epistemology*, 174.

9. So, to anticipate the follow-up criticism after the charge of circular reasoning, no, this does not run into the fallacy of special pleading either for the transcendental reasons Bahnsen gave above.

I assure you that at secular universities, when science and philosophy professors talk about proving God's existence, they always take for granted that proving God is like proving any other fact in the universe, even though they may not flag it, don't let you know they're doing it, or they may not even know they're doing it. We all have to use the same kind of logic, the same kind of empirical premises and so forth, and then we hope that we can get a generalization big or extensive enough to finally get to the supernatural. Of course, you never can. *This line of reasoning refuses to begin with the Creator-creature distinction.*

> If God is to be thought of at all as necessary for man's interpretation of the facts or objects of knowledge, he must be thought of as being determinative of the objects of knowledge. In other words, he must then be thought of as the only ultimate interpreter, and man must be thought of as a finite reinterpreter.[10] Since, then, the absolute self-consciousness of God is the final interpreter of all facts, man's knowledge is analogical of God's knowledge. Since all the finite facts exist by virtue of the interpretation of God, man's interpretation of the finite facts is ultimately dependent upon God's interpretation of the facts. Man cannot, except to his own hurt, look at the facts without looking at God's interpretation of the facts. Man's knowledge of the facts is then a reinterpretation of God's interpretation. It is this that is meant by saying that man's knowledge is analogical of God's knowledge.
>
> We must now consider more fully the question how one who has thus become convinced that analogical reasoning is the only type of reasoning that gives us truth at all, must

---

10. Bahnsen: If God and His existence are significant for the objects of knowledge, it must be because He has determined the objects of knowledge. If He determines the objects of knowledge, then He is the ultimate Interpreter, and since we think His thoughts after Him, we know things via reinterpretation.

face one who is convinced that univocal reasoning[11] is the only type of reasoning that can possibly bring one into contact with truth…We can start with any fact at all and challenge "our friends the enemy," to give us an intelligible interpretation of it.[12]

Start with any fact and tell your opponent, "Okay, give me an interpretation that is intelligible, that gives me a broader context and then a context beyond that one where absolutely everything fits so that it is all coherent, so that it all makes sense." What happens, you see, is that when you push out far enough the unbeliever is going to say that everything that happens is random. But if it's random, then you couldn't be very sure about, for instance, the mechanical principles you needed to utilize to fix the carburetor on a car. In a random universe there are no principles you can count on. You obviously won't get there immediately with the unbeliever, but eventually he will reach the unknown.

> Since the non-theist is so heartily convinced that univocal reasoning is the only possible kind of reasoning, we must ask him to reason univocally for us in order that we may *see the consequences*.[13]

Van Til is going to grant the non-theist's position to be true for the sake of argument. Now, what are the consequences of that approach? If those consequences are absurdity or the *impossibility* of the very

---

11. Bahnsen: Reasoning which does not honor the Creator-creature distinction. "Univocal" means to speak with one voice or to have everything have the same basic kind of meaning. Van Til uses this term in more of a metaphorical way to indicate that when we talk about God's reasoning and man's reasoning, we are reasoning in the same way. God and man are on the same level—there is no difference when both we and God approach the facts; there is no Creator-creature distinction.

12. Van Til, *A Survey of Christian Epistemology*, 176.

13. Van Til, *A Survey of Christian Epistemology*, 176.

thing they started with in their argument, then they have refuted themselves.[14]

> In other words, we believe it to be in harmony with and a part of the process of reasoning analogically with a non-theist that we ask him to show us first what he can do. We may, to be sure, offer to him at once a positive statement of our position. But this he will at once reject as quite out of the question. So we may ask him to give us something better. The reason he gives for rejecting our position is, in the last analysis, that it involves self-contradiction. We see again as an illustration of this charge the rejection of the theistic conception that God is absolute and that he has nevertheless created this world for his glory. This, the non-theist says, is self-contradictory. And it no doubt is, from a non-theistic point of view.[15] But the final question is not whether a statement appears to be contradictory. The final question is in which framework or on which view of reality—the Christian or the non-Christian— the law of contradiction can have application to any fact.[16] The non-Christian rejects the Christian view out of hand as being contradictory. Then when he is asked to furnish a

---

14. Philosopher Adrian Bardon wrote a stimulating paper pertaining to the delineations of performative transcendental arguments, fixating around the nature of self-stultifying propositions (those which are not rationally defensible) and self-falsifying propositions (those which are, if affirmable, untrue). Here we see a precursor-statement to Bardon's paper which was written some years after Bahnsen's death. Contentions have arisen over whether or not absurdity itself acts as a refutation to a particular worldview or if it has to be self-falsifying/impossible. More will be said of this dispute in the last chapter, and is treated extensively in the appendix.

15. Bahnsen: How can God be all-glorious and then create the world to bring Him glory? He already has all the glory.

16. Bahnsen: Here we are arguing about logic, the Law of Non-Contradiction. Van Til says that in the end it's not important *what appears* contradictory to you or to me. Ultimately, the question is within which framework that logic can have any meaning at all?

foundation for the law of contradiction, he can offer nothing but the idea of contingency.[17]

What we shall have to do then is to try to reduce our opponent's position to an absurdity. Nothing less will do. Without God, man is completely lost in every respect, epistemologically as well as morally and religiously.[18] But exactly what do we mean by reducing our opponent's position to an absurdity? He thinks he has already reduced our position to an absurdity by the simple expedient just spoken of. But we must point out to him that upon a theistic basis our position is not reduced to an absurdity by indicating the "logical difficulties" involved in the conception of creation. *Upon the theistic basis it must be contended that the human categories are but analogical of God's categories, so that it is to be expected that human thought will not be able to comprehend how God shall be absolute and at the same time create the universe for his glory.* If taken on the same level of existence, it is no doubt a self-contradiction to say that a thing is full and at the same time is being filled. But it is exactly this point that is in question—whether God is to be thought of as on the same level with man. What the antitheist should have done is to show that even upon a theistic basis our conception of creation involves self-contradiction.[19] (emphasis mine)

Van Til says that if someone wants to do damage to my position, come stand within my worldview and show that it's incoherent. He

17. Bahnsen: For those who remember my debate with Gordon Stein, you can now see where I got my stuff, right? Stein had to give a foundation for logic, but all he had was contingency. That's his worldview. Guess what? If it's a contingent universe, then there are no necessary laws of anything.

18. Bahnsen: When Van Til talks about salvation, he's not just talking about going to heaven; he is saying that you can't save morality, life in this world, you can't even save the intelligibility of your thinking if you're not a Christian.

19. Van Til, *A Survey of Christian Epistemology*, 176-177.

welcomes that. But if the unbeliever is going to stand within his worldview and say that our theological premises are inconsistent, why should I be concerned about that? Of course they're inconsistent… in *his* worldview! If you think that God is like any other natural object, and the way we know God is by the way we know everything else in the world, then it will seem like a contradiction to say that He is full of glory yet He is being filled with glory. But if God is not like every other object in existence, then in Christian theology we can believe that God manifests the fullness of His glory by bringing greater glory to Himself through saving people, creating the world, showing the wonder of the stars, and so forth.[20]

> We must therefore give our opponents better treatment than they give us. We must point out to them that univocal reasoning itself leads to self-contradiction, not only from a theistic point of view, but from a non-theistic point of view as well.[21]

This is crucial. Van Til says that the unbeliever sees contradictions in Christian theology. Well of course within his framework of thought they are contradictory. Van Til says we must do better to the unbeliever than he has done to us. We don't want to just say that his worldview is contradictory to ours because *x*, *y*, and *z*. *We want to show that their point of view is contradictory even on their understanding of logic! Take their own worldview and Van Til says that they destroy themselves.*

> It is this that we ought to mean when we say that we must meet our enemy on their own ground. It is this that

20. Here is an example of the difference between internal and external critiques of Christianity: the non-Christian, in setting out his critique of the Christian worldview, has implicitly categorized God and man together such that both are subject to the more ultimate laws of thought; the Creator-creature distinction has not been appropriately taken into account by the non-Christian critic.

21. Van Til, *A Survey of Christian Epistemology*, 177.

we ought to mean when we say that we reason from the impossibility of the contrary. The contrary is impossible only if it is self-contradictory when operating on the basis of its own assumptions. It is this too that we should mean when we say that we are arguing ad hominem. We do not really argue ad hominem unless we show that someone's position involves self-contradiction, and there is no self-contradiction unless one's reasoning is shown to be directly contradictory of or to lead to conclusions which are contradictory of one's own assumptions.[22]…Similarly, if we reason when we place ourselves upon our opponents' position, we cannot for a moment do more than argue thus for "argument's sake."

When we reason thus we are not reasoning on the basis of some abstract law of self-contradiction. We have seen that the very question between theists and antitheists is as to the *foundation* of the law of contradiction. When they criticize our position and think they have reduced it to the place where it falls under the law of self-contradiction, we do not give in to defeat or appeal to irrationality in the name of faith, but we challenge their interpretation of the law of contradiction. We hold that they have falsely assumed that the self-contradictory is to be identified with that which is beyond the comprehension of man. But this takes for granted that human categories are ultimate categories—*which is just the thing in question.* In order to bring this argument as closely to the non-regenerate consciousness as we may, we must seek to show that the non-theist is self-contradictory upon his own assumptions, as well as upon the assumption of the truth of theism, and that he cannot even be self-contradictory

---

22. Bahnsen: I don't think he should've put it in the way of saying to argue *ad hominem,* but what he is saying that we are arguing "against the man" by granting him whatever he wants and then we will argue against what we granted him.

upon a non-theistic basis, since if he saw himself to be self-contradictory, he would be self-contradictory no longer.

Now when this method of reasoning from the impossibility of the contrary is carried out, there is really nothing more to do.[23]

Essentially, what I'm saying to the unbeliever is, "Do you want to argue? Do you want to come onto the court and play the reason-giving game? Let's look at your worldview and my worldview. On your worldview—even given your assumptions—you can't even give reasons in the first place. But if you stand in my worldview I can save rationality, science, or whatever else you've been arguing." And Van Til says that once you've done that, there is nothing else to do. From an apologetical standpoint, what you've done here is taken the weapon away from the unbeliever. His method of arguing undermines arguing, so he can't play the game.

The Defense of the Faith

These things being as they are it will be our first task in this chapter to show that a consistently Christian method of apologetic argument, in agreement with its own basic conception of the starting point, must be by presupposition. To argue by presupposition is to indicate what are the epistemological and metaphysical principles that underlie and control one's method.[24] The Reformed apologist will frankly admit that his own methodology presupposes the truth of Christian theism. Basic to all the doctrines of Christian theism is that of the self-contained God, or, if we

---

23. Van Til, *A Survey of Christian Epistemology*, 177-178. Emphasis added.

24. Bahnsen: To reason by presupposition you have to lay out your metaphysic and epistemology and you have to make sure the unbeliever understands his metaphysic and epistemology.

wish, that of the ontological Trinity. It is this notion of the ontological Trinity that ultimately controls a truly Christian methodology.[25] Based upon this notion of the ontological Trinity and consistent with it, is the concept of the counsel of God according to which all things in the created world are regulated.[26, 27]

Christian methodology is therefore based upon presuppositions that are quite the opposite of those of the non-Christian. It is claimed to be of the very essence of any non-Christian form of methodology that it cannot be determined in advance to what conclusions it must lead. To assert, as the Christian apologist is bound to do if he is not to deny the very thing he is seeking to establish, that the conclusion of a true method is the truth of Christian theism is, from the point of view of the non-Christian, the clearest evidence of authoritarianism. In spite of this claim to neutrality on the part of the non-Christian the Reformed apologist must point out that *every* method, the supposedly neutral one no less than any other, presupposes either the truth or the falsity of Christian theism.[28]

You might want to make a mental note that Van Til is offering now a **bivalent structure** for arguments. He says that every method assumes the truth of Christian-theism or that it's not true. People will always say that Van Til has only refuted worldviews 1-5. What about worldviews 6-10? Van Til's point is that there are only two worldviews. Or, to put it better, every worldview either assumes the

25. Bahnsen: Our metaphysical view controls our epistemology and method.

26. Ephesians 1:11.

27. Bahnsen: We begin with God the triune God, God who is self-sufficient, God the Creator and sovereign Controller of all things.

28. Van Til, *The Defense of the Faith*, 121-122.

truth of Christianity or its falsity. The immediate objection to this is to point out that some worldviews are neutral and non-committal. Who's right and who's wrong here? Van Til is going to quote Jesus: "He who is not with me is against me." This is the interesting thing about this worldview: you don't get to sit on the fence and think about it; you either affirm it or you deny it. Now, you may be polite in denying it and granting that it might possibly be true, but from Van Til's standpoint to say that it's possibly true is to say that it's (tentatively) not actually true, so you're denying it.

This is Van Til's "Law of Excluded Middle":
when it comes to worldviews, it's either
Christian or non-Christian.

Van Til doesn't believe there are a zillion worldviews so let's get busy because by the time we die we have to have refuted each one of them. *Van Til's apologetic is not an inductive process of knocking down one after the other.* Van Til says all of them either assume that Christianity is true or that it's not. This is Van Til's "Law of Excluded Middle." When it comes to worldviews, it's either Christian or non-Christian.

> The method of reasoning by presupposition may be said to be indirect rather than direct.[29] The issue between believers and nonbelievers in Christian theism cannot be settled by a direct appeal to "facts" and "laws" whose nature and significance is already agreed upon by both parties to the debate. *The question is rather as to what is the final reference point required to make the "facts" and "laws" intelligible.*[30] The question is as to what

---

29. Bahnsen: I have Christianity and non-Christianity and I'm going to refute non-Christianity. If you know anything about logic, it's akin or like a disjunctive syllogism: *a* or *not-a*, not *not-a*, therefore *a*.

30. Bahnsen: You can't directly go to the facts and say that *x* proves Christianity

the "facts" and the "laws" really are. Are they what the non-Christian methodology assumes that they are? Are they what the Christian-theistic methodology presupposes they are?[31]

The answer to this question cannot be finally settled by any direct discussion of "facts." It must, in the last analysis, be settled indirectly. The Christian apologist must place himself upon the position of his opponent, assuming the correctness of his method merely for argument's sake, in order to show him that on such a position the "facts" are not facts and the "laws" are not laws.[32]

To summarize what Van Til is getting at, I'll say, "Okay, let me reason with you in terms of your worldview. I'm going to stand within your framework of thought. But within your framework of thought there are no laws and there are no facts so there can't be any necessity

---

and have the unbeliever go to the facts and say *y* disproves Christianity. Van Til says the question is rather whose reference point can make the facts or the laws intelligible to begin with. (Note that Bahnsen is not saying that he and Van Til are rejecting the use of evidences altogether. That is not the point here. The point is that an appeal to evidences will almost invariably be useless when there are conflicting worldviews at war with one another, worldviews which have different views as to what the facts are, what the nature of a fact is, how we should utilize our knowledge going to the facts, and so forth).

31. Bahnsen: People like to say, "Well let's just go to the facts and settle this," but we have to say, "Well what do you think a fact is? What do I think what a fact is? If you think a fact is just some kind of random event in a chance universe, then we can't go to the facts to settle anything. Facts don't settle anything because they're random in a chance universe. So when you say that we should go to the facts to settle something, you must be thinking of facts as a Christian thinks of facts in order that you can use them to argue against the Christian view!" In the Christian worldview God not only created all the facts of the universe in creation, He also interrelated them all and continues to uphold them in His sovereign providence. A fact could not be intelligible to a knower if it was not first part of a system of facts in terms of which it can be made contextually coherent. In the same book Van Til famously says, "Brute facts are mute facts."

32. Van Til, *The Defense of the Faith*, 122.

to anything. In a chance universe anything can change; there is no invariance and thus there is nothing that is law-like."[33]

Why can't there be facts in a chance universe? In a chance universe you can't individuate one thing from another. Everything is sound and fury signifying nothing—everything is random. Everything is the same and everything is different. Everything is so different that you could never draw a similarity between two things. You couldn't identify seeing a barn in the distance because that assumes that there is some continuing idea of "barnness". But in a chance universe there is just experience after experience after experience and you can't get any unity between the experiences, so there are no facts and there are no laws.

> [We] must also ask the non-Christian to place himself upon the Christian position for argument's sake in order that he may be shown that only upon such a basis do "facts" and "laws" appear intelligible.[34]
>
> To admit one's own presuppositions and to point out the presuppositions of others is therefore to maintain that all reasoning is, in the nature of the case, *circular reasoning*. The starting point, the method, and the conclusion are always involved in one another.[35]

---

33. Bahnsen, again, is using the typical Darwinian atheist as his hypothetical opponent, Darwinianism being the reigning atheistic ideology today. Quite obviously, a non-Christian who does not stipulate a chance universe (for whatever reason) would be dealt with differently.

34. Bahnsen: If you stand within the framework of Christian presuppositions, not only do you see that facts and laws are intelligible, but within this framework it is the only one where they can be intelligible.

35. See footnote 25 in Chapter 12. There are *many* types of circularity, one of which being that of internal coherence or consistency. For any philosopher to be consistent he is going to assume implicitly the very thing he's arguing for, he's going to give an argument for what he believes, and he's going to conclude with what he believed at the outset. This is nothing more than consistency, yet it is circular. A Christian is not going to (legitimately) believe in Buddhism at the outset, give an argument for Islam, and then conclude with Christianity. That's simply asinine

Let us say that the Christian apologist has placed the position of Christian theism before his opponent. Let us say further that he has pointed out that his own method of investigation of reality presupposes the truth of his position. This will appear to his friend whom he is seeking to win to an acceptance of the Christian position has highly authoritarian and out of accord with the proper use of human reason. What will the apologist do next? If he is a Roman Catholic or an Arminian, he will tone down the nature of Christianity to some extent in order to make it appear that the consistent application of his friend's neutral method will lead to an acceptance of Christian theism after all. But if he is a Calvinist, this way is not open to him. He will point out that the more consistently his friend applies his supposedly neutral method the more certainly he will come to the conclusion that Christian theism is not true.[36]

If I allow the unbeliever to reason in terms of his worldview, which he pretends is neutral, and I present all sorts of facts that show that Jesus very probably rose from the dead, if he accepts that conclusion from within that worldview, he will have to conclude most certainly that Christianity is not true. Why? Because within his worldview, if Jesus rose from the dead, it is because there is some very odd principle that operates in the biological realm that we haven't discovered yet. On his principles that is what it would have to be. He can't say that Jesus rose from the dead and that it's a miracle because given his "neutral" and natural method he has to say that we're not allowed to bring the supernatural into the picture. If you let him get away with using his

---

and *inconsistent;* it doesn't even make sense. A Christian assumes his Christianity at the outset of the arguments he gives for it, as does every single proponent of *any* particular philosophy or ideology. *Everyone* implicitly assumes the very thing they're arguing for.

36. Van Til, *The Defense of the Faith,* 122-124.

method, his method will destroy the Christian worldview. Even when it appears that he is agreeing with points in your worldview, he will, in fact, naturalize them. If you allow him to use his neutral method where he is the center of authority for what he believes, will he ever, if he is consistent with that, say that God is the center of authority? You can never get to that conclusion if you begin with the idea of a neutral method where man is the ultimate authority for what he believes.

So Van Til says that if you allow the unbeliever to continue in his pretended neutrality, you're just going to reinforce his rejection of Christianity. What looks like an acceptance of points of the Christian worldview is in fact the destruction of those very facts being received.[37]

Further down Van Til talks about appealing to the "true method which the natural man knows *but suppresses*."[38] Notice how he says "true method." He's not just appealing to the knowledge of the true God or the truth about God in creation. He also says that the natural man knows what the true method of thinking is, but he suppresses it.

> The natural man at bottom knows that he is the creature of God. He knows also that he is responsible to God. He knows that he should live to the glory of God. He know that in all that he does he should stress that the field of reality which he investigates has the stamp of God's ownership upon it. But he suppresses his knowledge of himself as he truly is. He is the man with the iron mask. A true method of apologetics must seek to tear off that iron mask.[39] The Roman Catholic

37. In principle. This obviously isn't a universal phenomenon as there are genuine, open-minded unbelievers who seek to (and subsequently do) convert to Christianity without premeditated rejection or vilification.

38. Van Til, *The Defense of the Faith*, 124.

39. Bahnsen: Van Til had great illustrations. Here is this guy who has this iron mask. My job as an apologist is not to flatter the mask and say, "You know, I think I could show in terms of the principles of your iron mask that there's really a face behind that iron mask." *Van Til says we need to tear that mask off!* Stop pretending to be autonomous. We're not.

and the Arminian make no attempt to do so. They even flatter
its wearer about his fine appearance.[40] In the introductions
of their books on apologetics, Arminians as well as Roman
Catholic apologists frequently seek to set their "opponents"
at ease by assuring them that their method, in its field, is all
that any Christian could desire. In contradistinction from
this, the Reformed apologist will point out again and again
that the only method that will lead to the truth in any field is
that method which recognizes the fact that man is a creature
of God, that he must therefore seek to think God's thoughts
after him.

It is not as though the Reformed apologist should
not interest himself in the nature of the non-Christian's
method. On the contrary, he should make a critical analysis
of it. He should, as it were, join his "friend" in the use of
it. But he should do so self-consciously with the purpose
of showing that its most consistent application not merely
leads away from Christian theism, but in leading away
from Christian theism leads to [the] destruction of reason
and science as well.[41]

An illustration may indicate more clearly what is meant.
Suppose we think of a man made of water in an infinitely
extended and bottomless ocean of water. Desiring to get out
of water, he makes a ladder of water. He sets this latter upon
the water and against the water and then attempts to climb

---

40. Bahnsen: Natural theology will flatter the unbeliever. "You know, you're
doing really well when it comes to natural reasoning. You're really good as a
historian (a doctor, or whatever else)." Van Til would say that you couldn't do
anything if you didn't already depend upon the God that you use your science and
history to argue against.

41. Bahnsen: What I want to show the unbeliever is that if they're consistent,
they can't possibly be a Christian. *But if you're consistent, you can't use logic and science
either!* In leading away from Christianity you lead away from the intelligibility of
everything.

out of the water. So hopeless and senseless a picture must be drawn of the natural man's methodology based as it is upon the assumption that time or chance is ultimate.[42]

One of the easiest illustrations one can make for this "man of water" illustration (which C. S. Lewis uses as well) is if the unbeliever is right that all we have is matter in motion so that physics explains everything, then the real question is if I am nothing more than matter in motion just like a rock is matter in motion, how, then, do I ever, as matter in motion, get to the point where I think of myself as matter in motion? Rocks don't think of themselves. How can self-consciousness be explained as matter in motion? That's a devastating critique.

Van Til says that on the unbeliever's position everything is water, everything is chance, everything has these material characteristics. How do you take water and make a ladder of water that you can put against the water so that the man who is made out of the same stuff can climb on the ladder of water out of the water? *How do you rise above matter in motion and now be an intellect who can talk about matter in motion?* You're nothing but matter in motion. The non-Christian position destroys itself.[43]

On his assumption his own rationality is a product of chance. On his assumption even the laws of logic which he employs

---

42. Van Til, *The Defense of the Faith*, 124.

43. Responses to this objection usually pivot around the aspect of ignorance: that we don't have an answer yet does not mean that there isn't one. The problem, however, is rather straightforward and easy to see—given this ontology of man and his mind, any answer that does arise, no matter how convincing and definite it may appear to be, is, and can only ever be, a product of the atoms in man's brain. Definitionally, every act of cogitation is reducible to atoms in motion. In which case, it is wholly irrelevant what answer is conjured concerning the problem of consciousness and the mind. There is no free will, let alone *a will* by which we can conjure rational arguments. *Everything* is deterministic on an exclusively-materialist and physicalist metaphysic.

are products of chance. The rationality and purpose that he may be searching for are still bound to be products of chance. So then the Christian apologist, whose position requires him to hold that Christian theism is really true and as such must be taken as the presupposition which alone makes the acquisition of knowledge in any field intelligible, must join his "friend" in his hopeless gyrations so as to point out to him that his efforts are always in vain.

It will then appear that Christian theism, *which was first rejected because of its supposed authoritarian character, is the only position which gives human reason a field for successful operation and a method of true progress in knowledge.*[44]

So far, I have only read eight pages out of two books.[45] It's all there, isn't it? This is absolutely brilliant. The expression of it can be improved on and cleaned up, to be sure, but it is nonetheless brilliant.

---

44. Van Til, *The Defense of the Faith*, 124-125. Emphasis added.

45. Eight pages out of the older editions Bahnsen is reading from.

CHAPTER 14

Van Til's Critics

After everything discussed concerning transcendental arguments and Van Til's transcendental apologetic, there has to be something wrong with it, right?

I'm going to break up the criticisms into two categories. The first group of criticisms is directed at Van Til's apologetic in general, and what they show is a lack of comprehension that it's a transcendental program. These criticisms would never be given if they had known what Van Til's transcendental program was in the first place. The second category of criticisms will be by those who *do* understand that it's transcendental and try to criticize it anyway.

Naïve Criticisms[1]

1. A Fideistic Apologetic

There are those who say Van Til's apologetic reduces to *fideism*. There is no rational argumentation possible according to Van Til. Everybody has their faith commitment, and beyond that there is no argument. If you understand the transcendental character of his program, that kind of criticism is absurd. Far from being fideistic, Van Til says we are going to argue from *any* given fact for the Christian worldview as the *only* possible truth in terms of which people can make sense out of experience. This is the exact opposite of fideism.

---

1. The headings and subheadings for this category of criticisms and the next are those of the editor.

2. No Argument Between Final Authorities

The unbeliever has his final authority, we have our final authority, and since we don't agree on final authorities then we just can't argue with each other.[2] But this is completely contrary to what Van Til says! Van Til says we *must* argue. Well how do we argue if there are conflicting presuppositions? *Transcendentally!* You have to ask which worldview has the preconditions for the intelligibility of any argument.

The point is that you can't exalt logic above God in authority if you're a transcendentalist.

---

3. Christians Shouldn't Use Logic[3]

Given Van Til's view of analogical knowledge and God's incomprehensibility, we shouldn't use logic. Logic is not authoritative for Christians. Okay, well how do we make sense of the criticism of Van Til rejecting logic when he over and over again in his writings affirms logic? What gives a critic of Van Til this impression that we shouldn't use logic? What Van Til is actually saying is that we should not use logic *as our final authority*. God is the ultimate authority in terms of which logic is intelligible. Now, does that mean that logic isn't required? Not at all. It means that logic is subordinate to something else, namely, the authority of God. Then some people will say, "Oh, well then God could change the laws of logic, right?" Not the Christian God. The Christian God doesn't deny Himself and the laws of logic are based on His character, so we don't have to worry about that. The point is that you can't exalt logic above God in authority if you're a transcendentalist.

---

2. This is the same criticism raised by John Warwick Montgomery's "Once Upon an A Priori" in the Festschrift for Van Til in *Jerusalem and Athens* edited by E.R. Geehan (Nutley, NJ: Presbyterian and Reformed, 1971), chap. 21.

3. The term 'logic' here is/can be synonymous with both logical thinking and laws of logic.

4. Van Til Rejects Evidences

Apart from just poor scholarship, why would someone think that Van Til rejects evidences?[4] What little might they run into from Van Til that gives them the idea that he is not in favor of evidences? Van Til says that if you think you can just go to the evidences in a naïve neutral way, it doesn't work. And to the degree that it works it simply reinforces autonomy.[5]

5. Arbitrary and Interchangeable Authority Claims

Also leveled by Montgomery in Van Til's Festschrift *Jerusalem and Athens*, Montgomery writes this parable that goes something to the effect of the Christian screaming, "I have my authority! It's the ultimate authority and you have to accept it and if you argue against me, you're violating the authority, you heretic! You have to accept it!" Montgomery says that on that basis someone else can come along and say, "I have my authority!" and so on and so forth. The idea here is that these authority claims are interchangeable so that everything the Christian says the non-Christian can say back and you're just left at a standoff. Well, the problem with Montgomery's analysis is that these are *not* interchangeable. Van Til says that we are comparing *concrete* worldviews, and the exact details of our Christian worldview are what have that authority (i.e., God, Him existing, Him giving us His inscripturated and authoritative Word, etc.). So the transcendental nature of Van Til's argument has not been comprehended or appreciated.[6]

---

4. See Thom Notaro, *Van Til and the Use of Evidence* (Phillipsburg, PA: Presbyterian and Reformed, 1980).

5. Bahnsen: Now does this mean that God never uses an impure apologetical witness to bring people to conversion? Of course not. Van Til doesn't think that his arguments are always the best-formulated either. God uses imperfect people— and even heretics!—to bring people to genuine faith.

6. See the second criticism, also leveled by Montgomery. Authority claims are not interchangeable because not all authority claims are transcendentals. The

6. Unbeliever's Could Know Nothing At All.
I don't know how intelligent people could make this mistake, but they do.[7] Van Til doesn't say that unbelievers don't know things. He says that they *couldn't* know things if their worldview was true. Our whole point is that the unbeliever *does know things*, and therefore since their worldview can't account for these things, they ought to give up their worldview!

So the preceding arguments, which are fairly standard in the literature against Van Til, all rest on a failure to appreciate the transcendental character of the argument. For the rest of this chapter and the next, we will turn to six more arguments against Van Til, but which do appreciate the transcendental nature of Van Til.

Transcendental Criticisms

1. The Inability to Refute All Worldviews.
This program of transcendental proof will never be successful because no matter how long you live and how much you write and how good your arguments are, you will never have refuted all of the alternatives. Here we have someone who understands that the argument is a

---

Christian God is the ultimate transcendental for intelligibility, so it is not as though anyone else can come along with their authority and proclaim it for what it is and think this ends in a stalemate.

7. Bahnsen: Alvin Plantinga is a brilliant philosopher. He may not always do it the way I would do it, but no one can doubt that he has a mind that God has given him. He is a smart man and extremely well-read. When I first met Plantinga I was still an undergraduate student in philosophy, and he had come to my college to present some lectures. I talked to him for a few minutes during a break and brought up the name of Van Til to get to some kind of "Where are you coming from about this?" sort of thing, and Plantinga basically said, "Since Van Til's apologetic requires me to think that unbelievers can't know about the digestive tract of a lion, I just don't see that it's realistic or practical at all." I asked him what made him think that was the case and he said that Van Til believes the unbeliever can't know anything and yet we all know that unbelievers do know things.

reductio ad absurdum argument,[8] but, they say, the only way we could say that our Christian worldview is true from the falsity of the others is if you refute all the others, and nobody can do that.

We have already gone over this criticisms. Van Til says that there are only two positions. So when someone says that we haven't refuted "all" of them, all he is saying is that we haven't used every illustration we could use yet. But I don't need to use every illustration. The point is that you either assume that Christianity is true or it's not. If you say it's not, let me show you what happens (i.e., you're reduced to absurdity).[9]

2. Another Possible Worldview?

How do we know that there is not another possible worldview out there that would work? This is not just that we haven't been able to refute all of the alternatives, we also haven't shown that our Christian worldview is the only necessary one because how could we know that another one isn't available that would do the same thing? I'm going to give two different kinds of answers to this, but they supplement each other:

The first answer to this is that in the nature of the case, there can only be one transcendental. To talk about two separate worldviews is nonsense in itself. It would be like saying that there are two ultimate authorities. There cannot be two ultimate authorities or else they're not ultimate, right? If somebody says that Christianity "does the job" such that we can make sense out of science, logic, morality, human dignity, and so on, but that there may be another worldview which does the job as well, you have to say that in the nature of the case you can't have two transcendentals for meaningfulness. Why? Because if there are two transcendentals, what have you lost? Unity. Coherence, unity, and continuity is the name of the game here. Meaningfulness

---

8. That is, we illustrate the transcendental status of q via an indirect reductio argument.

9. See pages 174-175 for review concerning Van Til's bivalent/either-or view of worldviews.

and intelligibility mean coherence which means there is *one* system of truth. If there were two transcendentals, you wouldn't have one system of truth; you would have two, and then what would you have to ask? What's the relationship between the two systems? If they are different, then you have lost unity. If they are the same with the names being changed, then we don't have to worry about it; this would be nothing more than a linguistic variation.

To summarize, the nature of the transcendental program is to find unity and coherence in all of our experience, so you can't have two ultimate authorities, you can't have two ultimate systems of truth, because if you have two, you no longer have coherence or unity. You have to then ask the question, "What is the relationship between these two?" The relationship is either that of identity (under different names) or diversity, and if they're diverse, then you no longer have coherence or unity in your worldview.[10]

To make sense of the claim that there are two systems by which facts can be made intelligible requires another system in terms of which you're saying that about the other two. But you see if these two transcendental systems are postulated by hypothesis, we can't get behind them to have the one that unites the two.[11] *To talk about there being two there needs to be one perspective in terms of which you can talk about the two. But these two that you're talking about are by definition ultimate!* And so there can't be a one that unites the two, even to talk about their relationship.

---

10. By way of metaphysical example, it would be like arguing that the creation of the earth and man (and all the facts of the universe) are ultimately a result of the Big Bang apart from God, but at the same time the earth and man and all the facts of the universe are a result of God creating them (and thereby all the implied truths such as being made in the *imago Dei*, inherent belief in God, etc.). They can't both be true; only *one* necessarily can if unity is to be salvaged. So it is, too, if one wants to endorse the position that multiple worldviews/metaphysical schemes can be true. Since Christianity transcendentally makes sense of intelligibility, then by default all other worldviews are false.

11. Bahnsen: By "unites" I simply mean to make intelligible that there are even two; to talk about there even being two.

When somebody says to you, "How do you know there can't be another one out there?," you say that in the nature of the case there can't be another one out there. There can only be one ultimate, transcendental worldview. If there were two, then it wouldn't be an "ultimate," transcendental worldview. You would have to have one behind it to make it even possible to talk about there being two.[12]

In the second, less philosophical approach, in the nature of the case the Christian worldview has to be the only worldview that works because it claims to be the only true worldview. That claim is either true or false. If it's true, then there aren't any other ones. If it's false, then Christianity is not a worldview that will work. If there is one transcendental and it is Christianity, then it must be the only one because internally it claims to be the only one. And if the Christian worldview really is a transcendental for meaningfulness, then its claims must be true. And one of its claims is that it's the only one! If that one claim is wrong, then the worldview as a whole is not true, in which case it can't be a worldview that is a transcendental for meaningfulness. *This criticism assumes that there can be two true worldviews. But on this assumption Christianity couldn't be true because Christianity says there is only one.*

You don't understand what a transcendental is if you think that there could be another one. In the nature of the case there can only be one transcendental.

---

12. To talk about there being two true worldviews as a route of stultifying presuppositionalism requires what Bahnsen calls a "meta-transcendental worldview" in terms of which you talk about the two worldviews being "satisfactory to do the job." But even if this could be conjured, who's to stop someone from arguing that there is/could be another "meta-transcendental worldview" that is also true? This would call for a "meta-meta-transcendental worldview" *ad infinitum.* In short, this second (albeit commendable) criticism (a) leads to infinite regression on hypothetical grounds, and (b) refutes itself on metaphysical grounds (fn. 10).

I appreciate and understand why those who are studying Van Til's transcendental method come up with these two objections. But if someone says that there may be another transcendental worldview, we have to tell them that you don't understand what a transcendental is if you think that there could be another one. In the nature of the case there can only be one transcendental.

3. David P. Hoover's Criticisms[13]

The paper that I am going to be looking at is "For the Sake of Argument: A Critique of the Logical Structure of Van Til's Presuppositionalism,"[14] and for the sake of time I will only be going over four basic shots against Van Til. Hoover then takes his time on another criticism of Van Til, but I will argue that he is really criticizing a formulation of what Van Til said rather than Van Til's system itself.

I. Hoover writes:

> How could a finite human intellect achieve the perspective necessary to run an argument of such great consequence? To repeat what was earlier cited from Van Til:
>
>> [...] the best and only possible proof for the existence of such a God is that his existence is required for the uniformity of nature and the coherence of all things in the world.
>
> But here the tacit assumption is made that the arguer has an acquaintance with "the uniformity of nature and the

---

13. Dr. Hoover is a mostly unfamiliar name in presuppositional circles. He wrote a paper on Van Til for an IBRI (Interdisciplinary Biblical Research Institute) and is (or at least was) a professor of philosophy at Covenant College in Lookout Mountain, Georgia.

14. David P. Hoover "For the Sake of Argument: A Critique of the Logical Structure of Van Til's Presuppositionalism" in *IBRI Research Report No. 11* (1982). Citations will be from the 2012 Kindle edition without page numbers.

coherence of all things in the world" such that the God of Christian theism is the *only* thing or being possessed of those properties and attributes sufficient to account for that world of experience. What is striking, however, is that no person this side of omniscience knows the cosmos in that required way. At very most Van Til is logically entitled to claim that the Christian's God is a *sufficient* condition to account for the world so *far as his knowledge goes*. Sufficient perhaps, but not necessary.[15]

Hoover is saying that no one who is short of omniscience can give you the transcendental. Well, Van Til agrees. So where are we going to get our transcendental? From God's revelation. *It has to be revealed.* Now, he won't like that answer, but that is what answers this particular objection he is raising. We're not claiming to be omniscient; we're claiming to know the One who is, and we are using the worldview He has given us.

Hoover gives us another aspect of this criticism when he says that "the tacit assumption is made that the arguer has an acquaintance with 'the uniformity of nature and the coherence of all things in the world.'" In the first place, that is not what we're claiming. I'm not familiar with all of the coherence in this world. So what am I saying? *I'm projecting as a principle that everything is coherent, that nature is uniform.* And in terms of those principles I reason, do scientific research, and so forth.[16] Hoover somehow has the idea that I'm supposed to be able to say as my first premise, "I know all of nature is uniform." But what I'm arguing is that if you're going to

---

15. Hoover, "For the Sake of Argument."

16. Notice how Bahnsen is incisively referring to transcendentals as principles in the same manner that Kant argued they ought to be treated as. From pgs. 123-124: [A transcendental] "should be entitled a *principle*, not a *theorem*, because it has the peculiar character that it makes possible the very experience which is its own ground of proof, and that in this experience it must always itself be presupposed." Kant was exactly right in his analysis.

act like all of nature is uniform, you need the omniscient perspective of the sovereign God. So in a sense Hoover has misunderstood the argument. I'm not claiming that I'm directly acquainted with this uniformity universally as if I'm omniscient enough to provide the transcendental. I'm saying that if you're going to act like that you, need to have the omniscient God speak to you at the beginning of your process.

II. Hoover criticizes what is, admittedly, a poor illustration. Van Til says that when I come into the house and see a floor, I can't argue for the beams under the floor in a direct manner. I have to say that the floor presupposes that it has beams. Of course every illustration has its defects, and Hoover jumps on this and says, "Wait a minute. You don't know that this floor is such that it has beams under it. It could be this kind of floor or that kind of floor. It could have no foundation at all; maybe it's right on the ground." Okay, so if you score a point here, of all the brilliant, helpful, and funny illustrations that Van Til had, this one backfired. That is *at best* what we have here. Here is Hoover's point:

> The floor, one might rightly suspect (although there is no logical necessity in one's doing so), *has some foundation or other*, but the nature of that foundation cannot logically be identified under the conditions that define Van Til's thought experiment about the floorboards.[17]

Getting beyond the fact that he's jumped on a faulty illustration, what Hoover is saying is that the system itself can only argue that there must be a foundation for our thought, but it can't tell you what the nature of that foundation is.

Earlier I explained that Van Til doesn't work from abstract questions and principles one-by-one up to the Christian worldview. Van Til is not trying to say, "Well first there must be *a* god, and

---

17. Hoover, "For the Sake of Argument".

now we're going to find out what kind of God it is." But that's what Hoover's criticism assumes. Van Til can, at best, say that there is a foundation, but he can't tell us whether it's the ground underneath, or whether it's beams, and so on. *But Van Til says that he is starting with the blueprint of the house.* He knows what kind of house this is and what kind of floor it is. Van Til is saying that given the blueprint of the house he knows what kind of foundation is underneath the floor. Van Til is not talking about some type of formal transcendental, saying that there must be something. No, he is saying that we must begin with the concrete transcendental of the Christian worldview.[18]

III. Third, Hoover criticizes something Van Til has said which he believes gets at the heart of Van Til's system, but earlier I said that I think what he is getting at could be viewed in a more charitable way.

Van Til is more explicit about his argument strategy and logical warrant in a remarkable statement against Buswell:

The argument for the existence of God and for the truth of Christianity is objectively valid. We should not tone down the validity of this argument to the probability level. The argument may be poorly stated, and may never be adequately stated. But in itself the argument is perfectly sound.[19]

---

18. In other words, presuppositionalists begin with the Bible—the blueprint of the universe. This blueprint was given to us by a specific type of God who has specific types of features or characteristics. We live in a specific type of universe created by this specific triune God, we are made in His image, we are all sinners against Him, He sent His Son to die for us, and so on. Again, Van Til's transcendental program is "concrete," not abstract. As Van Til says, "we must begin with the *actuality* of the Book" (pg. 153). We do not begin with speculation claims, nor do we begin with the probability of the Bible's truth so that at the very least we can say that we're not being speculative. We begin with its "actuality."

19. "Van Til, *A Christian Theory of knowledge*, 291."

...[we are being] assured, apparently by fideistic resolve, of what must be the case metaphysically, [and because it must be the case metaphysically] it does not much matter how one argues it.[20]

Hoover's interpretation of that statement is that Van Til, "by fideistic resolve," says that we have a sound argument, and because we know that it's true (fideistically), it doesn't make any difference how badly your formulation comes out. Now is that what Van Til is saying? Even if you don't like Van Til and reject his apologetic, isn't it much more reasonable to say that what he is talking about here is that arguments can always be made more precise, more adequate for different audiences, and so forth? That's what Van Til is saying.

IV. Hoover writes:

[H]ypothetical premises can never be made to logically yield more than hypothetical conclusions. Thus, [when Van Til's apologetic argues] "for argument's sake," the Christian necessarily both starts and finishes his argument at the level of hypothesis.[21]

Hoover is saying of Van Til's apologetic that *if*, for instance, experience is intelligible, then God exists. But the conclusion of the argument is resting on a hypothetical "if," so at best we have, hypothetically, God existing. He continues:

[I]n both cases, that of the Christian's position and that of the non-Christian's position, the provisional, or hypothetical, character of the opposing sets of presuppositions is the same. Neither, for the sake of argument, has the status of *being* true, only of being *provisionally* true "to see what will happen." The question, then, is how Van Til exhibits Christian theism's

20. Hoover, "For the Sake of the Argument."

21. Hoover, "For the Sake of Argument".

necessity given his ground commitment to the parity of logic, [that we're only arguing provisionally].[22]

When Van Til says that he is going to stand on the non-Christian's position "for argument's sake," he is taking the non-Christian's own assumptions and showing that they disprove themselves. But when we ask the unbeliever to stand on our position, we're asking them to assume that such a God as we have talked about exists. We want them to think through a position that says that Christianity is necessarily true. Now, if Christianity is necessarily true because of God's self-attesting authority, notice how we save science, logic, morality, and so forth.

My point here is that I think Hoover has misconstrued the way in which we are testing the Christian hypothesis. *We're testing the Christian hypothesis as the claim to being a transcendental necessity!* We're not testing it like any other hypothesis would be tested! We're asking the unbeliever to test the Christian worldview as a transcendental necessity, not to test the Christian worldview as a hypothesis.[23]

4. Herman Dooyeweerd's Criticism

In Van Til's Festschrift, *Jerusalem and Athens*, Dooyeweerd criticizes Van Til's apologetic by basically saying that his transcendental approach is no different from a "transcendent criticism." Well, it

---

22. Hoover, "For the Sake of Argument".

23. Hoover also fails to understand the logical formalities behind transcendental reasoning. In Chapters 7-9, Michael Butler went into great detail concerning not only transcendental arguments in contemporary usage, but also their form and structure, and what they may or may not intend to accomplish. At base, transcendental arguments often begin from some version of a conditional premise (if-then), to be sure, but the antecedent clause is immediately after asserted as being the case and the consequent conclusion drawn accordingly, and the illustration of the transcendental necessity of the conclusion (or consequent clause of the conditional premise) is an indirect reductio ad absurdum approach. Show that the denial of the transcendental reduces one to absurdity, but also show that the denial of such a transcendental nevertheless *requires it to be the case* in order for you to even deny it. So, far from Hoover's criticism here, transcendental reasoning is not strictly hypothetical.

is not a "*transcendent*" criticism; it is a *transcendental* criticism. A transcendent criticism is one which is given on the authority of God, who is beyond human experience. The reason Dooyeweerd says Van Til isn't engaged in transcendental analysis (just transcendent criticism) is because he says Van Til brings the Bible in at the very beginning of his argument. According to Dooyeweerd, a truly transcendental method must be "immanent," it must arise from within human experience, not from a transcendent source.

Per this criticism, I'm not going to go to unbelieving scholars and come in with a dogmatic, Christian point of view. I'm going to engage in his problematics. Given his way of thinking I'm going to challenge him that there must be transcendentals, and from within our analysis then we'll see that there must be, in the broadest sense, a ground motive of creation, fall, and redemption that we use in our thinking. But I won't be trying to prove the truths of the Bible specifically, and I certainly don't want to dogmatize about theology.

While Dooyeweerd does critique unbelieving thought, in the end Van Til says that if you don't begin dogmatically with the transcendent revelation of the omniscient God, and if your transcendental analysis is immanent in its context, then you're no different from what the autonomous man is doing, and you'll never rise higher in your conclusions than what the autonomous man could do.

Again, to belabor the point, Van Til says that he does not believe in reasoning formally and abstractly; he reasons "concretely," which means that he must begin with a concrete worldview given on authority at the outset. We don't go out there and talk about, for instance, the concept of cause and see what we all can ultimately derive from that.

CHAPTER 15

Van Til's Critics: John Frame

I will briefly go through a series of criticisms Frame makes, but the heart of his criticism is on page 76 of his book *Apologetics to the Glory of God: An Introduction.*[1] Before getting to the heart of the matter, Frame introduces transcendental arguments on page 69 and then on page 71. Having introduced the subject, he says, "but I have some questions."

I. Frame asks:

First, I question whether the transcendental argument can function without the help of subsidiary arguments of a more traditional kind. Although I agree with Van Til's premise that without God there is no meaning, I must grant that not everyone would immediately agree with that premise. How, then, is that premise to be proved?[2]

This isn't a devastating criticism, because as I understand the transcendental program, you have a general claim that is made and then you can illustrate that from any fact in human experience. So when Frame asks, "Well after you've made that claim how do you expect unbelievers to accept it?" *The answer is by illustrating it.* Is that supplementing it with traditional arguments? No, it's supplementing

---

1. John M. Frame, *Apologetics to the Glory of God: An Introduction* (Phillipsburg, NJ: Presbyterian and Reformed, 1994).

2. Frame, *Apologetics to the Glory of God*, 71.

it with illustrations of the transcendental challenge that nothing makes sense or is coherent in our experience apart from the Christian worldview.

II. Frame continues:

> Second, I do not agree that the traditional arguments necessarily conclude with something less than the biblical God.[3]

If the traditional arguments are interpreted according to the claims of those who make them—as autonomous attempts to make sense out of this world (e.g., we all see causation about us, everything has a cause, therefore this world must have a cause)—while Frame says that arguments of this sort don't necessarily conclude with something other than the Christian God, I would argue that it does. Why? Because if you are being autonomous in your reasoning, *the only kind of cause you could be talking about is a natural cause. You don't have the supernatural God of Christianity.*

On the other hand, if you mean in their heart of hearts that traditional apologists have been reasoning this way, but they have been thinking in terms of the framework of the Christian worldview so that they're concluding in their heart to the Christian God, I think that's true. They may have been trying to talk about God, but their interpretation of their arguments does not lead to God.

III. Frame says:

> It should be remembered that the traditional arguments often work. They work because (whether the apologist recognizes this or not) they presuppose a Christian worldview.[4]

---

3. Frame, *Apologetics to the Glory of God*, 71.

4. Frame, *Apologetics to the Glory of God*, 71–72.

Well, to this I would say that if they work because they presuppose the Christian worldview, then they ought not to be offered as denying that they presuppose the Christian worldview!

When the traditional apologist tells the unbeliever, "I'm not presupposing anything here! I'm not begging any questions!," and then the argument works because he was presupposing the Christian worldview, I don't see how John Frame can commend that. We should really be telling apologists like this, "Well you better be more honest about the banner under which you're flying." Now, should we always flat out say that we're presupposing Christianity? No. *But you shouldn't say the opposite of that and think that the argument works!*

IV. Frame states:

> ...I do not think that the whole of Christian theism can be established by a single argument, unless that argument is highly complex! I do not think that an argument should be criticized because it fails to prove every element of Christian theism. Such an argument may be part of a system of apologetics which as a whole establishes the entire organism of Christian truth.[5]

I know Frame is trying to be a good and improved Van Tillian, but this is crucial to Van Til. Van Til says we don't prove Christianity block-by-block. Now, Van Til doesn't deny that you can talk about this block and that block and answer specific questions about this block and that block. But his point is that in the transcendental argument we don't just assume a part of Christianity; we assume the whole Christian worldview. Why is that? Because it comes to us on authority and God says, "Who are you to disagree with Me?" Let God be true and every man a liar.[6]

---

5. Frame, *Apologetics to the Glory of God*, 72.

6. Romans 3:4.

Moreover, when he says you can't establish by a single argument every one of the Christian details, you can if the whole argument is about the whole enchilada at one time! That kind of argument doesn't have to talk about every detail. If the argument works and the whole worldview is being referred to by the argument, then the whole worldview is proven by that argument. If you have a principle that shows that the Christian worldview must be true, then that proves the whole Christian worldview.[7]

V. Frame writes:

> If we grant Van Til's point that a complete theistic argument should prove the whole biblical doctrine of God, then we must prove more than that God is the author of meaning and rationality. Ironically, at this point, Van Til is not sufficiently holistic![8]

Well, this interpretation seems to suggest that Van Til is only proving that God is the ground or author of meaning and rationality. But if we begin with a concrete worldview and we're proving that whole worldview from rationality, then of course we are dealing with a very rich thing, much more than God and causation and logic if you will.

VI. Frame claims:

> All of this suggests a further reason why there is no single argument that will prove the entire biblical doctrine of God...Since there is no single argument guaranteed to

---

7. Take the unity and diversity in the Godhead, for instance. This doctrine alone satisfies (either directly or through implication) the philosophical problems of unity and diversity that not even Islam and Judaism can satisfy. This principle (or fundamental truth), when argued transcendentally, necessarily implies the entirety of Christian-theism, and thus when argued transcendentally, simultaneously proves all the other points of the Christian worldview. We defend Christianity as a unit.

8. Frame, *Apologetics to the Glory of God*, 73.

persuade every rational person, there is no argument that is immune to such additional questioning.[9]

Therefore, Van Til's transcendental argument, like every other argument, is not sufficient, by itself, to prove the existence of the biblical God to everyone's satisfaction.[10]

I agree that not everyone is satisfied. When Frame tells us that not everyone will be satisfied with this argument, I'd say, "Yeah, because there might be something wrong with people who are not satisfied with this argument" (Romans 1).

There is probably not a distinctively "transcendental argument" which rules out all other kinds of arguments.[11] That is, the God we seek to prove is indeed the source of all meaning, the source of all possibility, of actuality, and of predication. The biblical God is more than this, but certainly not less. And we should certainly not say anything to an inquirer that suggests that we can reason, predicate, assess probabilities, etc., apart from God.

Must we bring this point up explicitly in every apologetic encounter? I would say no.[12]

In the margin of my copy of Frame's book I wrote in "I agree." I don't think we need to bring it up explicitly as though that is the only thing that comes out of our mouth. But I would say that everything we do talk about must *implicitly* assume it!

Getting to the heart of the matter Frame says that arguments of this transcendental kind are useful. "But," Frame says, "I have a

9. Bahnsen: I think that my beloved professor whom I respect has confused proof and persuasion here. (See Chapter 1 for review of this discussion).

10. Frame, *Apologetics to the Glory of God*, 73.

11. Bahnsen: That is, he doesn't think transcendental arguments are distinctive.

12. Frame, *Apologetics to the Glory of God*, 73-74.

question about them: Are indirect arguments really distinct from direct arguments?"[13] Well, yes. Why? Because a transcendental argument is not a deductive argument nor is it an inductive argument. It's not an inductive attempt to generalize from what I already understand to the conditions or principles of understanding. Nor is it a deductive argument from a proposition to a set of propositions to what those propositions imply. And so when he asks whether or not indirect arguments are distinct, of course they are! They're as distinct as the difference between what Descartes was doing from what Hume was doing from what Kant was doing![14] And if anyone suggests that Kant was really just trying to "out-Descartes" Descartes or "out-Hume" Hume, I don't think any competent philosopher would give you credit for that.

Now, you may say what Kant was trying to do was silly and that he never achieved what he was intending to achieve. You can say all those sorts of things, but to think that there is nothing distinctive about transcendental arguments is too big to be considered a mistake.[15]

Somehow Dr. Frame has gotten so far out of the range of what we're talking about that we can't call it a mistake. And I certainly don't like doing this because I have a high regard for the man and his intellect. With that being said I think there is perhaps something more that is going on here besides intellectual analysis. I think Dr. Frame has a good heart and would like to see Christian apologists drawn together and in that case is being led to soften the antithesis for the sake of what we can all accomplish together. Continuing, he says:

> Any indirect argument of this sort can be turned into a direct argument by some creative rephrasing.[16]

13. Frame, *Apologetics to the Glory of God*, 76.

14. See Chapter 2.

15. Bahnsen here and in his Seminary Apologetics Course (taught during the same year) when going over this same criticism references a famous line by Ludwig Wittgenstein: "For a mistake, this is too big."

16. Frame, *Apologetics to the Glory of God*, 76.

He grants that there may be rhetorical advantages to our way of putting it, but he says that if we are creative enough, we could rephrase a transcendental argument and turn it into one of the more standard-form deductive or inductive arguments.

Now I am going to read the "heart of the hearts" of the matter:

> But if the indirect form is sound the direct form will be too—and vice versa. Indeed, if I say, "Without God, no causality," the argument is incomplete, unless I add the positive formulation "But there is causality, therefore God exists," a formulation identical with the direct argument.[17]

That is, he takes the argument to be "Without God, no causality. But there is causality. Therefore, God exists." Why is it that without God there is no causality? Because it doesn't make conceptual sense to speak of causality.

In Chapter 10 I gave a written illustration that offers the framework for a presuppositional argument: take p and ask what the precondition for the intelligibility of p is. When somebody argues in the traditional way, it's tantamount to saying, "I see all kinds of causes out there in the world. Therefore, the world as a whole must have a cause, and that cause we call God." In this instance *I am making God an extension of my thinking about causation*—God is the big, first cause. But that is an extension of what I know about this world around me. But when I take causation and ask what the preconditions for its intelligibility are, I'm not saying God is a cause. I'm saying that without God you can't even make sense of what you're talking about.

So at this point, at the heart of Frame's criticism, I just have to flatfootedly say, "That's wrong. You have mistakenly thought that a transcendental argument can be rephrased as a deductive or inductive argument, and it cannot be. Now, you can rephrase a transcendental

---

17. Frame, *Apologetics to the Glory of God*, 76

argument and make one that sounds like a deductive or inductive argument, but the conclusion of a transcendental argument is not ever going to be that God is the first cause. The conclusion will always be that you can't even talk about causation without God. No discussion of causation makes sense apart from God and the Christian worldview.

One Final Criticism

With these three authors being addressed, we have seen that they have not successfully overcome Van Til's transcendental program or shown it to be weak. They may show that it needs to be spruced up and that we must do more work to illustrate it, but I don't think that they have shown that the program itself is fundamentally flawed or that the argument does not work as an argument. Now, there is one last criticism of Van Til that I will finish up with.

Somebody might read all of Van Til's material or some of my seminars and debates and so forth and say, "The problem with this is that Christian apologetics is supposed to be done by every Christian. That's what the Bible says. But it sounds like this approach can only be done by philosophy majors, and maybe even some of them struggle with it." I want to tell everyone from the bottom of my heart that if that criticism were true, I think it would be absolutely devastating. But I don't believe it is true. I believe that what we have been doing here today can be likened to an advanced course in systematic theology.

Sometimes systematic theologians talk about some heavy material. Take the Trinity for instance. Wouldn't we all say that an extensive discussion of the doctrine of the Trinity and the biblical presentation of that would call for a lot of mental stretching? And when we all got done probably none of us would walk away saying that we had it all down perfectly. We'd all be inclined to say that the more we understand about it, the more profound and complex it seems.

Now, that being true, does that mean we can't teach the Trinity to our children? Or, if we do, is what we are teaching our children fundamentally flawed because it doesn't have all the complexity, sophistication, and depth of a seminar on the Trinity? Of course not. The same truth is subject to communication at different levels of sophistication and intellectual maturity. But it's the same truth and it's the same method. We begin at a very elementary level about the Trinity and as they grow, they develop and deepen and make more sophisticated their understanding. Their concepts become more adequate to the real-world life that they must live through.

Can you teach children the transcendental argument? Yes. I wouldn't call it that (for obvious reasons), but without mentioning it by name or without mentioning anything philosophically sophisticated you can certainly teach what Paul says in 1 Corinthians 1:20: "has not God made foolish the wisdom of this world?"

You can say to your child, "You know, out there in this world there are people who try to teach in elementary schools about mathematics and they don't believe in God. And they think they're really smart people despite not bowing to the Lord Jesus Christ and they don't believe God exists." And then you can ask your child, "But if God doesn't exist, is what is true about $2 + 2 = 4$ on Tuesday have to be true on Wednesday as well if God doesn't exist?" Nine-year-olds can understand that. I can put it into philosophical jargon, but why bother? They can understand that in a chance universe things change all the time, so the truths of mathematics can change as well.[18]

---

18. The comebacks to this typically revolve around demarcating the absoluteness of mathematics (and logic) over against the material, contingent facts within the universe and how only the latter can be subject to chance. But this demarcation grants that the universe isn't really or ultimately chance as demarcation assumes at least some sense of regularity or uniformity, and thus this comeback fails to even critique Bahnsen's statement accurately. To this, more astute philosophers would perhaps critique this statement by pointing out that the fact that there is still a chance universe implies the absoluteness ("unchangingness") of mathematics, as

What we want to teach our children is that if we're not faithful to God, as you grow up you're going to run into people that tempt you to be arrogant and to act, as the Proverb says, like a fool. You know what the fool rejoices in? That his mind should reveal itself. He pours out folly. And what does the fool do when he pours out folly? He returns to it like a dog returns to its vomit.[19] When

---

the indefinite article implies the quantity of one, and thus there are things which are immune to mathematically-chance circumstances or events.

But this doesn't rebut Bahnsen's point either as the things which stand "immune to chance" (i.e., the (one, singular) universe as a whole) are not things *within* this chance universe, which was Bahnsen's point (viz. "*in* a chance universe things change all the time"). By definition, a chance universe would imply chance changes to those principles which we believe to stand immune to chance or change within the confines of the universe. To rebut this point by arguing that it's impossible for the laws or principles of mathematics to be subject to chance or change is to simply argue from the *impossibility of the contrary*. Sound familiar? This incisive, oppositional comeback would have to entail a transcendental argument for the impossibility of what Bahnsen has said. And it is either the case that Bahnsen is right, or it is not the case the Bahnsen is right by the sword of transcendental argumentation from the non-Christian.

However, what has the consistent albatross for the unbeliever been given his secular transcendental enterprise? Any argument made transcendentally is like a rock falling in a bottomless ocean—he has nowhere to put this "rock-solid" argument in a coherent, justifiable worldview. Moreover, as was also observed by Van Til, the unbeliever must come to the brute facts of the universe for the first time and rationalize them into his system. But this is a far stretch from definitively rebutting Bahnsen's point because, as Bahnsen explained, push the unbeliever far enough in his system and he can only ever resort to chance (which the unbelieving philosopher here rejects) or unknowability. But if reality is ultimately unknowable, there could always be a defeater that defeats his incorrigible belief that the laws of mathematics are absolute in the first place, despite it *seeming* impossible.

Thus, why argue transcendentally for them as a rebuttal against Bahnsen at all? All of this stands as a devastating illustration and application of how absurd the unbelieving position is. Unbelievers who read this controversial statement by Bahnsen *end up having no justifiable basis by which to criticize it to begin with.* They cannot make sense out of *anything* apart from reverence to God and His revelation.

19. Bahnsen: That is a statement about circular reasoning if you don't recognize it. The fool pours out his folly (he vomits this worthless stuff) and then he goes and eats his vomit. He's just so proud of his own way of thinking.

the Bible refers to that, it's teaching us some fundamental truths about how stupid unbelief is. To rebel against God is stupidity because when you rebel against God you become a fool and can't understand anything.

The fascinating thing about discussing the transcendental approach to apologetics is that it can keep one busy for over 200 pages of in-depth philosophical study, but it can also be taught to our children growing up without any of that. To me, this suggests that this is coming very close to the way the Bible teaches us we should reason and the way we should interact with people in the world because all of God's children—from children to PhDs in philosophy—should do it, and I hope that this book will have encouraged you to give you more boldness to show that you can do it where God places you and at the level of educational sophistication or at the level of communication you need for the people you're talking to.

The transcendental argument amounts to what Paul says in Romans 1: "Professing themselves to be wise they became fools, and their reasoning was made futile."[20] Has not God made foolish the wisdom of this world?

---

20. Romans 1:22.

Answering the Transcendental Criticisms of Van Til's TAG

Joshua Pillows

Author Note

The contents of this work do not comprise an extensive, exhaustive, or historical bibliographical survey pertaining to the issues of transcendental arguments and their criticisms. The sole focus will revolve specifically around (1) the presuppositionalist's particular use of transcendental reasoning (TAG), (2) the distinctive features of Van Tillian philosophy as TAG proceeds, and (3) answering the challenges presented against it as they have been historically promulgated.

Abstract

The motivation behind the current research derives mainly from the failure of contemporary and past presuppositionalists to adequately address the philosophical and transcendental criticisms directed towards Van Til's Transcendental Argument for the Existence of God (hereafter referred to as TAG). Given this shortcoming—which, with it, comes an atmospheric, looming doubt over the argument's legitimacy—and given that this work is not only intended for refutation but also practical conciseness, brevity concerning appropriate citations and expositions (where not as pivotal) will be stressed while simultaneously retaining the objective aspect of refutation. An overview of both Van Tillian presuppositional apologetics and TAG as operating under a *Christian* philosophy will first be embellished before finally turning to the list of transcendental criticisms levelled against presuppositional apologetics. Criticisms 1-4 are the same criticisms which Michael Butler dealt with in his published thesis over 20 years ago and will be addressed and refuted in the same chronological order from least-potent to most-lethal in a more elucidated and improved manner before addressing one final criticism that has, in recent years, surfaced in transcendental philosophy, and finally concluding that Van Til's controversial argument retains its objective force.

Answering the Transcendental Criticisms of Van Til's TAG

From its inception, Van Til's transcendental argument has been subjected to numerous criticisms, both transcendental and non-transcendental alike (Van Til, 2008, pp. 3-24). While the more generic criticisms against presuppositional apologetics have been answered sufficiently (e.g., concession to idealism, opposing the use of evidences, question-begging, etc.), the apparent neglect of the more philosophical issues allows them to act as a catalyst for the apologetic's impotency. Van Til never specifically addressed these now-modern criticisms, and Bahnsen, Van Til's protégé, likewise never dedicated any written, formal work to the venture of such refutation, though he has written a lengthy section in his last book pertaining to the nature and controversial climate of transcendental arguments (hereafter TAs) (Bahnsen, 1998, 496-529). Only in the months preceding his untimely death did he address them head-on in a recorded seminar, but even then it was not exhaustive (Bahnsen, Butler, 1995).

In the seminar, Bahnsen, with his renowned incisiveness and acuity, expounds on the following transcendental criticisms: the mere sufficiency of proving Christian-theism, the uniqueness of transcendental proof, and the metaphysical nature of transcendental reasoning—moving from a conceptual conclusion to metaphysics/ontology. Michael Butler, a co-speaker at the seminar, specifically addresses criticisms pertaining to the nature of TAG itself—that being whether it is really an indirect proof as opposed to direct (though Bahnsen addresses this as well), or if transcendental arguments today are really TAs since they are not strictly Kantian—and addresses all four of these problems in his published thesis years later (Butler, 2002, 65-124). These issues more-or-less constitute the standard fare of transcendental criticisms in academia, and with the premature death of Bahnsen (who is widely regarded as the champion of presuppositionalism), the climate concerning the legitimacy of presuppositional apologetics is one of uncertainty, the philosophical foundation of which is, at best, precarious.

CRITICS

This dubitability of Van Tillian presuppositionalism has led even those which identify/have identified as Van Tillians to adopt an alternative position, or rejecting the presuppositional position altogether. For instance, Bàlint Békefi, a Reformed Christian, has expressed his doubts on Van Til's apologetic in his recently published paper "Van Til versus Stroud: Is the Transcendental Argument for Christian Theism Viable" in which he focuses his criticism against TAG upon the charge of moving erroneously from conceptual necessity to metaphysical necessity without presenting the horns of a dilemma (Békefi, 2017, 136-160).

Michael P. Riley's doctoral dissertation revolves around this same problem and, more specifically, attacks Michael Butler's answer to it (Riley, 2014). The same criticism and direct attack are likewise posed by Bryan Sims in his dissertation (Sims, 2006). Both men are cited by Békefi to further enforce the notion that even within Christendom, the argument from "brother Van Til" ought to be regarded as a failure.

Of course, the criticisms from the secular world (or non-Christian world, broadly speaking) outnumber those within the Christian "camp." Pertaining to the above three critics, what could ostensibly be considered as the most lethal criticism of moving from conceptual necessity to metaphysical necessity finds its origin in secular philosopher Barry Stroud (1935-2019) who levelled charges against another secular philosopher, P. F. Strawson (1919-2006), for utilizing a TA to (allegedly) draw a metaphysical conclusion (Stroud, 1968; Strawson, 1959). While this criticism was never intended to be used against Van Til, it nevertheless has been fully legitimized against TAG and attests to the precariousness of transcendental ventures in today's philosophical climate.

Stephan Körner has focused his criticism on the problematic nature of uniquely proving a particular schema, and it perhaps resonates most frequently in academic literature after the "Stroudian" objection (Körner, 1974). How is one to uniquely prove their position transcendentally alone? Would we not all have to share the same schema to come (at least theoretically) to an agreed-upon conclusion? Or could one inductively refute all real and hypothetical worldviews? Human finitude renders this an impossible feat.

A secular attempt at proving a uniquely and commonly held schema amongst all peoples comes from Donald Davidson (though his argument was specifically intended to prove that there is no such thing as a conceptual scheme, but, as Butler points out, this is tantamount to arguing that there is only one) (Davidson, 1984). Succinctly put, Davidson argues that if there were more than one conceptual scheme, translations between languages should be impossible. Moreover, we could not even relate to other peoples' experiences if our concepts of the world were different. To therefore speak of a diversity of conceptual schemes is meaningless and incoherent. While this criticism may have merit on its own grounds, it would still only prove a conceptually-necessary transcendental conclusion, thus leading the critic back to Stroud's objection.

Finally (keeping with the theme of brevity), A. C. Grayling gives a concise and commendable overview of this chaotic climate in the *Blackwell Companion to Philosophy* (Grayling, 2010, 768-771). Not only are the preceding argument without an answer (allegedly, anyway), he also additionally hearkens back to the exact nature of TAs, illustrating that there are transcendental-type arguments (polar concept arguments) utilized by several different philosophers which themselves slightly differ from what one would call a contemporary "conceptual TA." And given that contemporary TAs differ from Kant, we come to an ever-evolving lineage of TAs in which the "genome" progressively departs from Kant, the Father of TAs. We're thus left with several criticisms levelled against transcendental argumentation as well as the charge that TAs *themselves* in the modern sense are simply spurious and should not be regarded as such to begin with.

Presuppositional Apologetics Exposited

Van Til's apologetic has often been viewed as an anomaly in Christian apologetics, especially considering its late development in the Church. However, Van Til's utmost desire was to formulate an apologetic that was consistently biblical (Reformed) and not founded on the foundation of autonomous philosophical presuppositions which ultimately end in ruin. Often, his new transcendental perspective has come off as a flat-out rejection of the historic proofs, as if Van Til regarded himself as the most pietistic apologist of Christianity next to Paul. This most certainly was not the case. It was Van Til's contention that the historic proofs proved to be unfaithful in starting their defense of the faith on a foundation which assumed the self-sufficiency of human reason and not from the authoritative and infallible scriptures. For instance, in *The Defense of the Faith* (Van Til, 2008, 110):

Following Aristotle's general method of reasoning Thomas Aquinas argues that the natural man can, by the ordinary use of his reason, do justice to the natural revelation that surrounds him. He merely needs some assistance in order that he may also see and react properly to the supernatural revelation that is found in Christianity.

This assumed self-sufficient and alleged neutral authority of human reason as pitted against the authority of God's revelation ought wholeheartedly to be rejected. The Creator-creature distinction *must* be acknowledged; the Bible as come from the Creator supersedes the intellectual endeavors of men:

> But to engage in philosophical discussion does not mean that we begin without Scripture. We do not first defend theism philosophically by an appeal to reason and experience in order, after that, to turn to Scripture for our knowledge and defense of Christianity. We get our theism as well as our Christianity from the Bible. The Bible, as the infallibly inspired revelation of God to sinful man, stands before us as that light in terms of which all the facts of the created universe must be interpreted. (28-29, 129)

Van Til did not reject the historic, theistic proofs for Christianity, but argued only that they ought to be construed in a way that acknowledges the truths of Scripture as pertains to the natural man (Rom. 1:18-32), the infallible authority of God's revelation (2 Tim. 3:16-17), and acknowledging the Creator-creature distinction (Prov. 1:7; cf. Gen. 1:1; Ps. 36:9). God is not to be brought down to the probability level, subject to the rational inquiries and judgments of apologists and natural men alike:

> Accordingly, I do not reject "the theistic proofs" but merely insist on formulating them in such a way as not to compromise the doctrines of Scripture. That is to say, if the theistic proof is constructed as it ought to be constructed, it is objectively valid, whatever the attitude of those to whom it comes may be. (255)

Van Til contended that the only objective and consistently biblical apologetic would be to reason on a *presuppositional level*, always founded upon the self-authoritative Word of God as the Christian's ultimate authority and exposing the intellectual folly of the natural man's system of thought by showing the transcendental necessity of Christian-theism:

> ...a consistently Christian method of apologetic argument, in agreement with its own basic conception of the starting point, must be by presupposition. To argue by presupposition is to indicate what are the epistemological and metaphysical principles that underlie and control one's method. It is not as though the Reformed apologist should not interest himself in the nature of the non-Christian's method. On the contrary, he should make a critical analysis of it. He should, as it were, join his "friend" in the use of it. But he should do so self-consciously with the purpose of showing that its most consistent application not merely leads away from Christian theism, but in leading away from Christian theism leads to the destruction of reason and science as well. (121-122, 124)

For Van Til, therefore, Christianity alone is the only worldview which makes sense of the rational endeavors of men. By arguing presuppositionally on the non-Christian's ground, we can indirectly prove the absolute necessity of presupposing Christianity's truths, thus qualifying as an "objectively valid" proof. Moreover, this sort of apologetic renounces any sort of pretense to neutrality as if the sanctified Christian and the natural man are on the same metaphysical, epistemological, and ethical levels. It acknowledges the fundamental *antithesis* between Christian and non-Christian not simply in terms of salvation, but also in terms of mindset (i.e., the Christian has been saved by God and thus operates under new presuppositions; the non-Christian is totally depraved and worships himself rather than God, wanting nothing to do with his Creator, and exchanging the truths about God for a lie (Rom. 1:23)).

The transcendental apologetic of Van Til amounts to nothing short of conversion. It unashamedly stands on the foundation of Scripture, following the theology of Augustine: "I believe in order to understand." The transcendental challenge truly aims at bringing "every thought captive to the obedience of Christ" in that it gives no leeway to the non-Christian's philosophy of life as apologists such as Aquinas have done throughout the ages. By comparing the presuppositions of both the Christian and the non-Christian, it can objectively be shown that Christianity supplies the transcendental necessities needed for the intelligibility of human experience. Thus, Van Til argued for the proof of God's existence from the fact that without such a system as incorporates Him, there can be no intelligibility to human experience. Christianity is the *only* philosophy of life that accounts for such uniformity, for possibility and necessity.

COMPARING PRESUPPOSITIONS

Since the presuppositional Christian rejects the pretense of open-minded neutrality when considering the existence of God and the truths of Christianity, argumentation will naturally proceed by comparing antithetical systems of Thought between the believer and unbeliever. Whose fundamental assumptions (presuppositions) pertaining to metaphysics, epistemology, and ethics justify the intelligibility of human experience? Van Til again (Van Til, 2008):

> The answer to this question cannot be finally settled by any direct discussion of "facts." It must, in the last analysis, be settled indirectly. The Christian apologist must place himself upon the position of his opponent, assuming the correctness of his method merely for argument's sake, in order to show him that on such a position the "facts" are not facts and the "laws" are not laws. (122)

Van Til contends that the presuppositions of all non-Christian Thought do not explain or justify the transcendentals for intelligible human experience. However, by illustrating the presuppositional truths of Christian-theism, we can demonstrate that Christianity *does* justify (or give answers) to intelligibility. By standing on the authoritative Word of God as the backing of our apologetic, the presuppositionalist argues that by denying this very worldview you're reduced to philosophical absurdity, unable to make sense out of anything whatsoever. Either one justifies intelligible experience and therefore facts, or one fails to justify intelligible experience and with it any fact of existence, from something as simple as boiling noodles to advanced considerations in quantum mechanics.

TRANSCENDENTAL CONSIDERATIONS

As Van Til stated above, this "analysis" is (and must be) settled in an indirect fashion, not directly by appealing to one or more agreed-upon facts. Since neutrality is not only immoral from a Christian perspective but also philosophically and theologically impossible, an appeal to facts simply takes for granted the undergirding antithetical philosophical positions or worldviews maintained by both parties of the debate. Since an appeal to facts operates under a "direct" line of argumentation, and since an appeal to facts is inadequate in defending the truths of Christianity, the "indirect" line of transcendental argumentation must therefore be utilized.

Relating to the debate over whether TAs are really distinct in their nature, there is also debate over how a TA should properly be formulated. Should the argument itself be formulated deductively to procure a certain (though perhaps unsound) conclusion? Should it be formulated inductively in a more modest fashion at the expense of certitude? Or should it be formulated as something other? Numerically, should it be formulated as an enthymeme? Should it be formulated as a syllogism? Or should it incorporate more than two premises and a conclusion? While these insights into argument-formulations most certainly have relevant status concerning the topic of TAs, and while debate may proceed concerning the legitimacy and efficacy over differing forms, the ultimate considerations pertain to the contents of the argument itself.

The Distinctives of Transcendental Argumentation

Michael Butler astutely observes that unlike traditional forms of argumentation, TAs in particular reference the *contents* of the premises (Bahnsen, Butler, 1995). Strictly speaking, in a deductive argument the content of the argument itself is irrelevant, only that the conclusion logically follows from the premises. Likewise, strictly speaking, in an inductive argument, the argument itself isn't purporting to prove a particular type of conclusion, only that the conclusion follows with probability from the premises. However, in TAs, the aim is to specifically prove the existence or truth of a *transcendental*. Of course, the argument must be both valid and sound, but the conclusion is a distinct type of propositional truth which the premises intend to prove. Butler says (Bahnsen, Butler, 1995):

> Transcendental arguments, although they do refer to a form of argumentation, … include the type of conclusion that is drawn in the argument itself…In the debate on transcendental arguments there are some who say that when you compare a transcendental argument with a deductive argument, all you're doing is comparing two different forms of argumentation. There is something to that, but that is not all that is happening between the two…it is a mistake to say that deductive, inductive, and transcendental arguments are all the same just with different forms used. [Specifically], it is a category error in that you are categorizing all three of the arguments under the same rubric without giving further qualifications.

Thus, the first distinctive of transcendental reasoning lies in its content, not its form per se—the conclusion is a *transcendental*.

The second distinctive of transcendental reasoning is found in recognizing that TAs themselves operate symbiotically with reductio ad absurdum arguments. That is, given the nature of TAs in proving necessary preconditions, the negation of said preconditions results either in self-falsification or self-stultification, both conclusions of which are only inferred via a reductio argument. In contradistinction, deductive and inductive arguments are not necessarily tethered to the use of an additional argument to prove their respective conclusions. This, however, should not be seen as a defect, only as another distinct aspect to transcendental reasoning.

The third distinctive of transcendental reasoning is observed in its indirect character. Analysis of deductive and inductive arguments once again shows this distinction—both of these arguments utilize facts or considerations within the universe and directly draw a conclusion *as an extension* from the premises, itself non-transcendental in character; the line of reasoning is strictly linear in scope as a chain is linked one link at a time.

However, since TAs (a) prove a specific type of conclusion, and (b) concomitantly utilize reductio arguments, the charge of its identicality to deductive and inductive arguments is, as Butler put it, simply a category error. While the transcendentalist argues positively in the sense of putting forth his premises, and while the argument may be said to be linear (or "direct") in the sense of logical validity and "direct" inferential patterns, the ultimate proof of the transcendental conclusion is reliant upon the reductio argument of assuming its negation for the sake of the argument—this assumption of the negation defining its indirect character. Without such a utilization, the TA could only be said to be inferentially and directly valid or invalid at base with the aspect of soundness left wanting.[1]

---

1. See the syllogism below. If a TA omits the symbiotic reductio argument, the syllogism, depending on the contents of the x and y, will (a) either be consistent (valid) or inconsistent (invalid), and (b) be a direct, linear argument like inductive and deductive arguments. Without the illustration-aspect of the reductio

The fourth distinctive of transcendental reasoning lies in its inherent circularity. Given that transcendental considerations are considerations which inquire about *necessary* preconditions for intelligible experience, such necessary preconditions must be (and cannot help but be) assumed even upon arguing for or against them. While this aspect of transcendental argumentation is (or has been) positively recognized widely—especially as it pertains to this work, by Stroud (Stroud, 1977, p. 106), Jaakko Hintikka (Hintikka, 1972, p. 278), Bahnsen and Butler, (Bahnsen, Butler, 1995), Grayling (Grayling, 2010), and Kant himself (Kant, 1781) (among others)—it mustn't be conflated with the *petitio principii* fallacy which most are too presumptuous to wield in the venture of criticizing presuppositional apologetics. A brief analysis of TAs—whatever form they take—will illustrate that the truth of the conclusion is nowhere assumed in any of the premises; however, the argument itself must assume the transcendental in question in order to even be postulated to begin with (viz. the Law of Identity, as a transcendental, must be utilized to put forward any argument, thus having to be assumed in order to even argue for it transcendentally).

The Formulation of TAG

Turning to TAG more specifically, and following in line with Bahnsen, we will formulate the skeleton of Van Til's transcendental argument as the following syllogism (Bahnsen, Butler, 1995):

1. For x to be the case, y must be the case because y is a necessary precondition for x.

2. x is the case.

3. Therefore, y is the case.

Bahnsen and Butler make the conscientious decision to formulate TAG distinctly from a deductive or inductive form presumably

---

argument, we could never confirm the actual truthfulness of the argument itself, nor categorize TAs as indirect arguments.

to belabor the point that TAs are distinct from either line of argumentation.[2]

One of the fundamental aspects of TAs lies in the fact that x is agreed upon by both parties. To argue over the preconditions of a fact that is not even believed by both opponents seems at least to bring with it a lack of conduciveness to the venture and purpose of transcendental argumentation; it is of course necessary that a point of contact be found within the argument itself, regardless of whether there is disagreement over the conclusion. Thus, the two qualifications for the first premise of a TA are (a) that the fact in question, x, is believed by both parties, and (b) that the "because" clause is at some point (though perhaps not chronologically) proven via a reductio argument.

However, some presuppositionalists see merit in electing to utilize a purely deductive formulation of TAG that does not follow the prescribed formulation above. For instance:

1. If the negation of Christian-theism is self-defeating, then Christian-theism is true.

2. The negation of Christian-theism is self-defeating.

3. Therefore, Christian-theism is true.

Here the affirmation of x in the antecedent clause of the conditional (2) would not be agreed upon by both parties, contrary to the first formulation which does take a fact that both sides acknowledge to be the case. While this is a stark difference between the first form given, (2) is still proven ultimately via a reductio argument in which some point of contact could be found, thus still sharing the aspects of transcendental argumentation. This hearkens back once again to what exactly constitutes a "proper" TA: should a TA utilize an agreed-upon fact and inquire about its preconditions as well as a

---

2. (1) could easily be translated into a conditional if-then premise, thus making the argument deductive, but in form only as modus ponens.

reductio argument? should a TA only require a reductio without the necessity of appealing to an agreed-upon fact? James Anderson illustrates that TAs are a "family" of arguments much like the other traditional arguments for the existence of God are and have been formulated:

> ...there is no definitive formulation of the transcendental argument, just as there are no definitive formulations of the ontological, cosmological, and teleological arguments. When philosophers discuss "the ontological argument," for example, what they're typically referring to is a family of theistic arguments that have a common theme or goal, namely, showing that the existence of God follows from the very idea of God. Likewise for "the cosmological argument" (a family of arguments from contingency or change in the universe) and "the teleological argument" (a family of arguments from apparent design in the universe). I suggest that "the transcendental argument" should be understood along similar lines; specifically, as a family of theistic arguments from the possibility of human thought and experience. (Anderson, 2011, 1)[3]

However, since these considerations draw away from the subject of this paper, it is not currently indispensable for a definitive solution to be procured, only that TAG as the Bahnsenian strain of presuppositionalism formulates it falls within the strictures of historic uses of TAs.

---

3. This paper responds to David Reiter's objection which states that TAG does not prove that God necessarily exists, but maybe that he actually exists. Reiter predicates his argument off of three different formulations of TA; however, all of which are unessential for a transcendentalist (again observing that transcendental formulations can be fluid) and do not conform to the formulation Bahnsen and Butler give (though his "Pattern II" perhaps aligns most with what Bahnsen would contend).

Narrow versus Broad TAG. Since Van Til's apologetic maintains that not a single fact can be known or justified if it were not for God's existence, x can be substituted for any given fact of experience, from the seemingly innumerable number of atomic facts in the universe (boiling noodles, quantum mechanics, etc.) to the number of different philosophical issues (one-and-many, unity-and-change, etc.). Whatever the subject matter may be, the general (or "broad") syllogistic form of TAG remains unaltered. What *is altered* is the corresponding reductio argument that supports the premise that y is a necessary precondition for x.

To argue for the necessity of God's existence to boil noodles would need only to show that God's existence explains the uniformity of nature, the reliability of sense perception and cognitive function, identity, etc., all of which are prerequisites (transcendentals) for the possibility of boiling noodles, and that to deny this truth reduces one to absurdity. To argue for the necessity of God's existence based on a particular philosophical problem such as the one and the many would naturally require the incorporation of different and more premises to fulfill the task of illustration. This, again, warrants the observation that while the contents of TAG are fluid, the overarching structure remains the same.

Moreover, a presuppositionalist could elect to bypass the particular nuances of experience and instead argue that the intelligibility of experience as a whole (which would entail all facts simultaneously) owes its explanation to God's creative decree by which uniformity, consciousness, knowledge, truth, moral absolutes, etc. are explained; therefore, Christian-theism is true. Thus once again, whatever election the presuppositionalist takes, the argument of TAG itself remains the same, regardless of how narrow or broad the argument may be constructed, or how poorly it may be *stated* (Van Til, 2015, 77).

Answering Criticisms

As was addressed in the Abstract, Michael Butler's work (Butler, 2002), while being the long-running staple of defending the transcendental aspects of Van Til's apologetic, has received the brunt of these anti-TAG criticisms since its publication, especially as it pertains to his answer against the Stroudian objection. All of the criticisms he addressed will be treated in like manner, though with some elucidation, embellishment, and improvement; following this will the fifth and final criticism be addressed.

1. THE NATURE OF TAG

The first objection in Butler's paper pertains to TAG not being a distinct type of argumentation, instead being reducible to the traditional arguments given throughout Christian history. He writes:

> Specifically, some have argued that TAG is not a unique argument form but is reducible to the more traditional arguments for God's existence. John Frame especially has advanced this criticism in his recent writings on apologetics (Butler, 2002, 77).

Crucial and central to the aspect of transcendental reasoning is its indirect character. That is, by assuming the opposite of the transcendental in question, upon pain of absurdity and/or self-defeat, the transcendental is proven objectively in such indirect fashion. Butler cites the same passages from Van Til as the section expositing the presuppositional method (above) where Van Til instructs us to assume the "correctness" of the unbeliever's position for argument's sake to show him that not only is his position philosophically untenable, but *relies* on Christian-theism ultimately for its grounding (Van Til, 2008).

Still, John Frame has advanced the criticism that TAs can be utilized either indirectly or directly as the traditional proofs are, thus necessitating the conclusion that TAs are not, in fact, distinct in form (though still perhaps in character). Frame writes: Are indirect arguments really distinct from direct arguments? In the final analysis, it doesn't make much difference whether you say "Causality, therefore God" or "Without God, no causality, therefore God." (Frame, 1994, 76)

Butler makes two astute observations from this quotation. First, in referencing a quotation from another book of Frame's, Butler argues that Frame here is specifically reducing a version of TAG to the traditional cosmological argument, which "is certainly something Van Til would take issue with" (Butler, 2002, 78). Succinctly stated, the/a traditional cosmological argument argues that since there are causes in the world, and since they are all contingent and cannot regress infinitely, there therefore must be a first uncaused cause which we call God. There are, unfortunately, many non-Christian assumptions within the traditional proofs (which Frame here ostensibly reduces TAG to) and which the reader should be acquainted with: they begin neutrally, assume autonomy, proceed directly, argue probabilistically, and conclude deistically. The cosmological apologist could, of course, cite the fact that a first uncaused cause is a prerequisite/ transcendental to explaining the infinite number of contingent causes within the universe, but this is not how the argument has been historically formulated. Thus, for Frame to move TAG to the level of a traditional proof is simply erroneous. Bahnsen decisively illustrates this from his last seminar:

> [Earlier] I gave a written illustration that offers the framework for a presuppositional argument: take p and ask what the precondition for the intelligibility of p is.
>
> When somebody argues in the traditional way, it's tantamount to saying, "I see all kinds of causes out there in the world. Therefore, the world as a whole must have a cause, and that cause we call God." In this instance *I am making God an extension of my thinking about causation* – God is the big, first cause, but that is an extension of what I know about

this world around me. [However], when I take causation and ask what the preconditions for its intelligibility are, I'm not saying God is a cause; I'm saying that without God you can't even make sense of what you're talking about. (Bahnsen/Butler, 1995)

In terms of the broader philosophical considerations of inductive, deductive, and transcendental reasoning and their respective differences, transcendental reasoning is not an attempt at inferring a generalized conclusion from personal experience in a "bottom-up" inferential pattern, contra inductive reasoning; nor is transcendental reasoning an attempt at arguing from a set of general premises and their respective implications to a conclusion in a "top-down" inferential pattern, contra deductive reasoning. Thus, Frame both theologically and philosophically fails to accurately critique the use of transcendental reasoning.

Second, Butler picks up on Frame's usage of "Causality, therefore God" and "Without God, no causality, therefore God" and construes them as two enthymemes[4]:

The first ... enthymeme ... when spelled out reads: "There is causality and therefore God exists (for without God there could be no causality)." The second is also enthymematic which when spelled out reads: Without God there is no causality (but there is causality) therefore God exists." Understood this way, Van Til would have no disagreement. (Butler, 2002, 78)

This analysis brings us back to the partial fluidity of constructing a TA. Both enthymemes would fit the argument-form given by Bahnsen and Butler, the only difference being that through enthymematic utterance or postulation, the argument is more

---

4. Arguments in which one or more premises are left unstated or are just assumed.

direct in character.[5] Thus, Frame has erred in taking a reductionistic approach to TAG in construing it as one of the traditional proofs. If, however, Frame never intended on reducing TAG to a traditional proof, the "directedness" or positively-formulated nature of the/an enthymematic statement or dictum should not be conflated with the direct-indirect dialectical usage in discussions over TAs. A mere positive assertion in an argument alone does not constitute a "direct" line of reasoning per se, and this is particularly the case in TAs utilizing symbiotic reductio arguments as the catalyst for their indirect character.

Lesser Framean Criticisms

In the same book, Frame gives a series of criticisms concerning his "questions" about TAG (Frame, 1994, pp. 71-73), which Bahnsen addresses head-on in the seminar. Since he handles these criticisms with succinct acuity, what follows will simply be the transcript of Frame's criticisms/questions and Bahnsen's responses (Bahnsen/ Butler, 1995):

> First, I question whether the transcendental argument can function without the help of subsidiary arguments of a more traditional kind. Although I agree with Van Til's premise that without God there is no meaning, I must grant that not everyone would immediately agree with that premise. How, then, is that premise to be proved? (Frame, 1994, 71)

Well, this isn't a devastating criticism because as I understand the transcendental program, you have a general claim that is made and then you can illustrate that from any fact in human experience. When Frame asks, "Well after you've made that claim how do

---

5. The term "direct" here is used in a declarative sense, not in an inferentially linear sense as has been used in this work to delineate between direct and indirect forms of argumentation.

you expect unbelievers to accept it?" the answer is by illustrating it. Is that supplementing it with traditional arguments? No, it's supplementing it with illustrations of the transcendental challenge that nothing makes sense or is coherent in our experience apart from the Christian worldview.

> Second, I do not agree that the traditional arguments necessarily conclude with something less than the biblical God. (Frame, 1994, 72)

If the traditional arguments are interpreted according to the claims of those who make them—as autonomous attempts to make sense out of this world (e.g., we all see causation about us, everything has a cause, therefore this world must have a cause)—while Frame said that arguments of this sort don't necessarily conclude with something other than the Christian God, I would argue that it does. Why? Because if you are being autonomous in your reasoning, the only kind of cause you could be talking about is a natural cause. You don't have the supernatural God of Christianity. On the other hand, if you mean in their heart of hearts that traditional apologists have been reasoning this way, but they have been thinking in terms of the framework of the Christian worldview so that they're concluding in their heart to the Christian God, I think that's true. They may have been trying to talk about God, but their interpretation of their arguments does not lead to God.

> It should be remembered that the traditional arguments often work. They work because whether the apologist recognizes this or not, they presuppose the Christian worldview. (Frame, 1994, 71-72)

Well, to this I would say that if they work because they presuppose the Christian worldview then they ought not to be offered as denying that they presuppose the Christian worldview! When the traditional apologist tells the unbeliever, "I'm not presupposing anything here!

I'm not begging any questions!" and then the argument works because he was presupposing the Christian worldview, I don't see how John Frame can commend that. We should really be telling apologists like this, "Well you better be more honest about the banner under which you're flying." Now, should we always flat out say that we're presupposing Christianity? No. *But you shouldn't say the opposite of that and think that the argument works!*

> I do not think that the whole of Christian theism can be established by a single argument unless that argument is highly complex! I do not think that an argument should be criticized because it fails to prove every element of Christian theism. Such an argument may be part of a system of apologetics which as a whole establishes the entire organism of Christian truth. (Frame, 1994, 72)

I know Frame is trying to be a good and improved Van Tillian, but this is crucial to Van Til. Van Til says we don't prove Christianity block-by-block. Now, Van Til doesn't deny that you can talk about this block and that block and answer specific questions about this block and that block. But his point is that in the transcendental argument we don't just assume a part of Christianity; we assume the whole Christian worldview. Why is that? Because it comes to us on authority and God says, "Who are you to disagree with Me?" Let God be true and every man a liar.

Moreover, when he says that you can't establish by a single argument every one of the Christian details, you in fact can if the whole argument is about the whole enchilada at one time. That kind of argument doesn't have to talk about every kind of detail. If the argument works and the whole worldview is being referred to by the argument, then the whole worldview is proven by that argument. If you have a principle that shows that the Christian worldview must be true, then that proves the whole Christian worldview.

If we grant Van Til's point that a complete theistic argument should prove the whole biblical doctrine of God, then we must prove more than that God is the author of meaning and rationality. Ironically, at this point, Van Til is not sufficiently wholistic. (Frame, 1994, 73)

Well, this interpretation seems to suggest that Van Til is only proving that God is the ground or author of meaning and rationality. But if we begin with a concrete worldview and we're proving that whole worldview from rationality, then of course we are dealing with a very rich thing, much more than God and causation and logic if you will.

All of this suggests the further reason why there is no single argument that will prove the entire biblical doctrine of God...Since there is no single argument guaranteed to persuade every rational person, there is no argument that is immune to such additional questioning. Therefore, Van Til's transcendental argument, like every other argument, is not sufficient by itself to prove the existence of the biblical God to everyone's satisfaction. (Frame, 1994, 73)

I think my beloved professor whom I respect has confused proof and persuasion here. I agree that not everyone is satisfied. When Frame tells us that not everyone will be satisfied with this argument, I'd say because there might be something wrong with people who are not satisfied with this argument.

There is probably not a distinctively transcendental argument which rules out all other kinds of arguments. That is, the God we seek to prove is indeed the source of all meaning, the source of all possibility, of actuality, and of predication. The biblical God is more than this but certainly not less, and we should certainly not say anything to an inquirer that suggests that we can reason, predicate, assess probabilities apart

> from God...Must we bring this point up explicitly in every
> apologetic encounter? I would say no. (Frame, 1994, 73-74)

In the margin of my book, I wrote "I agree." I don't think we need
to bring it up explicitly as though that is the only thing that comes
out of our mouth. But I would say that everything we do talk about
must *implicitly* assume it![6]

Frame's criticisms, though valid, have not wreaked any
significant havoc on Van Til's transcendental program, and from
a Christian perspective they ought to be appreciated given not
only his relationship and acquaintance with Van Til, but also his
intellectual sympathies and contributions to the apologetic despite
his disagreements. The transcendental argument Van Til has
formulated cannot be reduced to a traditional proof (along with its
unbiblical philosophical assumptions), cannot be argued directly,
and thus cannot be deductive or inductive in character despite the
legitimacy of formulating it in such manner.

2. THE UNIQUENESS PROOF OF TAG AND THE EXCLUSIVITY OF CHRISTIANITY

The second criticism Butler deals with centers around whether
or not TAG proves the exclusivity of Christianity, not merely its
sufficiency. TAG may "get the job done" in proving that Christian-
theism provides the preconditions of intelligible experience, but
we're still left wanting over whether or not it is both sufficient and
exclusive. How is this to be done? Particularly, Butler quotes the
Lutheran John Warwick Montgomery and his criticism in Van Til's
festschrift. Montgomery writes:

> Even Van Til's trenchant decimations of non-Christian
> positions are rendered ineffective by his ultimate

---

6. The transcript of Bahnsen ends here.

presuppositionalism, since all the non-Christians whom Van Til chooses to criticize could employ his own two-edged sword against him, crying: "Such criticisms are irrelevant, for right reason—true interpretation of fact and genuine application of the standards of consistency—begins with the commitment to *my* presuppositional starting point!" And even if it were possible in some fashion to destroy all existent alternative world-views but that of orthodox Christianity, the end result would still not be the necessary truth of Christianity; for in a contingent universe, there are an *infinite* number of possible philosophical positions, and even the fallaciousness of infinity-minus-one positions would not establish the validity of the one that remained (unless we were to introduce the gratuitous assumptions that at least one *had* to be right!). (Montgomery, 1971, 387-388)

From this paragraph, three different criticisms can be ascertained: first, denying the disjunction of a contradiction (viz. rather than "*a* v -*a*" it ought to be "*a* v *b*" (and/or *c*, *d*, etc. *ad infinitum*); thus secondly, the impossibility of refuting all other non-Christian worldviews; and third, that all possible and existent worldviews could theoretically be false. How, then, is the uniqueness of Christian-theism as proved by TAG to be defended?

Bahnsen explains that on Van Til's Christian philosophy, there really are only two different worldviews: the Christian worldview and the non-Christian worldview (hence the disjunctive contradiction):

Van Til doesn't believe that there are a zillion worldviews out there so let's get busy because by the time we die we have to have refuted each one of them. Van Til's apologetic is not an inductive process of knocking down one after the other. Van Til says all of them either assume that Christianity is true or that it's not. This is Van Til's "Law of Excluded Middle":

when it comes to worldviews it's either Christian or non-Christian. (Bahnsen/Butler, 1995)

Van Til's justification for this particular type of disjunct comes from Jesus' words in Matthew 12:30 and Luke 11:23 where He declares that those who are not with Him are inevitably against Him. While this justification may be written off as cliché and illegitimate at proving the contradictory nature of the disjunct to non-Christian Thought, to point out the obvious, Van Til is operating on a distinctly Christian philosophy, not one which proceeds from the ruin of autonomous human reason.

In Christian philosophy and theology Christ is described as many things, both metaphorical and literal. Metaphorically, Christ is described as the vine (John 15:5), the door (John 10:7), an angel (Ex. 23:20-21; Is. 63:9), and a good shepherd (John 10:11). Literally, Christ is the Word of God (John 1:1), God Himself (John 8:58), a prophet (and fulfillment of prophecy) (Luke 24:19; Acts 3, 7; Is. 9:6), a mediator and High Priest (1 Tim. 2:5), King (John 18:36; Rev. 19:16), and the Alpha and Omega (Rev. 1:8; 21:6; 22:13). However, Van Til's justification for the contradictory disjunct more specifically revolves around Christ being the embodiment of Truth (John 14:6; 17:17 cf. 1:1). As such, the fact remains that *if* a proposition is either true or false, it cannot be both (despite Postmodern and skeptical adherence to relativism and subjectivism). Thus, as the nature of truth stands broadly, and the nature of the truth of Christianity narrowly, it *is* either a v $-a$, necessitating a disjunction of a contradiction—either it is true that Christianity is the case or it is not true that Christianity is the case, agnosticism tentatively amounting to the latter.

Critics will predictably retort that they don't adhere to such a philosophical stricture, thus the contradictory nature of the disjunct as pertains to Christian-theism has not so much been proven as it has simply been postulated. Such critics, however, embarrassingly take for granted the fact that their criticism itself proceeds from *its own philosophy* which he likewise hasn't proven. This, then, invokes the conversation to turn to a discussion of presuppositions and transcendental considerations which, when carried out, show the necessity of Christian-theism's truth, thereby necessitating all the truths in Scripture, one of which entailing that the disjunct Christ proclaimed is ultimately contradictory in nature.

Tethering this first criticism to the second (the impossibility of refuting all non-Christian worldviews), we see therefore that induction is not necessary to prove the exclusivity of the Christian worldview. Moreover, for a critic to assert that the transcendentalist is really an inductivist at heart speaks volumes of his ignorance in transcendental considerations. Kant rightfully writes that the conclusion of a transcendental argument "should be entitled a *principle*, not a *theorem*, because it has the peculiar character that it makes possible the very experience which is its own ground of proof, and that in this experience it must always itself be presupposed" (Kant, 1781, A 737/B 765). Thus, a transcendental is not *itself* a theorem which finds its legitimacy through a linear chain of reasoning, subject to certain paradigmatic truths of reality; a transcendental is a *principle*, a fundamental or foundational truth of reality itself that is "its own ground of proof, and that in this experience it must always itself be presupposed." Transcendentals are the very preconditional truths by which reasoning about theorems (or worldviews in the case of apologetics) can even proceed, not the other way around; the venture of transcendental reasoning does not amount to a smorgasbord of contrary or contradictory conclusions about differing transcendentals. In the nature of the case there can only be one type of transcendental which, as a *necessary truth*, definitionally cannot conflict with other necessary truths. Thus, Montgomery is simply mistaken in analyzing the transcendental program as, at best, an inductive survey of viewpoints, or, at worst, a relativistic guessing game. If such necessary truths are supplied by Christian-theism—which entails the existence of the Triune God who is the very embodiment of truth itself—and if such a Christian worldview entails its exclusivity apart from any transcendental considerations (cf. Is. 43:10; 44:6), the impossibility of contrary or contradictory truths necessitates the exclusivity of the Christian worldview supplying these necessary truths or transcendentals.

As for Montgomery's third criticism about the theoretical possibility of all worldviews being false, Montgomery confuses or conflates on the term "worldview." Van Til unwaveringly argued that his proof for Christianity was a "concrete" proof (Van Til, 2008, 48-49). That is, Van Til did not argue that Christianity could only be conceptually conceived; TAG proves Christianity *metaphysically*. And since there can only be one actual reality, Christianity, again, stands exclusively true. Bahnsen explains it transcendentally this way:

> ...in the nature of the case, there can only be one transcendental...to talk about two separate worldviews is nonsense in itself. It would be similar to saying that there are two ultimate authorities.[7] There cannot be two ultimate authorities or else they're not ultimate, right? If somebody says that Christianity "does the job" such that we can make sense out of science, logic, morality, human dignity, and so on, but that there may be another worldview which does the job as well, you have to say that in the nature of the case you can't have two transcendentals for meaningfulness. Why? Because if there are two transcendentals, what have you lost? Unity. Coherence, unity, and continuity is the name of the game here. Meaningfulness and intelligibility means coherence which means there is *one* system of truth. If there were two transcendentals you wouldn't have one system of truth; you would have two, and then what would you have to ask? What's the relationship between the two systems?

---

7. Or two "ultimate realities." It's "nonsense" because it would be tantamount to saying something like the Earth exists and it's also true that the Earth doesn't exist at the same time and in the same sense. Such metaphysical contradictions would be the case if there were two true worldviews.

If they are different then you have lost unity. If they are the same with the names being changed then we don't have to worry about it—this would be nothing more than a linguistic variation...

To make sense of the claim that there are two systems by which facts can be made intelligible requires another system in terms of which you're saying that about the other two. But you see if these two transcendental systems are by hypothesis, we can't get behind them to have the one that unites the two. *To talk about there being two there needs to be one perspective in which you talk about the two. But these two that you're talking about are by definition ultimate!* And so there can't be a one that unites the two, even to talk about their relationship.

So when somebody says to you, "Well how do you know that there can't be another one out there?" you say that in the nature of the case there can't be another one out there. There can only be one ultimate, transcendental worldview. If there were two then it wouldn't be an "ultimate", transcendental worldview; you would have to have one behind it to make it even possible to talk about there being two. (Bahnsen/Butler, 1995) (emphasis added)

Montgomery's criticisms constitute a more forceful, metaphysical challenge as opposed to Frame's mere formal complaints. Through both theological and philosophical exposition and elucidation, it stands that Montgomery's criticisms, although commendable, do not fully understand or grasp (a) the metaphysical-entailment of Van Til's transcendental program, (b) the exclusive status of transcendental considerations, and thus do not constitute a legitimate refutation.

3. THE MERE SUFFICIENCY OF THE CHRISTIAN WORLDVIEW

Butler then addresses a criticism which specifically targets the sufficiency of Christian-theism while simultaneously rejecting the second criticism concerning the issue of a plurality of worldviews/realities. That is, Christian-theism may be a sufficient answer to justifying intelligible experience, but it is not indispensable, for there could be a worldview which apes the Christian worldview in every way with some theo-philosophical differences and still satisfies justifying the transcendentals of experience, thereby itself being true and entailing the error of proponents for Christian-theism.

This criticism comes in two forms: first, the *Fristian* form which utilizes the Bible as the grounding for its worldview with alterations in the Trinity (such as adding or removing a person such that it can ape the Christian worldview); second, a form which is postulated apart from the Bible but still draws from it in such a way as to comprise a transcendental worldview (i.e., a one-and-many grounding as the Trinity is). How, then, is the truth of Christianity to be maintained in TAG? How do we (a) know, and (b) prove transcendentally that Biblical truths as pertain to orthodox, trinitarian Christianity are, in fact, necessary?

Remarkably, from an exegetical perspective this criticism fails in an immediately-straightforward way. In terms of *proof*, Brant Bosserman writes:

> [E]very personal distinction in the Godhead must be facilitated by, and appear within the overarching context of a third, and only a third person. For, if the number of divine persons were decreased to two, then the relationship between those two persons would have to appear within an impersonalist void, since there is no third, divine and personal context to be found. If the number of divine persons were multiplied beyond three, then the relationship between

any two divine persons would have to be facilitated by an additional "group" of divine persons (which is not, properly speaking, a "person"). Each individual person of the Trinity would fail to comprehend the entire divine life in and by Himself, and that which comprehended the whole of the Godhead and his self-relationship would not be a person, but an impersonal dynamic. Hence, in the Christian system, where God is a personal Absolute, it can be concluded that the oneness and threeness of God mutually necessitate one another. (Bosserman, 2014, 20-21)

In terms of *knowledge*, Butler writes:

The only way to know that God is a Trinity is that He revealed it to us—mere speculation or empirical investigation would never lead us to this conclusion. But the Fristian worldview, which is, ex hypothesis, identical to Christianity in every other way, asserts that its god is a quadrinity. But if Fristianity is otherwise identical to Christianity, the only way for us to know this would be for the Fristian god to reveal this to us. (Butler, 2002, 118)

Following this quotation, Butler likewise dissects the exegetical implications of such a worldview, illustrating that a tinkering of the Trinity would warrant an *entire alteration* of Scripture since Scripture in its entirety attests to the Trinitarian nature of God. Thus, it is not as easy as altering the Trinity for the Fristian without overhauling the entire Canon. It would therefore fall upon the Fristian (who, mind you, is postulating this criticism ex hypothesis) to re-exegete all of Scripture in order to maintain his criticism.

Moreover, since God *has* revealed to us His Trinitarian nature, the only refutation required by the presuppositionalist would be an exegetical exposition of Scripture—the same as any other ordinary theological debate between Christians (whether it be over baptism, eschatology, covenantal views, etc.). Thus, exegesis alone constitutes enough *proof* to refute the Fristian as just another Christian heretic, and revelation from God is enough to refute the notion that we know about this Fristian god—we fully *know* and can fully *prove* the Trinity.[8]

The other route of minimally drawing from the Bible to formulate an alternative worldview (or perhaps not at all) will naturally be dealt with differently from exegesis. In both cases, Bahnsen's response revolved around the origins of the opponent's worldview. "Where did they get their worldview from?" Bahnsen repeatedly referred to the block-by-block fashion of erecting said worldview: anyone positing a worldview that is built up block-by-block, aspect-by-aspect is ultimately utilizing his or her mind as the *ultimate* arbiter

---

8. An astute critic would perhaps hearken back to Montgomery's criticism. He argues (among other things) that anyone can make the claim for the legitimacy of their particular worldview, and, so we are erroneously told, there would therefore be no definitive refutation of contrary worldviews to Christianity—everyone has their own worldview-interpretation. Pertaining to the relevence of this particular criticism, a Fristian could respond by exegeting through the scriptures as well to draw his particular conclusion, thus, at the very least to a certain degree, proving Montgomery's point. Two obvious problems arise from this response: (a) Montgomery's viewpoint fails to recognize and therefore articulate the difference between proof and persuasion, a problem Frame likewise succumbed to. While ideally we would harbor the ability to persuade others to the Faith, apologetics centers around a defense and therefore proof of the veracity of Christianity. That apologists cannot inherently persuade other people is not a defect to the edifice of apologetics itself—one might as well regard all people as failures given our innate inability to naturally persuade anyone over *any* subject; (b) Montgomery either disregards or overlooks the double-standard of this particular criticism. Montgomery's criticism itself proceeds from a certain subjective interpretation, in which case who is he to dogmatize it since, after all, anyone else with contrary viewpoints could just disagree with his analysis under the paradigm of their interpretive scheme as is apparently the problem with TAG? While the Fristian may still maintain their position exegetically, a biblical exegesis—regardless of contrary opinions—proves Trinitarian theology; epistemic or conceptual disagreement (from the Firstian here) do not dictate truth, and the failure of the apologist to *persuade* the Fristian opponent exegetically does not detract from his faithful and biblical *proof*—the only thing God asks of Christians in the apologetic enterprise.

or authority for the grounding of their worldview, thus predicating the worldview off of a subjectivistic reference point:

> ...what determines this off-brand Christian worldview? One answer is to say that they took the Bible and they edited it, getting rid of all the stuff they didn't need. Well, if this is the case then he didn't really start with the Bible because the Bible says that every "jot and tittle" must be there. So we ask them again. They would have to say that maybe they didn't start with the Bible as their authority but they got their ideas from the Bible. But if this is the case, then each and every one of them has to be built up block-by-block individually which brings us right back to the rock in a bottomless ocean scenario—the unbeliever cannot take individual elements—logic, uniformity in nature, morality, a human mind—and bring them together. And so as it turns out, anyone who wants to take Christianity and edit it down has an authority outside of the Bible (that person's mind) by which he is living. And by that authority he edits the Bible. (Bahnsen/Butler, 1995)

Thus, what we're left with is an objective authority in Christianity in which the mind is merely the *medium* by which we reach the ultimate authority (God/Revelation) standing over against a subjective, finite, individualistic authority from either a knock-off Christian or non-Christian, both utilizing their mind not simply as a medium, but as *an ultimate authority*: objectivity versus subjectivity. Exactly how much credence, therefore, should the critic receive?

Butler's answer resonates Bahnsen's in that the Fristian (or any other knock-off opponent) must "spell out" every intricacy of their worldview in order for it to receive any ounce of credibility. This is certainly problematic for a secularist who begins subjectively without any sort of objective tether to knowledge and truth (i.e., the Creator-creature distinction). Van Til illustrates the problem of subjectivity and finitude in unbelieving thought this way:

Modern philosophy in practically all of its schools admits that all its speculations end in mystery. Speaking generally, modern philosophy (and science) is phenomenalistic. It admits that ultimate reality is unknowable to man. All systems of interpretation are said to be necessarily relative to the mind of man. And so it seems at first sight that modern philosophy ought, on its own principles, to admit that there is a dimension of reality that is beyond its reach and about which it ought therefore to be ready to listen by the avenue of authority. (Van Til, 2008, 148)

Thus, a purely secular attempt at formulating a knock-off worldview which justifies the transcendentals of experience is doomed to failure from the start; as Bahnsen would say: "If you begin with an egocentric picture, don't be surprised when you end in an egocentric predicament." This in turn requires the secular attempt to gravitate once more to the authority of Scripture with alterations (narrowly speaking, as the Fristian does), or religion (broadly speaking, with a Creator-creature distinction). But, of course, the hypothetical Fristian worldview cannot withstand exegetical scrutiny, and the broad appeal to religion which acknowledges a Creator-creature distinction would either (a) operate too close to Christian-theism, or (b) be too generic of an ad hoc, ex hypothesis counterargument.

Since this particular critic knows his postulated worldview *proceeds from sheer hypothesis*, there is no already-established holistic, unified system which justifies the transcendental preconditions of experience. To try and explain and prove every facet of experience ad hoc in a block-by-block, concrete, metaphysical fashion is futile and definitionally impossible given human finitude—all potential and/or actual defeaters cannot be known, precluding absolute conclusions in the same way as operating TAG in an inductive fashion, attempting to refute every actual *and possible* worldview sequentially until only Christian-theism remained. Here, Dr. Montgomery is absolutely correct.

In contradistinction to hypothesizing, the Christian worldview is predicated from (a) revelational-objectivity, (b) millennia of history, and (c) metaphysical "concreteness." That is to say, the Christian has tangible justification (the Bible, historical evidence, etc.) from a God who *has* revealed Himself to all people, including the hypothesizing critic (e.g., the Bible, natural revelation, innate or constitutional revelation, the very existence of God). This begs the question as to why the Fristian criticism has received any credibility to begin with in charging TAG with proving a mere plausibility. Apart from exegesis, the refutation of a Fristian objection proceeds in the same fashion as the previous one: in the nature of the case there can only be one true, objective reality—metaphysical contradictions are an impossibility. And since Christianity has material proof which supplies the transcendentals of experience, is exegetically proven, is not argued for ex hypothesis, has a tangible book and millennia of history, then (a) by default it is the only worldview, thus (b) all stipulated hypotheticals therefore fail to relegate Christianity to the level of mere sufficiency. Why entertain a metaphysically false hypothetical when we are already in contact with the metaphysical Truth?

4. MOVING FROM CONCEPTUAL NECESSITY TO METAPHYSICAL NECESSITY[9]

The questionable move from conceptual proof to metaphysical proof is widely regarded as the most lethal criticism against TAs broadly and thus TAG specifically. The objection arises when we observe that just because we must psychologically think a certain way does not necessarily entail that the external world aligns with our conclusions. Christian-theism may be a transcendentally-necessary worldview, but how do we prove it as a *metaphysical* necessity and not merely a conceptual one? How is this bridge to be linked? Such was Stroud's

---

9. The events between Stroud and Strawson that were briefly mentioned on page 212 will not be embellished here given, to a degree, its lack of relevance; what will be embellished, of course, is Stroud's objection and dilemma in and of itself.

argument against Strawson and the final criticism Butler addresses as it pertains to TAG.

When the critics of TAG were first addressed, attention turned specifically to criticisms of Butler's response to this objection by Bryan Sims and Michael Riley in their dissertations. Specifically, Butler's answer runs as follows:

> It is a serious error to conceive of the Christian worldview as nothing more than a mere conceptual scheme that organizes our experience. Certainly Christianity does, in some sense, organize our experience, but it does more than this. The Christian worldview is much richer than the conceptual scheme that is the precondition of, say, reidentifying particulars. Christianity provides us with a detailed metaphysical, epistemological and ethical system. The foundation of this system is an absolute personal God who has created all things including man. This God, moreover, has given man his word so that he may know the truth. The Christian worldview, thus, not only provides a way to organize experience, but it tells us that a sovereign God has revealed truths about the world to us. (Butler, 2002, 122-123)

Sims's response revolves around the circularity of Butler's answer: However, Butler seems to assume the very thing he asserts, namely the metaphysical truthfulness of the Christian worldview based on God's existence (Sims, 2006, 56 note 8). Riley's response exposits more on the sentiments of Sims:

> Indeed, I think that Butler's suggestion not only fails to answer Stroud's dilemma: it may in fact exacerbate the problem. To increase the richness of the world-directedness of one's transcendental argument, as Butler clearly seems to suggest, hardly seems an advisable move when the very possibility of any kind of world-directed argument is precisely what is at issue. It seems that Stroud's response here would

> remain unchanged: no matter how rich the conception of the worldview that one finds necessary by transcendental argument, it is always possible to insist that we merely must *believe* that a sovereign, personal, absolute, Creator God exists, that he has created a world that he says is independent of him and of us. (Riley, 2014, 22)

In short, a mere postulation or assumption of a particular worldview/metaphysical scheme does not in and of itself qualify as a legitimate refutation. It still *needs to be shown* that the Christian's metaphysic is, in fact, the correct metaphysic or reality.

From this problem of moving conceptually to metaphysically Stroud offers the horns of a dilemma: one must either adhere to some version of verificationism by which we can "verify" the nature of the external world at the cost of rendering TAs superfluous, or one must embrace idealism in which all facts are known by the mind given that the real *is* the mental. Since both philosophical positions have proven to be untenable throughout the history of philosophy, Stroud concludes that we are ultimately confined to a Kantian divide with no seeming route of escape. Dr. Grayling confirms the situation:

> The primary importance of transcendental arguments resides in the fact that we have to reflect on our concepts and beliefs from the internal perspective of having to use them even as we investigate them. There is no external point from which we can view our conceptual scheme; like Neurath's sailors we have to rebuild our ship at sea. (Grayling, 2010, 771)

From only these brief considerations there is enough material to turn to the immediately-straightforward, hypocritical, and fallacious problem the Stroudian position and its adherents face against TAG.

Riley, Sims, and Békefi all concur that a mere postulation of the Christian worldview does not in and of itself refute Stroud. It seems rather obvious given a mere postulation assumes a conjunctive lack of justification. Thus, the Christian's metaphysic needs to be explicitly proven, and TAG, these men would object, does not draw metaphysical conclusions on its own. "What, then, are you to do, Butler?" The astute thinker here should see the blatant, metaphysical double-standard: why does the Christian presuppositionalist bear the burden of proving their metaphysic but not Stroud? Stroud's criticism proceeds from a particular secular, egocentric view of the world and, as Grayling reinforced: ... we must reflect on our concepts and beliefs from the internal perspective of having to use them even as we investigate them. *There is no external point from which we can view our conceptual scheme* (emphasis added) (p. 771). Stroud, Grayling, most other secular philosophers, and even Christian sympathizers of Stroud have all simply taken for granted that Stroud, too, has his egocentric presuppositions by which his argument proceeds just as Butler, the presuppositionalist, had his presuppositions when he gave his response. To demand explicit metaphysical proof from one side while arbitrarily taking for granted the metaphysical truth of the other without the need for first proving it is to simply commit oneself to the fallacy of special pleading.

The typical comeback by Stroudians is to argue that an egocentric metaphysic as Stroud (and Kant) adhered to is the default position unless or until one proves otherwise. But, of course, this ad hoc response is nothing more than mere philosophical speculation without warrant. Does he have any objective proof that the Christian's metaphysic is not the default position? That egocentrism is the default position? Of course not. If he is postulating an egocentric picture, then any proof he conjures up will just be subjected to the scrutiny of egocentrism.[10] The Stroudian critic has to somehow

---

10. Including, ironically, verification principles as one of the potential escapes from the objection. Consistent or generic skeptics such as Stroud would naturally be skeptical about everything; and yet Stroud the skeptic proposes that a verification principle could be a plausible solution for escaping egocentrism and therefore saving knowledge. Well, what happened to adhering to a skeptical paradigm? If a secular, skeptical philosopher is truly a skeptic, he would likewise call into question the validity of said verification principle. Perhaps a skeptic may

prove that their egocentric, Kantian, metaphysical position is the "default" position and not the metaphysic of Christianity; ironically, this cannot *objectively* be done if one is *subjectively* confined to an egocentric predicament.

Proponents of Stroud's criticism have simply taken for granted that philosophical-neutrality is nothing more than a myth. No one is without their presuppositions, their commitments, their biases (which includes the domain of metaphysics). This truth, in turn, warrants a worldview apologetic that analyzes competing presuppositions, competing epistemologies, competing metaphysical schemes; and the only way by which a worldview can be proven objectively is via the medium of transcendental considerations. Since the Christian worldview supplies the transcendentals necessary for escaping egocentrism (entailed by the Creator-creature distinction), we can therefore attain objectivity and thus disagree with and refute Grayling when he concedes that "There is no external point from which we can view our conceptual scheme." Bahnsen illustrates this incisively in laying out two pictures of knowers:

One [picture] says that God created us and our minds, and God also created the world that we know with our minds. This is the Christian view of things. As a diagram we can put God above the mind of man and the world, and since He is the Creator, we can put arrows going from Him to both the mind and the world; He is the cause of the human mind and the way it operates, and the cause of the world (the world includes the human mind) and the objects of knowledge. God made the mind and the objects that the mind knows. Therefore, our conceptual scheme is automatically in touch/

be convinced of such a principle(s) and alter his entire philosophy, but as Stroud's *skeptical* challenge stands, he seems to take for granted the ostensible objectivity of the principles of metaphysical verification, thus himself (subjectively) defining and delineating the bounds of certain propositions exempt from skepticism, which, in turn, leads to a second special pleading fallacy.

automatically corresponds to the objects of experience on this presupposition. If this is your beginning outlook or perspective, then you already begin with the idea that our conceptual scheme (or the human mind and the way it works) is in connection with the objects of knowledge. And what is the connecting link? God. Now, I realize that some philosophers will just say to this that we are doing theology. Okay, fine, but if you won't do theology with me then let's see what happens to your philosophy. Another approach says that we can't know anything about God at the outset. All we can know is that we have a human mind, we assume its sufficiency, and we are pretty sure that there are objects out there that the mind can know. Everything here is loose and disjointed. The objects of knowledge are not connected to one another by God's creative, sovereign, foreordaining work. Nor are the objects automatically connected to the mind of man in his conceptual scheme. In fact, all minds are loose and separate as well. God is not brought into the picture here because we don't want to do theology in the place of philosophy after all, right? We'll just do philosophy autonomously. We begin with man and then work out from man, and this mind also operates on a conceptual scheme. The skeptic comes along and asks, "How do you know there is a connection between your conceptual scheme and the objects in the world?" This worldview by definition cannot answer the skeptic *because it begins with a separation between minds and the objects in the world.* There's no connecting link. And any attempt to bridge the dividing link is going to be easily criticizable by the skeptic. *If you begin with an egocentric picture don't be surprised when you end with an egocentric predicament.* If you start your philosophy with man, you end up with man separated from everything in the universe. How do you know there's any connection between your thinking and what's outside the mind? The skeptic can push even harder and ask how we know there is anything at all outside of our minds. Autonomous philosophy—which says we don't want to bring God into the picture—if pushed hard enough becomes solipsistic. If you leave God out of the picture you leave man separated from everything. Not only can you not know if there are other objects outside of your mind, if that's the case then you couldn't even know that there are other minds outside of your own mind! So when the skeptic raises the question: "How can you be sure your conceptual scheme corresponds to the world outside of us?" our answer as Christians is that this is our presupposition; that is the picture we begin with. We don't face the problem that you're raising. But your problem is a really good one for those who start with man without God in the picture. For those people who want to do Godless philosophy then the skeptic is on very good grounds to push them. But then again, as we have just seen, as a skeptic you have to say there is no rational justification for rationality, so we can dismiss you, too. (Bahnsen and Butler, 1995) (emphasis added)

Thus, again, the side that endorses a Kantian divide where we do not (or even cannot) begin our experiences with the external world is predicated on skepticism. But if it's an ultimately skeptical worldview, then the skeptic (assuming he still has the logical desire to be consistent) *must likewise be skeptical about the legitimacy of his own starting point!*[11] This Stroudian skeptic countering TAG has no

11. In line with their being consistently skeptical about verification principles. The horns of our counterargument, therefore, amount to (a) one remaining consistently skeptical about both verification principles and the very starting point they're taking for granted unjustifiably, thus never escaping an absurd philosophy and embracing special pleading, or (b) (at least) attempt to obtain some degree of epistemic and/or metaphysical justification by which to rationally rebut the presppositionalist (contra the skeptic confined to irrationality)—here, however, running into the helplessly subjective reality of secular Thought, thus never attaining rationality at all. Both options attest to Scripture's teaching of the

right to assume the truth in advance that his metaphysical viewpoint of egocentrism, subjectivism, skepticism, and solipsism as if it's an indisputable given—for all he knows, the presuppositionalist's metaphysic is correct "from the outset" and therefore we should turn the tables and instead call into question the legitimacy of Stroud's metaphysical skepticism.

Riley, Sims, and Békefi, *as Christians*, should have known better than to start their philosophies—or, at the very least, this criticism—on any other foundation than the revelation from the very God whom they worship. Their firm commitment here to autonomous presuppositions is, ironically, a blessed illustration of the prodigal son: by "leaving behind" their Christian presuppositions, they, as Van Til once remarked, ended up *intellectually* at the swine trough, evidenced by endorsing a double-fallacious criticism. If they had simply "stayed in the father's house," they would never have succumbed to the foolish outcomes of secular Thought. Especially telling for presuppositionalists who give credence to Stroud, in addition to unknwowingly embracing fallacious reasoning, is their evidenced-ignorance of the rudimentary aspects of the apologetic, namely, ignoring or overlooking what Bahnsen coined as "unargued philosophical bias." Stroud's presuppositional commitments were just as biased as the presuppositionalist's—the predication for the rejection and impossibility of neutrality. And while presuppositionalists such as Békefi argue in favor of Stroud, they seem to overlook his own unargued philosophical bias. A prudent presuppositionalist would consciously and conscientiously stand on this fundamental tenet of the apologetic, not so willingly, hastily, and erroneously seeing merit in a skeptical philosophy. Philosophical problems pertaining to one particular metaphysic do not of necessity carry over to all metaphysical views.

---

foolishness of worldly "wisdom."

The Symbiotic Nature of TAG and Scriptural Verification

A further complication arises, however, when considering the Christian's justification for direct realism—knowing that we are in-touch with the external world. He has not yet definitively rendered Stroud's argument impotent. Thus far analysis has only revolved around the fallacious double-standard of Stroudian proponents taking for granted (a) the truth that Stroud's metaphysical viewpoint is the "default" position, and (b) that verificational propositions are, according to subjective standards, exempt from the skeptical enterprise. When pressed on this belief that we *do* begin with contact of the external world as God has created it and us, its justification lies not in TAG itself, but in revelation. It is through Scriptural, natural, and innate revelation via the imago Dei by which we know with certainty that we are always in contact with the external world— revelation has "verified" the metaphysical situation, both for Stroud/ non-Christians and Christians alike. But if this is the case, then it would be tantamount to arguing through a form of verificationism, the first horn of Stroud's dilemma, thus making TAG superfluous and entirely unnecessary. With the Scriptural verification principle (hereafter SVP) as our metaphysical backing, how do we circumvent the dichotomizing of TAs and VPs and therefore this horn of Stroud's dilemma to save TAG? The Bible most certainly does not endorse a metaphysic of idealism, and thus the presuppositionalist is now backed into the corner of the other horn—verificationism and thereby the nullification of the use of TAG altogether. The answer— reinforcing the underlying theme from the opening pages—lies once more in the delineation of secular philosophy over against Van Tillian Christian philosophy. In the same way that Stroud introduced a delineation between different types of TAs, so, too, ought we be scrupulous in analyzing the nature and delineations of VPs.

The opposing worldviews pertaining to secular and Christian philosophies should make it rather obvious that the SVP and VPs generically cannot be considered cognates given their antithetical paradigms. This, then, naturally brings into question the exact nature and scope of this horn of the dilemma. Every TA which fell under the secular paradigm would succumb to this horn—there is no use in transcendental considerations so long as there is the option for a direct appeal to a principle(s). This much we know for certain. What we do not know for certain is whether a Van Tillian (or, more broadly, a religious) view of VPs likewise succumbs to Stroud.

The first of two major distinctions between VPs and the SVP concerns *quantity*. In 20th-Century verificationism, Popper's verification principle of falsificationism was singular; the logical positivists was dualistic.[12] The singular SVP is also, in another sense, pluralistic as well if we look at it broadly. Christianity and TAG are predicated off of numerous verifying principles within the pages of Scripture. Naturally, this would seem to *endorse* the horn rather than nullify it. If the transcendentalist has a plethora of principles he can appeal to within the Canon, then it seems more incumbent for him to disregard Van Til's transcendental program in favor of scriptural verification. So, it seems that the nature of quantity is not a reliable avenue of refuting Stroud.

The second major distinction between VPs and the SVP concerns *quality*, and this category, in turn, invokes different aspects over the nature of quality itself (as opposed to quantity which solely concerns numerical extent). The *logical quality* of the logical positivists' verification principle was openly and obviously that of self-refutation. The logical quality of Popper's falsificationism similarly succumbed to self-frustration. Conversely, the logical quality of Scripture's verifying principles is that of holistic harmony

---

12. Popper argued that the only meaningful statements are those which are testable and therefore falsifiable, taking for granted that he likewise harbors beliefs which he considers immune from revision. The logical positivists of the Vienna school in the early 20th Century argued that the only things we could verifiably know to be true are empirical proofs, or those truths which are analytically or definitionally true (apart from experience). This, thesis, however, does not even live up to its own criterion and therefore refutes itself.

or unity. The propositions within the pages of Scripture—concerning genealogy, history, prophecy, wisdom literature, and more—form an infallible, inextricable whole from beginning to end. Thus, as it stands on verificationist terms, Scripture has an advantage over both quantitative and qualitative differences against secular uses of VPs. But this, again, would seem to endorse Stroud's horn rather than refute it.

The ultimate consideration as pertains to the nature of the SVP, however, concerns *content quality*. We can see the similarities between *content* and *logicality* in that the content of any given theory or system can either be logical or illogical. But whereas logical considerations concern consistency (or lack thereof), *content quality* extends beyond mere consistency-considerations and focuses on the truth-factor of propositions—the entailments of both logical validity and soundness. For one, the content(s) of Scripture are not brute facts or merely stipulated principles as was the case with the logical positivists and Popper. Scripture (and its principles) comes from a divinely-intelligent and conscious Source—the one, true, living Triune God. Here we see a fundamentally distinct aspect of the Van Tillian's SVP that goes beyond mere quantity and quality (as broadly defined). Moreover, many principles in Scripture are *prescriptive* rather than merely descriptive—another commendation of its content quality. As pertains to the *propositional content quality* in the SVP concerning TAG, we can list just a few of Scripture's "principles":

Metaphysical Principles:

- God created everything, including man, and placed him in contact with the created order (Gen. 1-2)
- God made man in His image as a moral, conscious being to live in this universe and obey Him (Gen. 1:26; Rom. 2)
- Therefore, man's faculties are reliable, though tampered by sin (Rom. 1; cf. 2 Pet. 1:18-19)

- God is providential and therefore upholds His universe (Rom. 8:28; Gen. 3:21)
- God will uphold the universe into the future (Gen. 8:22)
- God is One-in-Many (Gen. 1:26, "et al")
- God is eternal, perfect, and necessarily exists (aseity) (Rev. 22:13; Lev. 19:2; Ex. 3:14)

Epistemological Principles:

- Man is a knowledge-bearing creature (Gen. 1:26; Lev. 19:2;)[13]
- The fear of the Lord/revelation is the *beginning* of knowledge (Prov. 1:7)
- If you reject God's revelation you have no basis for knowing anything: you're a fool (Ps. 14:1; Prov. 28:26), darkened in understanding (John 8:12; Eph. 4:17-18; 5:8), and are vain in your philosophy (Col. 2:8)
- Knowledge of the truth is only attained by adherence to revelation (John 17:17; cf. Prov. 4:20)
- Man's faculties are still reliable, though tampered by sin (Rom. 1; cf. 2 Pet. 1:18-19)

Ethical Principles:

- God is absolute, holy, and perfect (Ex. 3:14; Lev. 19:2)
- Therefore, His law is also absolute, holy, and perfect (Lev. 19:2)
- As His creatures we are therefore held accountable to absolute moral standards (Rom. 2)

---

13. The observance also of *Wisdom* Literature in the Bible quite literally assumes or presupposes man's cognitive ability to harbor knowledge, thus also presupposing the epistemological nature of man's constitution.

The Stroudian will once again praise the Van Tillian transcendentalist for his willingness to compromise his position; yet the above observations only serve to strengthen the argument for the indispensable role of the Bible in TAG. The quality of the principles being presented should not be disregarded.

When taking into consideration these principles, what is the Van Tillian left with? If these principles were run through a philosophic machine, what would come out the other end? As it turns out, these principles just entail Van Til's transcendental program! If these principles were in fact run through such a machine, *the end result would simply be a formula for TAG*. Which is to say, in effect, that there is an inextricable, symbiotic relationship between TAG and its verifying principle of Scripture. I cannot proceed to use TAG without the backing of Scripture as its verification principle. And yet, if I concede Stroud's horn and simply operate on the SVP, I'm left exactly with what TAG is: the verification principle the presuppositionalist uses as the foundation of TAG itself entails the use of a transcendental argument. Not only does God's Word layout or "describe" a transcendental program, *it prescribes it*, necessitating the Christian's adherence to it. These considerations lead us to the conclusion that the entailments of the SVP run entirely antithetical to the verification principles postulated throughout the 20th Century by secular philosophers in every respect, save perhaps quantity.

TAG has always been predicated on scriptural truth. There is a reason Van Til endorsed a revelational epistemology: if I remove scriptural truths (SVP/revelation) from TAG, TAG succumbs to Stroud's challenge and proves only a "modest" *conceptual* necessity; that is, in attempting to avoid the verificationist horn of the dilemma it just end up succumbing to Stroud's overarching objection, that being TAs only prove conceptual conclusions. But if I remove TAG and simply focus on the SVP, I'm forced back into transcendental considerations. *You cannot use TAG without Scripture and Scripture Itself entails TAG in its pages.* Thus, Stroud's challenge is fundamentally incompatible with a Van Tillian philosophy, irrespective of disagreements between them. In fact, it is so fundamentally incompatible that it ultimately amounts to a commitment of the fallacy of a false dichotomy—the third fallacy Stroud is now faced with. A Stroudian still seeking to prove otherwise would need to show on a Van Tillian's own terms how it remains illegitimate. When a Van Tillian's VP (Scripture) itself entails propositions which are necessary preconditions (transcendentals), then Stroud's dilemma is of no effect and cannot be retorted in any sense since the SVP entails transcendentals, which in turn entails TAG, and this in turn leads to the conclusion that the SVP *definitionally* withstands his challenge—there cannot be any further forthcoming responses when the VP of TAG itself comprises transcendental propositions.[14] This runs contrary to any VP stipulated by worldly philosophy: in the VPs analyzed, the principles themselves didn't entail transcendental necessities; they were, rather, stipulated by men operating under a futile, "vain" philosophy (Col. 2:8); moreover, the intelligent source these principles originated from was (a) fallible, finite, and subjective, and (b) only intelligent because they were made in the image of God whose revelation itself comprises the transcendentals necessary to even get their autonomous philosophies off the ground. They depended on the transcendental truths in Scripture (SVP) in order to argue against Christianity.

The apparent resilience or immunity of Stroud's dilemma against transcendental philosophy is, quite literally, apparent given the underlying presuppositions of Stroud and his proponents. In truth, back of all postulated viewpoints, arguments, criticisms, etc. is an

---

14. Put another way, Stroud's argument is predicated on an either-or predicament between TAs and VPs. Fundamentally speaking, these two are not cognates—they share no similar aspects or attributes. That is, one is an argument, the other is a principle. Within a Van Tillian philosophy, TAG is an argument, and the SVP is a network of principles, following in the same vein as Stroud. But these principles *themselves comprise the entire argument of TAG*, amounting to an indispensable symbiotic relationship. Thus, within a Van Tillian philosophy, Stroud's argument is predicated on a false dichotomy.

underlying philosophy which acts as the engine for the proponent to argue his position. Every arguer has his presuppositions, and every argument has a particular philosophy ascribed behind it. The sheer antithesis between secular, Stroudian philosophy and Christian, Van Tillian philosophy is as antithetical as the salvific status between both parties, and this dichotomy is likewise illustrated in each philosophy's corresponding verification principle. The Christian's VP is distinctly unique in both its quantity (as being able to be categorized as a singularity (one book) or a plurality (the propositions in the book)) and transcendent and transcendental quality. It is through this analysis that a rightful and definitive refutation of Stroud can proceed.

5. TRUE IN ALL POSSIBLE WORLDS?

The implications of Stroud's challenge would entail that a position's self-stultifying nature (absurdity or self-frustration) does not necessarily entail its falsity (self-falsification). While this delineation can and should be dispelled given the preceding material (namely, that self-stultification equates to self-falsification at least in worldview considerations since Christian-theism is provable and only one worldview/metaphysic can be true), a critic may question whether or not this truth extends to all possible worlds. For if not, and if other TAs *could* procure such a conclusion, then TAG may not prove what it intends to prove. Two questions will be examined: (1) does the truth of TAG (entailing the absoluteness of God such that nothing could exist without Him) still apply to all possible worlds?; (2) is this question even meaningful to begin with?

David Reiter in particular has expressed this concern (Reiter, 2009). He inquires, in the absence of a clearly distinct staple version of TAG, whether or not the transcendental program proves that God *necessarily* exists or simply *actually* exists.[15] If TAG proves that

---

15. If the latter is proven, this would be tantamount to an Anselmian ontological argument which, of course, deviates from the nature TAG (though

God does "actually" exist and His existence justifies the intelligibility of human experience—a statement which sounds exactly like what a Van Tillian presuppositionalist would argue—does that actuality apply to the realm of hypotheticals? Does its scope remain strictly within the realm of the "actual" while other TAs, such as Descartes's cogito dictum (properly formulated) which boasts hypothetical applicability in all possible worlds akin to that of a 1st place award holder, leave supporters of TAG to ruefully spectate from the sidelines with a mere "actual" TA?

It should first be observed that existence and/or conclusive propositional applicability in all possible worlds assumes necessity, for by definition failure for a truth to apply to any world—ours as actual or one hypothetical—would relegate the status of such an existent or proposition to the level of contingency.

Second, and perhaps more obvious, who or what determines the nature and extents of necessity and contingency, of possibility and impossibility? The objection to TAG concerning the exact extents of its hypothetical legitimacy already presupposes some understanding or another over the extents of both possibility and necessity. Van Til alludes to this issue throughout the corpus of his writings:

> For the natural man the idea of possibility is on the one hand identical with chance and on the other hand with that which the natural man himself can rationalize. For him only that is practically possible which man can himself order by his logical faculties. (Van Til, 2008, 164)

He even criticizes those Christians who do not acknowledge a revelational epistemology:

---

he concedes that the proponent of TAG could utilize an Anselmian approach at the expense of forfeiting the *necessity* aspect of transcendental arguments, thereby rendering TAG superfluous).

[Leibniz] was not less a rationalist in his hopes and ambitions than was Parmenides. He does not hesitate to make the "possibility of knowledge depend upon a knowledge of possibility." Yet, Leibniz questions whether man can ever attain to the perfect analysis, which would carry him back, without finding any contradiction, to the absolute attributes of God. (Van Til, 2008, 138)

In contradistinction to this, the Calvinist holds that God is the Determiner of necessity, possibility, and impossibility:

Every fact of history, Calvinism holds, happens according to the secret counsel of God. Using epistemological language we may express the idea by saying that the universals that bind the particulars of history, as well as these particulars themselves, have their origin in God. (Van Til, 1969, pp. 112-113)

Thus, the eternal, self-existing God is the Orderer of all facts and thereby the Determiner of necessity and contingency, of possibility and impossibility, contrary to the philosophies stipulated by non-theistic systems of thought: [Non-theism] has assumed the existence of the objects of knowledge and the possibility of their having meaning apart from God (Van Til, 1969, 6). We thus once more come face-to-face with the antithesis of worldviews at hand and, once again, observe that the only way by which to rectify the issue is, in the last analysis, proving which worldview constitutes the transcendental justification for the intelligibility of human experience.

Non-Christian thought does not believe in the indispensable existence of God; Christian-theism does. Christian-theism does not believe in any aspect of chance in the universe; non-Christian thought does (regardless of one's subjective perspective—without God chance is ultimate). Non-Christian thought believes there is ultimate mystery behind the impersonal and chance aspects of reality; Christian-theism does not. What, therefore, one deems as necessary, contingent, possible, and impossible in all worlds—what one deems as self-stultifying or self-falsifying and impossible—*is determined by one's worldview.*

Interestingly enough, this truth has also been recognized in secular thought in the 20th and 21st Centuries amidst the precariousness of transcendental philosophy. Briefly, Adrion Bardon, in his well-known article pertaining to transcendental arguments, writes: "Depending on one's background assumptions, a wide range of propositions could count as performatively inconsistent..." (Bardon, 2005, p. 72), and elsewhere that what people deem as self-stultifying only obtains "given other background presuppositions implied by their views" (Bardon, 2005, p. 74). Kuhn's philosophy of "paradigms" in the philosophy of science likewise acknowledges (and in this case particularly predicates itself of off) one's auxiliary assumptions (Kuhn, 1962). To therefore pretend neutrality and objectivity with respect to possibility and impossibility, to contingency and necessity, is as much a futile venture as attempting to do it anywhere else in philosophy.

Once more, we must invoke the rightful, metaphysical observation that since unbelieving thought cannot live up to the transcendental challenge, and since Christian-theism does, then any proposition which in effect conflicts with Christianity and the existence of the Triune God is, by definition, false. When an unbeliever argues that the denial of the "self" is performatively self-falsifying in all possible worlds but not the existence Triune God of Scripture (since a Quadrinity within another, though perhaps similar theological system likewise satisfies the transcendental challenge), his argument is legitimized *so far as his subjective knowledge is concerned.* The subject of man's finitude has been touched on enough to understand quite straightforwardly that the problems of finitude, ultimate mystery, and the ultimate impersonalism of the universe do not warrant an absolute conclusion. Van Til rightfully pointed out that non-Christians must come to the brute facts of the universe for the first time; the ultimate irrationalism of the universe is to somehow be understood rationally by an agent/agents who have no objective justification for their rational ontos to begin with.[16] Herein lies the rational-irrational dialecticism of all worldviews which reject the Creator-creature distinction: non-Christians cannot bring the irrational and rational aspects of the universe together. And if the unbeliever does not possess exhaustive knowledge of this world and universe—which implies they have interpreted every single fact and interrelation therein accurately—one ought to see that his more audacious claim that the truth he is purporting would apply to *other* worlds is abjectly asinine.[17] Since revelation from the Triune God is harbored by all men, and since the natural man already rejects this metaphysical truth in this world, their meaningless postulations into hypothetical worlds testifies to the foolish, darkened, and vain philosophy utilized by unbelieving Thought: "Like a dog who returns to his vomit is a fool who repeats his folly" (Prov. 26:11).

Hearkening back to the two questions (1) does the conclusion of TAG apply to all possible worlds?; and (2) is this question meaningful to begin with?, we must observe with respect to the first question that how one answers this question is entirely dependent upon

---

16. This includes every religion which, at least in theory, rejects a Creator-creature distinction. If there is no distinction between god(s) and men, then the two parties explore the facts of the universe in a parallel fashion, *both* subject to *having to learn* the bruteness of the universe.

17. At this juncture, unbelievers will predictably appeal to such truths as being *a priori* or definitional to save absoluticity, the obvious problem being that deductive inferences from *self*-evident truths are, once more, purely subjective from an autonomous perspective, and definitional truths are purely analytic, saying nothing of the external world. As Bahnsen has said of unbelieving epistemologies: if the indubitability of beliefs are solely *internal to me* (rejecting analogical reasoning), notice how the basis of that indubitability is *purely subjective*. To apply the philosophical and definitional standards of deduction, analyticity, and absoluticity in this universe to other "worlds" which are, as of yet, still relegated to the level of hypothesis, all while dealing with *pervasive skepticism in this world*, exacerbates the already asinine conclusion. The unbeliever has no claim to objectivity if he cannot even obtain objectictiveness in this universe (or "world").

one's worldview. While the natural man may argue that the *cogito* dictum applies to all possible worlds upon pain of self-falsification, the worldview by which he predicates his assertion off of is itself without metaphysical justification. His argument, therefore, is without content.

Whether or not it's meaningful to talk of transcendental necessities in other possible worlds, the preceding considerations force us to answer in the negative. Since what one deems as possible or impossible is determined by that person's worldview, to speak of the reaches of transcendental conclusions to other possible worlds (such as the *cogito* dictum) leads both parties back to worldview considerations anyway; thus, why talk about possibility and necessity in other possible worlds if we are going to inevitably turn the discussion to worldview considerations? From a discussion of worldviews, the transcendentalist should first answer the fool according to his folly, lest he be wise in his own eyes (Prov. 26:5), which was done in the preceding paragraphs; and once the fool's folly has been exposed on his worldview, we proceed to layout the Christian worldview, not answering the fool according to his folly, his foolish standards (Prov. 26:4). It will then be observed that it is the *Triune God* who is the determiner or standard of possibility and impossibility, of necessity and contingency. While the unbeliever stands on his foolish, subjective, irrational worldview, arguing over the extent and legitimacy of certain transcendental conclusions to possible worlds unjustifiably, his lack of objective standards concerning possibility and impossibility, necessity and contingency, and the Christian's certain Objective Standard concerning them leads us to conclude that this discussion of hypothetical worlds—in the same vain as dealing with hypothetical worldviews against the Fristian objection—is meaningless. The transcendental charge concerning necessity, contingency, possibility and impossibility in hypothetical worlds is completely void on the opponent's worldview.

Final Remarks

The aim of this work was to act as further elucidation and refutation of the various philosophical criticisms levelled against Van Til's TAG that Bahnsen and others may not have directly addressed, or, if they have, to supplement them in such a way as to continue the legacy of Van Til's biblical contributions to apologetics by offering definitive refutations to opponents of presuppositionalism in the 21st Century while striving to maintain brevity for the sake of practicality. The criticisms addressed comprised what are considered to be the most lethal charges brought against TAG, the first four drawn from Michael Butler's thesis in which he likewise deals with them in his own way. The fifth criticism, though reminiscent of the Fristian objection, when treated in a transcendental, worldview fashion, nullifies the notion that the limits of possibility and impossibility can be known and defined apart from the Triune God and His revelation to man. The non-Christian has no objective basis to determine such limits; the Christian does.

Other transcendental criticisms against TAG have been presented by Herman Dooyeweerd (Dooyeweerd, 1971, pp.74-88) in which he accuses TAG of being a "transcendent" proof, not transcendental, David P. Hoover (Hoover, 1982) who, though insightful, simply misunderstands multiple aspects of TAG, Gordon Clark (throughout many of his writings) who particularly questions what Van Til's transcendental formulation even is (a topic discussed multiple times now), as well as his notion of analogical reasoning, neither of which exhibit any serious charges against it (at least compared to the ones addressed in this work, and Van Til and Bahnsen addressed all three men in their works). As such, I have intentionally omitted them from consideration given their simplistically-misguided nature (as opposed to something more philosophically rigorous), especially when considering that outside of academia, the transcendental criticisms levelled by ordinary anti-presuppositionalists and anti-Christians are more-or-less resemblant of the criticisms addressed in this work, not the ones postulated by Dooyeweerd and Hoover specifically.

It should be noted that criticisms pertaining to the methodology and tenets of presuppositionalism (e.g., neutrality, common grace, revelation, authority, evidence and interpretation, etc.) are characteristically distinct from transcendental considerations and as such would warrant a work of their own, the upshot being that while, quantitatively-speaking, there would naturally be more criticisms correlating to the number of doctrines/tenets embedded in presuppositional methodology, the criticisms pertaining to transcendental arguments in particular are inherently more philosophic and therefore more rigorous and difficult to deal with. Thus, answering the critics as pertains to methodological or doctrinal aspects of presuppositionalism is not as intellectually daunting and more straightforward in nature and scope.

While it would be ill-advised to argue that TAG remains objective based on the now-absence of presented defeaters, TAG should be seen as unhindered and objective in light of the *nature of transcendental reasoning itself*. To conclude an argument with metaphysical proof of a transcendental is to achieve the highest level of proof one could ever hope to attain since nothing could ever supersede the status of such a principle(s). Any objection to TAG and the existence of God requires God's very existence to argue against them. That is the power of transcendental proof and existence. Van Til truly has given us a biblical and objective proof for the existence of God.

Soli Deo gloria

INDEX

Subjects

abstract principles 25, 35, 38, 38n. 12, 39, 46-47

analogical reasoning 40-41, 167-170

apologetics 116-117

    Christian 33

Arminian 55, 178-180

authority 154-156, 159, 185

    Bible 151, 153-156, 158-159, 193n. 18, 196

    God 184, 199

    ultimate 150, 187-189

autonomous 46, 111, 119, 198

    autonomy 18-22, 111, 185

blockhouse methodology 148-149, 155-156, 192, 199

British Empiricism 60-63, 67, 122

Calvinist 178

circular reasoning 124-125, 157n. 25, 165-166, 177

conceptual schemes 81-83, 93-111, 118-121, 123-125

Continental Rationalism .... 58-60, 66-67 conventionalism 74

Cosmological Argument 29-33

Creator-creature distinction 161, 167-168, 171

Critical Philosophy 57, 64-66

deduction 46

    deductive reasoning 46, 49-52, 84-85, 202

direct/indirect argumentation .. 127-128, 175-176, 187n. 8, 202-204

egocentric predicament 68, 110n. 19, 119. 121

Foundationalism 72-74

proofs 23-26

epistemology 14, 16

ethics 14

evidence 185

facts

    and reason 17-20

    brute 146, 161

    interpretation of 160-162, 167-168

    nature of 146-150, 160-162, 175-178

faith 17-20, 151-152

fallacies 30

    ad hominem 14

    begging the question 30

    composition 30

    equivocation 30

genetic 14

special pleading..30

fideism 18, 183

induction 32

inductively 26

inductive reasoning 32, 51, 65, 84-85, 202

idealism 145

idealists 62n. 9, 145, 150

knowledge..16, 63-64

of 16

laws of logic 38-39, 169-172, 182, 184

logical Positivism 73

"man made of water"... 180-181

metaphysics 14, 16

method of implication 45, 163

neutrality 30-32, 174, 178-179

persuasion.. 14-17, 201n. 9

picture of knowing............................... 46-49, 117-121

Pragmatism.............................. 16n. 5, 26n. 7, 74-76

preconditions for intelligibility 28-29, 54, 68-69, 76, 184, 203

presuppositions 27, 50, 52n. 18,53, 68, 118-120n. 7, 123, 125, 127, 145, 198-199

reasoning by................................173-178, 180-182, 195

Problem of Evil .... 52-53 proof..14-17, 21-29, 77

reason 17-20, 64

revelation 48, 111, 132-133, 136, 139, 191, 193n. 18, 196

"rock in a bottomless ocean"............. 101-102n. 7, 121, 156, 160, 206

Roman Catholic 178-180

skepticism...............28-29, 58, 63, 68, 71-72, 74, 99-111, 120-121, 151-152, 161-162, 165

   skeptic............. 63, 71-72, 76, 93-96, 98-111, 115-117, 120-121

solipsism 00, 111, 119

"starting points" 155n. 23, 162-163

subjectivism 58-59, 68n. 15, 69, 161-162, 165

   subjective 69

transcendental...............................45, 68, 83, 124, 145, 187, 189-190

   idealism..68

Transcendental Argument for God (TAG).......31-33, 49-55, 76, 129, 131-207

transcendental arguments 13-14

   contemporary.....................................80-82, 87-90, 93

   generally 84-90, 99-111, 125-130

   program/method...... 9, 42, 45, 50, 54-55, 69, 123-144, 163-164, 203-204

worldviews........ 28n. 12, 111, 148-153, 155-162, 170-173, 185-189

   Christian...32, 39, 120-121, 156-162, 179, 189-193, 198-200, 204

INDEX

Names

Aristotle 43, 47, 89n. 14,

Austin, J. L. 100

Bardon, Adrian 169n. 14

Berkeley, George 23, 57, 62-63

Calvin, John 132, 139

Davidson, Donald 107-109

Descartes, René .... 21-22, 57-60, 101n. 7, -102, 202

Dooyeweerd, Herman 196,

Frame, John 197-207

Grayling, A. C. 99-107, 110-111, 124-125

Hepp, Valentine 146

Hintikka, Jaakko 89

Hoover, David P. 190-195

Hume, David 23-25, 57, 63, 65, 70, 122, 202

Kant, Immanuel 24, 30, 47-48, 57-58, 63-71, 87-90, 99-100, 122-124, 145-147, 150, 191n. 16, 202

Kuyper, Abraham 151-152

Leibniz, Gottfried Willhelm 22, 57, 59

Locke, John 23, 47-48, 57, 62, 122

Montgomery, John W. 157n. 28, 184-185

Plantinga, Alvin..65n. 11, 186n. 7

Plato 15, 47

Quine, Willard Van Orman..61, 107n. 16

Ridderbos, S. J... 139

Russell, Bertrand 21-22

Ryle, Gilbert... 75, 101

Schopenhauer, Arthur 31

Spinoza, Baruch..22, 57, 59-60

Strawson, P. F.. 93-99, 102-103

Stroud, Barry 96-98, 103

Van Til, Cornelius 35-55, 111, 129-148, 150-207

Wittgenstein, Ludwig...100, 202n. 15

Glossary

Apologetics—the vindication of the Christian philosophy of life against the various forms of the non-Christian philosophy of life. "Apologetics" is derived from the combination of two Greek words: *apo* ("back, from") and *logos* ("word"), meaning "to give a word back, to respond in defense."

Atomism—the metaphysical view that reality is made up of a number of fundamental, indivisible components (atoms).

Autonomy—From the Greek *auto* ("self") and *nomos* ("law"), effectively meaning a "self-law" or "law unto oneself," endorsing therefore the supremacy and/or legitimacy of man's mind and cognitive abilities without reference to God.

British Empiricism—a school of philosophy which argued that there are no innate ideas, and that knowledge is only obtained, and traced back to, observation.

Coherentism—a view of justification which holds that the justification for our knowledge is found within a web or cluster of beliefs as opposed to a linear chain of regression.

Conceptual Scheme—a cognitive or mental system through which we interpret our experience, bringing to bear on our experience our conceptual resources.

Continental Rationalism—a rationalist view held by certain philosophers in Continental Europe in the 17th and 18th Centuries, believing that: 1. There are self-evident truths from which we can deduce substantial conclusions about reality; and 2. We should search for certainty in our knowledge where mathematics is the ideal of knowledge.

Conventionalism—the belief that fundamental principles are held to, and predicated upon, the ideals of the society one lives in.

Deduction—a method of argumentation which guarantees with certainty the truth of the conclusion.

Dualism—the metaphysical view that reality is composed of mind (internal) and matter (external).

Epistemology—from the Greek *episteme* ("knowledge") and *logos* ("word"), is the branch of philosophy pertaining to the theory and considerations of knowledge.

Ethics—the branch of philosophy pertaining to how we should live our lives; morality.

Fideism—(literally *"faith-ism"*), referring to faith which is itself ungrounded or independent from considerations of reason; blind faith.

Foundationalism—a view of justification which holds that knowledge is predicated off of certain "foundational" axioms by which we can draw conclusions about reality.

Induction—a method of argumentation which argues with probability for the truth of the conclusion.

Logical Positivism—a view held in 20th-Century Vienna which holds that the only things meaningful for conveying truths are those things which are either empirically observed or statements which are true by definition or analytically (i.e., all bachelors are unmarried). The positivists aimed at holding no metaphysical assumptions at the outset, wanting to get away from all the speculation around it.

Metaphysics—from the Latin *metaphysika*, is the branch of philosophy pertaining to the nature of reality: the origin, structure, and nature of what is real.

Monism—the metaphysical view that reality is composed of one, singular substance.

Ontology—the branch of metaphysics concerned with the nature of being within reality.

Particulars—individual, material entities suspended in space.

Phenomenalism—the doctrine that human experience is solely confined or restricted to one's experiences via their senses, exemplified particularly with the contemporary, secular usage of transcendental arguments being almost exclusively and subjectively conceptual.

Phenomenology—a branch of philosophy concerned with the structure of one's consciousness/conscious experience.

Pragmatism—a school of philosophy which argues that the success of certain procedures defines rationality, not self-evident truths like the Continental Rationalists, nor conclusions drawn from sensations like the British Empiricists.

Presupposition—an elementary or foundational assumption pertaining to the nature of reality (metaphysics), knowledge (epistemology), or how we should live our lives (ethics). Presuppositions have the highest authority in one's worldview (web of beliefs), surpassing the level of mere assumptions.

Rationalism—a term subjected to a number of different definitions: the rationality of man's mind being the highest authority of reason; a school of philosophy adhered to by the Continental philosophers which is structured and predicated on foundational, fundamental, indubitable axioms or starting points, allowing for the possibility of knowledge; generically, the reasoning or cognitive abilities of man's mind.

Skepticism—the view that some or all knowledge is impossible to attain, and that all (relevant) knowledge-claims, therefore, are subject to questioning and scrutiny.

Solipsism—the view that only one's mind is sure to exist.

Transcendental—a necessary precondition for the intelligibility of human experience; in Kantian philosophy, something which is presupposed or necessary for knowledge of experience; a priori.

Transcendental Reasoning—a type of reasoning which seeks the preconditions or presuppositions necessary for the intelligibility of human experience.

Transcendental Idealism—Kant's particular transcendental program; the view that knowledge is a product of the phenomenal experience of one's mind through 12 categories.

Universals—abstract entities which correspond to, and unite, their particulars, allowing for a person's conceptual scheme to understand, organize, and interpret them.

Worldview—a network of presuppositions regarding the nature of reality (metaphysics), knowledge (epistemology), and how we should live our lives (ethics).

References

- Anderson, J. (2011). "No Dilemma for the Proponent of the Transcendental Argument: A Response to David Reiter," *Philosophia Christi* 13:1.

- Anderson, J. (2005)."If Knowledge Then God: The Epistemological Theistic Arguments of Plantinga and Van Til," *Calvin Theological Journal*.

- Bahnsen, G. L. (1998). *Van Til's Apologetic: Readings & Analysis.* Phillipsburg, NJ: Presbyterian and Reformed Publishing.

- Bahnsen, G. L., Butler, M. (1995). *Transcendental Arguments: 1995 Summer Seminar.*

- https://www.cmfnow.com/mp3/apologetics

- Bardon, A. (2005). "Performative Transcendental Arguments," *Philosophia* 33:69-95.

- Békefi, B. (2017). "Van Til versus Stroud: Is the Transcendental Argument for Christian Theism Viable?," *An International Journal for Philosophy of Religion and Philosophical Theology.*

- Bosserman, B. (2014). *The Trinity and the Vindication of Christian Paradox.* Eugene, OR: Pickwick Publications.

- Butler, M. (2002). "The Transcendental Argument for God's Existence," *The Standard-Bearer: A Festschrift for Greg L. Bahnsen.* Nacogdoches, TX: Covenant Media Press.

- Davidson, D. (1984). "On the Very Idea of a Conceptual Scheme," *Inquiries into Truth and Interpretation.*

- Dooyeweerd, H. (1971). "Cornelius Van Til and the Transcendental Critique of Theoretical Thought," *Jerusalem and Athens.* Presbyterian and Reformed Publishing.

- Frame, J. (1994). *Apologetics to the Glory of God: An Introduction.* Phillipsburg, NJ: Presbyterian and Reformed Publishing.

- Grayling, A. C. (2010). "Transcendental Arguments," *Blackwell Companions to Philosophy: A Companion to Epistemology.*

- Hintikka, J. (1972). "Transcendental Arguments: Genuine and Spurious," *Noûs,* 6:3.

- Hoover, D. (1982). "For the Sake of Argument: A Critique of the Logical Structure of Van Til's Presuppositionalism," *IBRI Research Report No. 11.*

- Kant, I. (1781). *Critique of Pure Reason.*

- Kuhn, T. (1962). *The Structure of Scientific Revolutions.* Chicago, IL: University of Chicago Press.

- Körner, S. (1974). *Categorical Frameworks.* Oxford: Blackwell.

- Montgomery, J. W. (1971). "Once Upon an A Priori," *Jerusalem and Athens.* Presbyterian and Reformed Publishing.

- Reiter, D. (2009). "A Dilemma for the Proponent of the Transcendental Argument for God's Existence," *Philosophia Christi,* 11:2.

- Riley, M. (2014). "Barry Stroud's Argument Against World-Directed Transcendental Arguments and Its Implications for the Apologetics of Cornelius Van Til." PhD dissertation, Westminster Theological Seminary.

- Sims, B. (2006). "Evangelical Worldview Analysis: A Critical Assessment and Proposal." PhD dissertation, Southern Baptist Theological Seminary.

- Strawson, P. F. (1959). "Individuals: An Essay in Descriptive Metaphysics," Oxfordshire, England, UK: Routledge.

- Stroud, B. (1968). "Transcendental Arguments," *The Journal of Philosophy*, 65:9.

- Stroud, B. (1977). "Transcendental Arguments and 'Epistemological Naturalism,'" *Philosophical Studies*, 31.

- Van Til, C. (2008). *The Defense of the Faith*. Phillipsburg, NJ: Presbyterian and Reformed Publishing.

- Van Til, C. (2015). *Common Grace and the Gospel*. Phillipsburg, NJ: Presbyterian and Reformed Publishing.

- Van Til, C. (1969). *A Survey of Christian Epistemology*. Phillipsburg, NJ: Presbyterian and Reformed Publishing. https://bit.ly/46pvOow